D1267098

TOM O'BRIEN'S

TIMING THE TRADE

TOM O'BRIEN'S

TIMING THE TRADE

HOW PRICE & VOLUME MOVE MARKETS

TOM O'BRIEN

Tiger Financial News Network, Inc.
Largo, Florida

Published by Tiger Financial News Network, Inc.

Warning and Disclaimer: There can be no assurance of profit in stock, commodity and mutual fund trading. Losses can and do occur. As with any investment, you should carefully consider your suitability to trade and your ability to bear the financial risk of losing your entire investment. It should not be assumed that the methods, techniques, or indicators presented in this book will be profitable or that they will not result in losses. Past results are not necessarily indicative future results. Examples in this book are for educational purposes only. This is not a solicitation of any order to buy or sell.

The information contained herein has been obtained from sources believed to be reliable, but cannot be guaranteed as to accuracy or completeness, and is subject to change without notice. The risk of using any trading method rests with the user.

A portion of the above notice is from a Declaration of Principles jointly adopted by a Committee of the American Bar Association and a Committee of Publishers.

All charts herein are presented through permission and courtesy of CyberTrader®, a Charles Schwab Company. Neither Tom O'Brien nor Tiger Financial News Network, Inc. is affiliated with CyberTrader® or Charles Schwab & Co., Inc.

Cover photo by ©Mark Harris
Cover design by Michael Comey

Chapter 1 quote excerpted from *The Four Agreements Cards* by don Miguel Ruiz.

Printed in the United States of America

ISBN 13: 978-0-9763529-0-7

10 9 8 7 6 5 4

For my Father.

He taught me the only limitations in life

are the ones you place on

yourself.

Acknowledgements

No man is an island unto himself.
~ John Dunne

Timing the Trade involved a tremendous collaboration of talent, inspiration and undying dedication... a huge team effort! The following people were instrumental in its creation:

Angela O'Brien - My love, for her vibrant thoughts, ideas and support.

Warren Hampton, CPA - For his single-minded commitment and assistance, particularly the countless hours he spent sifting the nooks and crannies of my trading mind to craft this book's message.

Katelyn O'Brien - For her commitment to mastering the process necessary to prepare the text for delivery to the printer.

Michael Comey - For his devoted efforts and application of uncanny, out-of-nowhere graphic design talents to craft the book's cover, charts, and diagrams.

Marvin Thoroughman - My "point man", for keeping the office going in a forward direction at all times.

Ed O'Brien - For his devotion to production excellence and his creative abilities that help us fulfill our mission.

Dale Petts - For his help with creating the Confluence Calculator.

Bud Rolfs and Basil Chapman - For their commitment to provide continuing education to the TFNN community each and every day.

Tigers and Tigresses - This book would not have been possible without your support throughout the years. Thank you! You cats are the greatest!

Contents

Introduction

The concept of supply and demand has been with us since our very first existence on this planet; whether we were looking for food, shelter, clothing or whatever, the demand that we created was always met with the notion of supply. The meeting of these two forces would in turn create the concept of price. The methods of payment have changed over the centuries, be they in animal skins when we first started traveling over this great planet, to gold and silver coins in Roman and medieval times, to paper and electronic money today. What has not changed however, are the dynamics of supply and demand and their impact on price.

When I got out of the Marines in early 1970, I embarked on quite an entrepreneurial venture. I drove around the city of Boston and sold food from a truck called O'Bie's ARK (short for "A Roaming Kitchen"). Talk about a lesson in supply and demand . . . I got it in spades! Originally the truck was used as a flight line truck for the Air Force so it was one heck of a monster, all steel, and you could see it coming a mile away, especially after I painted it red, white and blue.

My (ad)venture with O'Bie's ARK started in March of that year when I financed the truck for $5,000. I just couldn't wait for the first day where I'd actually take home cash and not have to use proceeds to pay for the truck. In the beginning of June that day finally arrived, I was so jazzed! It was about the 90th day of cranking it out (it was a seven-day-a-week business) and on this very day I was going to go home with cash that I would get to stick in my pocket (remember, it's not what you make, it's what you keep). As I was trucking down the road of what looked to be a nice summer day in Boston to my lucrative spot on the beach, I dreamed of the cash I was going to take home at the end of the day – cash that I didn't have to throw back into the truck since I had paid it off. I pulled up to my spot, opened the

ARK up for business and within thirty minutes the skies opened up with the rain gods deciding that they, on this glorious day, were going to enrich the earth and not me.

On that "glorious" day, I sold one bag of potato chips for $.10, yes ten cents. The law of supply & demand was at work . . . in fact, it never sleeps. A few weeks later the temperature started to reach the high 80's and business began to pick up. I noticed that for every degree over 87° my soda sales would go up by 20 to 30%, it was unreal. By midsummer the lines up to the ARK were longer than Noah's line of animals! Oh, and by the way the ARK was the only source for food or drinks on the beach. Talk about supply and demand! Needless to say O'Bie's ARK not only got me on my financial way, it taught me the importance of supply & demand (especially the notion that you need demand in order to make money and that demand can be a very fickle creature).

The O'Bie's Ark lessons were invaluable to me in the 1980's when I became a flight consolidator buying and selling huge chunks of unfilled airline seats. Thanks to the Boston heat and thirsty patrons of the old ARK days, my lessons in supply & demand helped me better grasp the economic dynamics of the travel industry. In fact, I felt like I practically *was* the market; I simply had a better feel as to how much product was available and just how badly customers wanted it . . . definitely a competitive advantage!

In the early 90's I started to trade the equity markets and soon realized that it was a lot tougher to get a handle on the supply and demand dynamics, especially with gauging where certain supply and demand curves were intersecting (real price). In 1998 I went on a hunt looking for any resources to help with my dilemma. I ran across a book written by Richard Wyckoff and I laid out over $850 for it. Except for my beautiful wife and children, this is one of the best investments I ever made. Richard Wyckoff was a master at uncovering where supply and demand curves seemed to intersect. With his theories and others that I had learned along the way, such as Fibonacci expansion and contraction, I was gradually compiling an amazing chest of trading power tools that have helped me to this very day.

This book may seem at first blush like a technical analysis book, but in reality it's meant to be an everyday user's guide to understanding price moves in the market. Sure, you'll see plenty of charts and theories which individually have seen entire books devoted to them. The charts are presented to give you a picture, give you clarity. The theories are offered, not in too much detail for individual analysis, but for collective use in a trading discipline. Combined, the charts and theories will help you understand where you should be getting in and out of trades, how and why; and when you master this understanding, you'll be flowing in harmony with the market, be it up or down . . . remember: *harmony with the market.*

The purpose of *Timing the Trade* is to teach you how to interpret and anticipate movement in the markets and how to effectively react to them. There are road signs in the market each and every day and these signs have *everything* to do with volume and price; thanks to these signs you'll get a better grasp on supply & demand and ultimately price! The market for any commodity, equity or good can be boiled down to a range of numbers. *Timing the Trade* will teach you to recognize not only the range of numbers, but the range of movement and how to effectively trade price moves!

Timing the Trade is essentially an *approach* (combined with a focused discipline) that bases its present decision making in contemplation of future moves by paying attention to the past, particularly in the context of interpreting volume and its relationship to certain prices.

You'll want to use this book as a working guide. Realistically, it takes a considerable amount of time to fully understand and appreciate market dynamics in order to make correct and consistent trading decisions that result in profit, year in and year out. Hopefully you'll use this text as a reference tool and give it years of wear and tear.

Just as "life is a mystery to be lived, not a problem to be solved", understanding the true inner workings of the stock market is something of a journey. So hang on and enjoy the ride!

How to Read this Book

It does not matter how slowly you go, so long as you do not stop.
~ Confucius

Timing the Trade has evolved over the years from my experience in testing the many different technical systems in the marketplace.

I found that the most consistent way of analyzing the market was by using Fibonacci analysis, essentially price expansion/contraction theory. Together with the MACD (moving average convergence/divergence) indicator, this regimen would keep my account positive most of the time. The problem with using just Fibonacci alone was that it didn't always give me true direction on the market. It wasn't until I factored in the implication of volume that I not only felt more confident about where the market was heading but I could also understand it in a very simple sense – more buying: you are going up; more selling: you're heading south. This was where I could see the battle lines setting up at various swing points. You could actually see the bears and bulls preparing for war. I was starting to understand that these battle lines would give signals whether the market would continue, either up or down. You would see either the bulls or bears slightly wounded or rolled out flat like a piece of hot steel. Each one of these signals proved to be valuable road signs letting me know the strength and weakness of the market at all times.

Timing the Trade has been structured to teach you to grasp the clearest and most concise picture of any market, starting with the larger picture, then dissecting stock and market signals down to the point of executing or walking away from a trade. The concepts in *Timing the Trade* are conveyed as simply as possible using straight-forward language along with diagrams and charts to help crystallize their meaning. Whether you are just starting in the business or have been trading for twenty years you'll assimilate a whole new way of not only looking at the market, but understanding how and why the market moves.

The book's chapters have been judgmentally sequenced to facilitate your understanding of *Timing The Trade*; you should be able to notice how the chapters build upon the critical concepts.

I suggest that you make a clean sweep and read through the entire book without stopping at any particular chapter or overfocusing on any one concept; you'll garner a real appreciation for the layout of the book, not to mention *Timing the Trade*'s complexities and simplicities. When you're done reading, put the book down. Let your mind digest the material; it's amazing how much more information we retain if only we give our minds a well-deserved break.

After a few days, go back to the book and devote time and energy to each individual chapter. You should make sure that you understand each chapter's concepts with crystal clarity (studying the text, diagrams and charts) before moving on to the next. I suggest you do this at your own pace but set aside an hour to an hour and a half for each reading. This should put you at optimal shape to comprehend the subject matter and help cement the concepts.

I suggest you pull out a trusty No. 2 pencil and take notes of the points you find important. I find that when you do this, your mind tends to transcend to a higher level of clarity. This is where your studies will start flowing in harmony with your understanding of the market.

One of the most important concepts in *Timing the Trade* is exercising sufficient patience to await clear road signs before placing your hard-earned capital at risk. When you master the discipline of patience as well as risk & money management, the technical aspects of *Timing the Trade* will prove their worth.

You should use *Timing the Trade* as a reference book, checking back when you have any questions about the different concepts or face any uncertainties in your trading. Regardless, you'll want to consume this material, let it melt into your mind and psyche, and then trust yourself to make the right trading decisions.

This book is also about empowerment. Suddenly you'll find yourself with greater understanding, exercising greater patience and trading with greater confidence. You just might feel inspired to help spread the gospel of *Timing the Trade* and tell a friend or relative about the importance of volume, etc. Regardless, I'm confident that the time you invest in this book will translate into great dividends down the road for you.

I want you to understand that trading is a business that takes a firm commitment of time, energy, and patience. I want you to enjoy this book and more than anything, make money!!

> *A true Master is not the one with the most students,*
> *but one who creates the most Masters.*
>
> ~ Neale Donald Walsch

1

Let's Get Cookin'!

The journey of a thousand miles begins with one step.
~ Confucius

[music intro]

GROOWWWLLL!!

Welcome folks! This is Tom O'Brien from TFNN, Tiger Financial News Network, we go three hours a day, five days a week; we go 24 hours a day on the net at TFNN.

Always remember, whatever you think about you bring about, whatever you focus on grows. Make it a great one!

Let's take a look at one of our four agreements:

"Always do your best.

Take action without expecting a reward.

Do your best and take action because you love to, not because you expect a reward. When you take action without expecting a reward, you enjoy every action, and you can even receive greater rewards than you imagined."

Market-wise, let's take a look at it folks:

The Dow closed up 4
The NASDAQ up 9
The S&P's traded up 3 to 1221.21
Gold closed down 2.50 to $424.60
Oil traded up 1.50 to $60.75
The Dollar index traded down 1.05 to $88.28
Bonds down 16 ticks to 116.20

Give me a call folks, I want to know what's going on in your world. In the world of the S&P's, we traded up three, hugging the June17th highs, building cause to make the run for the March 7th highs. Volume today came in at 1.4 billion vs. 1.4 billion yesterday. We are going to need volume to the tune of 1.8 to 1.9 billion as we take out the 1229.11 mark on the SPX; that will tell us we have conviction on this move.

Excerpt from "The Tom O'Brien Show"

I'm the host of a daily radio show where for three hours people call in and ask my opinion on stocks and market action. I also interview some of the best traders and market timers in the world. Not only do I have a radio show, but I own a company that conducts seminars across the U.S. where we have trained thousands of traders. We also publish dynamic newsletters with market analyses and recommended trades for our clients with a track record for everyone to see on our web page. I place my reputation on the line with every trade I recommend. I live and die not quietly, but in full view of anyone within earshot of radio stations or computers worldwide. What you will learn here consistently makes money.

So why should you buy and read this book? Simply, this book outlines a trading approach based on ideas that have worked for over 100 years. Some of it is from books and articles written before the First World War. This stuff worked before computers, before most people had cars, this stuff still works. As a radio host I also get access to the best current traders that let me know their best indicators and practices. Frankly, I test what they propose and add what works to my system. Like an onion, each chapter will reveal another layer of a total system that can feed you for life.

Ok, how is it done? I first need to point out that the tools of my trade (and basically what I hang my hat on) involve the continually evolving science of technical analysis, not to mention sound judgment and money management. In contrast to fundamental analysis which focuses on the financial and business welfare of a particular entity, market, or economy, technical analysis offers predictions on future price movements based on different angles, interpretations and permutations on historical price and volume movements belonging to the trading activity of an individual stock or commodity, group of stocks or an overall market. I basically focus all my energy on looking at price and volume movements and look to those variables to give me road signs for future price movements. "Where is this stock (or market) headed based on the way it has traded in the past?" Basically, I get an understanding of what the equity is doing now, what it's telling me, and what it may do in the future.

I don't pay too much attention to Company XYZ's business model, past and future earnings and revenues, management, etc. I will however pay attention to reported insider trading activity (chief officers buying or selling stock) which demonstrates owners' and managers' conviction and faith in their own enterprise (are they getting in or are they getting out?). Other than that, price and volume are in my opinion where it's at! And if there are clear signals, I take steps to take advantage of those signals and set up a trade, provided the risk/reward scenarios are favorable.

What follows is a brief, perhaps accelerated summary of how I analyze and dissect a stock's or market's trading activity in order to better understand how it will probably behave in the future and then the steps I take to capitalize on its anticipated trading behavior to effectively "time the trade". In essence, this chapter should serve as a brief introduction to my analyses and trading style, as well as a segue to the major concepts outlined in this book. (Note: entire chapters are devoted to key terms highlighted in bold print.)

Reading a Chart & Identifying the Trade

The best way to look at a stock's historical trading pattern is through the use of a chart. A stock's chart is essentially a snapshot of trading activity for a given period of time. I typically use a six-month time frame when looking at price and volume activity to understand a stock's movement for the next month or so. I then move on to a bigger time frame to help me understand where it may want to trade in a longer time frame. Remember, to get the bigger picture, use a longer–term chart.

I am assuming that you, as the reader, already have a basic understanding of stock charts, know what a stock chart is and the basic information that it is meant to convey. You should know that price is always plotted along the vertical axis and the horizontal axis denotes a particular time interval (i.e., day, month, etc.). The bottom of the chart (especially the charts we'll be dealing with) should include a representation of the volume (typically marked with vertical bars) for that time interval. The exact volume is derived through the use of a data feed drawn from the internet or included in the charting service you might be subscribing to. There are many charting services available for free on the internet as well.

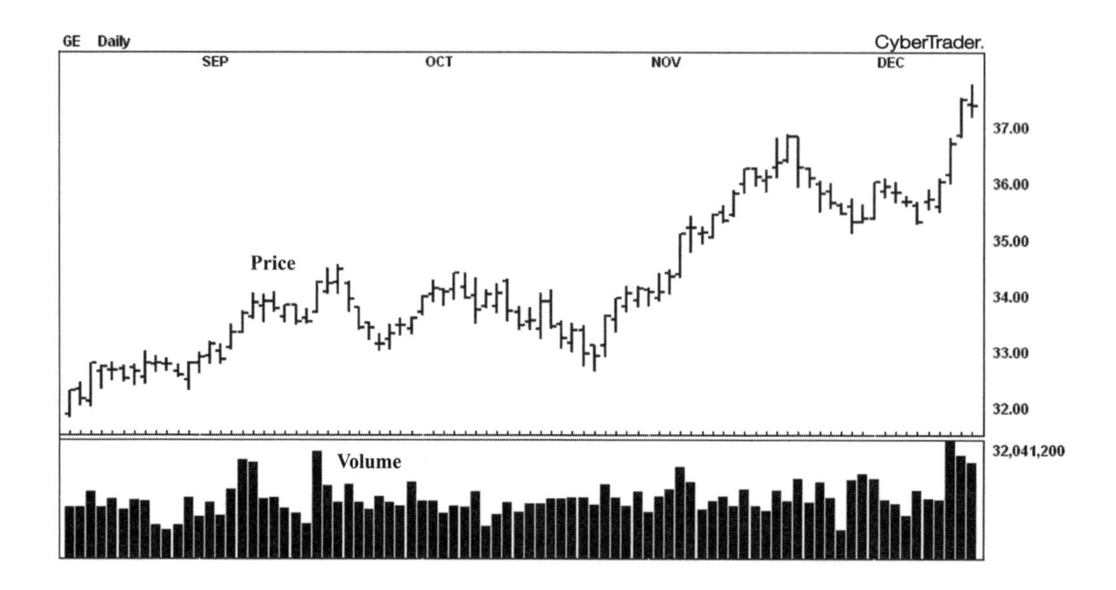

Figure 1-1: ***Basic Six–month Chart Showing Price & Volume – General Electric Company (GE)***

Price movements are typically reflected above volume amounts which are expressed with vertical bars.

Typically with the six-month chart in front of me, I immediately look for the stock's "lay of the land", the more important clues being the stock's **quality volume** and its **real price**. Where is strength and weakness insofar as volume is concerned? What are the highest & lowest price points? Where is the last day with big volume on the way *up*? Where is the last day with big volume on the way *down*? Is the stock rising in price in tandem with strong volume and pulling back on lighter volume? Or conversely, is the stock going down on strong volume and retracing or pulling up on lighter volume? With these variables, I can determine a stock's quality volume, its real price and pretty much grasp its "lay of the land".

Next, I look for the stock's road signs.

Where are the stock's **swing points**? Where was there a sudden shift in price direction and where was a great amount of money made and/or lost? It is very important to ascertain the exact trading volume with these swing points because other volume amounts when compared to the swing point's volume will be crucial to the context of identifying, entering and exiting future trades.

A stock's swing points may also lend clues to its **support & resistance** levels. Are there price levels that this stock may have trouble piercing through? If and when those price levels are pierced through, what are the next support & resistance levels? You will be basing your most important decisions at these price points.

What is the current trend of the stock? Is the stock trending up? Is it trending down? Is the stock consolidating and awaiting an explosion to the upside or downside? Is the stock trading in a **channel**? Has it signaled that it wants to break out of its channel? As the stock is approaching the boundaries of its channel, what's happening to trading volume? Is it weak or strong?

Has the stock demonstrated any price **gaps** between its opening prices and its previous closing prices? Do these gaps lend to support & resistance levels? Will they get filled?

Does the stock have any significant **candlestick** formations that signal a reversal or continuation in price direction? Can you spot any doji, engulfing patterns, hammers or hanging men?

I haven't gone into much detail with these major concepts but don't worry, I will soon. Much of it may sound fairly "Greek" right now, but I'm mentioning these here to give you a flavor as to how I read charts as well as the road signs I look for and the tools I use to effectively time the trade.

Setting up the Trade

After grasping a stock's lay of the land and taking notice of its obvious road signs, I then move to set up a trade, if it is practicable.

Is the market you are trading in moving up, down, or consolidating? What is the sector doing?

Is the stock creating an **ABC structure**? Is it an ABC up or an ABC down? Are there small ABC's within the overall ABC?

Is the stock expanding or contracting in a **Fibonacci** sense? What are its .618, .50 and .382 retracement levels? What are the stock's potential expansion levels? Is it at a 1:1, 1:1.382, 1:1.50 or 1:1.682 expansion and what should I expect next?

After identifying the possible ABC structure and checking the Fibonacci retracement levels, I perform a **confluence** calculation to help determine the appropriate entry price as well as a **stop** price, since confluence can help uncover powerful **support** or **resistance** levels.

I'm ready to fire off the trade, but not just yet. I look to the **3x3 DMA** & **MACD** to give me the final go-ahead.

I can, at any time during this process, cancel or flat out pull the plug on trading this stock. In most cases, I don't trade it because the **risk/reward** scenario just isn't favorable.

Throughout this entire process, I remain vigilant to a powerful principle I regard as **cause & effect**. This is very important because you can't have one without the other. If there is sufficient *cause* vis-à-vis volume, then there should be sufficient *effect* vis-à-vis price. If a stock has been consolidating for a long period of time (cause) then the breakout should be relatively as great (effect). If there are compelling signals and reasons to enter a trade and I've correctly calculated my entry and exit points, all under good risk/reward parameters (cause) then the trade should be successful (effect).

Again, it seems like I've raced through the motions as to how I analyze a stock, identify and set up a trade . . . and I have . . .but only to give you a brief introduction and whet your appetite to the major concepts you're about to learn. So let's get cookin', with gas!

2

Quality Volume™

Nothing else in the world... not all the armies...
is so powerful as an idea whose time has come.
~ Victor Hugo

Volume is it!

Volume is the gospel I preach, the air I breathe and the song I sing. It is what I primarily base all my stock and commodity analyses and trading decisions on. There are other matters in everyday life with which I can use volume in some way or another. An example would be volume's usefulness in analyzing local real estate prices, "are there many houses up for sale with no one buying?" etc. But with stock trading, volume is it! Without volume, you can't get a clear read on where the supply and demand curves may be intersecting and where prices may be heading. I can't do without knowing what volume is and neither should you. I hope that if you can only learn and benefit from just one concept in this book . . . by all means, let it be the importance of volume!

What is volume? Well, I am hoping that you are savvy enough with the capital markets that you already have a general idea, but just in case: volume (as it regards stock trading) is essentially the amount of shares that are exchanged back in forth in any given time period, usually expressed as a daily amount. In grade school, we were taught that volume was typically the amount of liquid or air that any three dimensional shape or container could hold. Remember hearing those formulas for volume in grade school? Remember height times pie times radius squared or something like that? Well don't worry; in stock trading, volume is a little different since we do not have any container from which to draw measurements. Trading volume gives us a straightforward amount of shares bought and sold; one number (for each transaction), plain and simple, end of story.

> ***Definition:*** **volume** – the amount of shares bought and sold for any given stock or market during any given time frame (typically expressed as a daily amount).

Let's use "driving a car" to demonstrate the importance of volume (throughout this book I will do my best to keep the concepts clear and simple, and in so doing, you'll see me use everyday examples as analogies in order for you to better grasp or crystallize these concepts). Let's say you crank up your car and hit the gas pedal. Well, gas is what makes you go. Easy enough, right? Well, trading volume is pretty much similar to gas, as it concerns price movement. As you have more volume, there should be movement or acceleration in price direction, be it up or down. There are definitely reasons why prices may not move with high volume or why they might move with little volume. We'll get into those reasons shortly, but remember that volume is the amount of gas that goes into a stock or market.

Now as I mentioned before, volume is the amount of shares bought and sold in a given time period. One half of the transaction equation includes a buyer and the other half, the seller. Without the buyer, you have no transaction and the same can be said for the seller. So by extension, volume helps gauge the demand and supply for a stock in a very direct sense provided there is clear direction in price movement. High volume in a rising stock reveals a high demand for it, while high volume in a declining stock reveals a high supply of shares with relatively low demand.

How does price move? Well, if there are many people who want (high demand) shares of XYZ and there are only so many shares (low supply), people will bid up the price, i.e., cause the price of XYZ shares to rise. Conversely, if there are many sellers of XYZ shares (high supply) and very few buyers (low demand), then people will drop their prices in order to unload their shares. Sound simple? Yes. Does it always happen this clearly? Not always. If you don't have clarity, your best bet is to stay away from the stock.

The Truth in Volume

Perhaps volume's greatest usefulness lies in its ability to reveal the truth and genuineness of price movements (Is this stock really going up? Or is the move not real?). Stock prices go up and down every minute of the trading day and volume gives you verification whether the price moves are real. Is price moving in a natural sense (i.e., is the movement being caused by legitimate buying and selling forces) or are prices moving in an unnatural sense (i.e., are there operators in the stock that are extending its price in order to accumulate or unload their shares at their price)? We'll get into real and unreal price moves later as we cover quality volume.

> ***Definition:*** **operator** – any individual trader or institution with the ability to manipulate a stock's price beyond the stock's natural price point (based on supply and demand) in order to gain an advantage in anticipation of a major price move. Operators usually have more information than the individual investor (remember: all market action comes from interests that are better-informed than the individual investor).

Another one of volume's greatest benefits is its ability to predict a certain technical event such as a breakout. As an example, suppose a stock in a downtrend has been trading in a particular channel for some time (we'll cover channels in a later chapter). Let's say the stock is approaching the upper boundary of the channel and just might pierce it while staging a fabulous breakout to the upside. With volume on your side, you'll be able to tell (at least with some greater probability) whether the breakout will be a likely event. In our case, if volume is strong while the stock is approaching the upper boundary of its channel, then it is likely that the stock will pierce the channel and may even continue upward. If volume is light, then you can count on the stock not piercing the channel and in fact continuing its downward trend within its channel. If it does pierce the channel, odds are the move will be short-lived with the stock soon returning back into the channel.

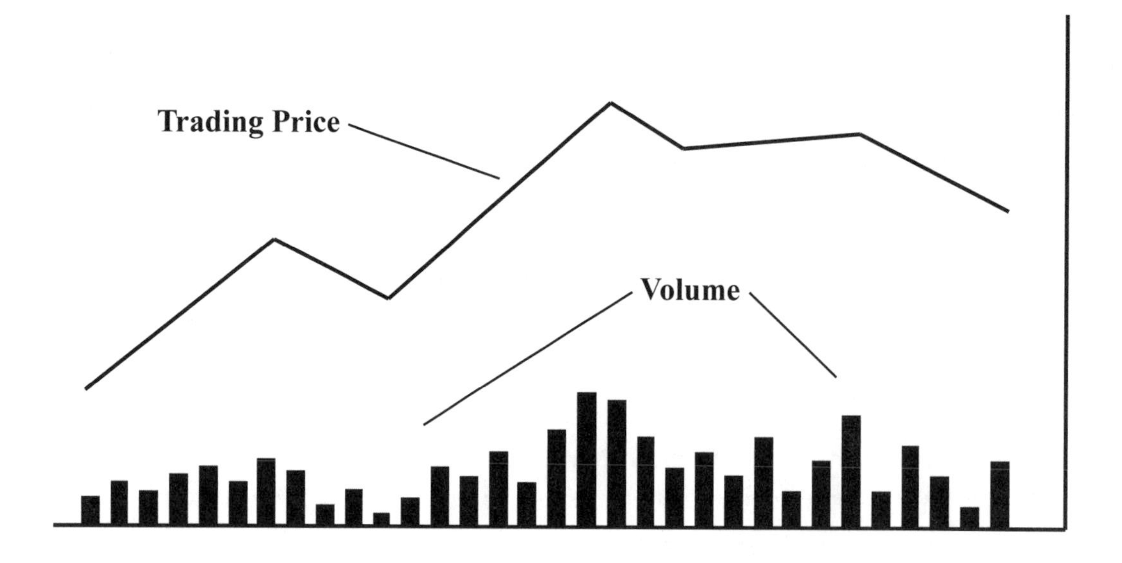

Figure 2-1: ***Trading Price & Volume***

Quality Volume™

Why is quality important? The answers are definitely more than obvious. Without quality, where would we be in this world? What would life be like? Would you be happy with a car that breaks down at least once a week? In trading, you'll definitely run into instances where the concept of quality in volume will lead to meaningful moves in price. Here's an example: let's say YES (Your Excellent Stock – throughout this book, YES will serve as our hypothetical stock, appearing in several examples and diagrams) has been moving through $20 to $25 and it's been going up every single trading day on roughly 1 million to 1.5 million shares of volume. We should all know that most stocks in upward trends do not continue rising without a pullback or a breather, i.e., stocks do not go up in a straight line forever. YES suddenly begins to pull back on lighter volume, say 700,000 shares. This is foremost what I look for in all price moves: significant moves on strong volume with pullbacks on lighter volume. I call this quality volume. Why? Because the buying and selling activity is *genuine*: the strong move in price is accompanied by strong volume and your verification of the reality of the move is demonstrated by light volume on the pause, breather, retracement, pullback, etc. Take a look at Figure 2-2; notice the pullbacks occurring on lighter volume.

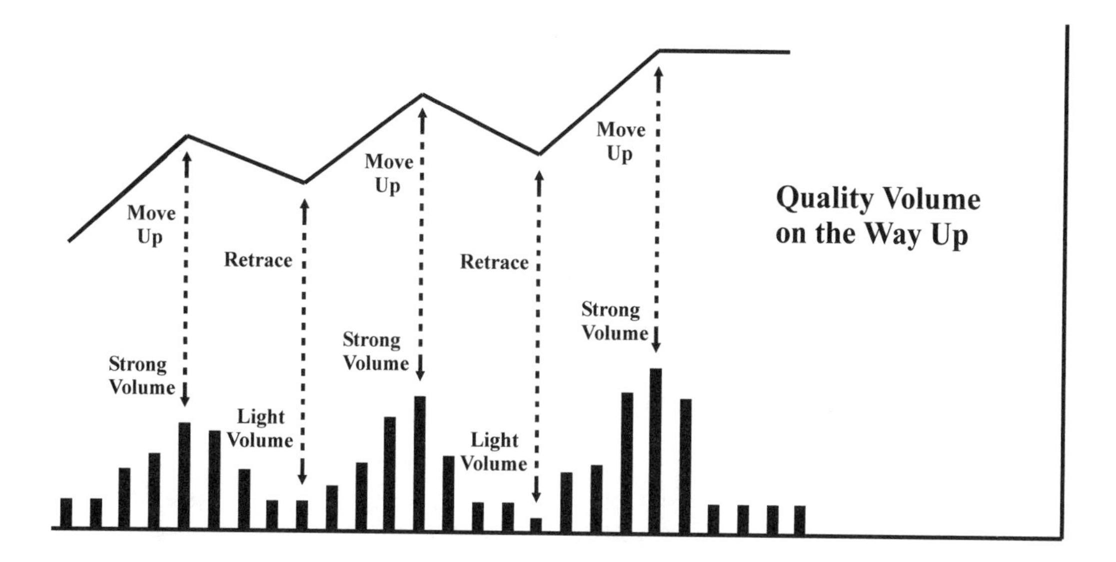

Figure 2-2: ***Quality Volume™ on the Way Up***

The same can be applied to a stock that is decreasing in price. A price move down (downtrend) that is accompanied with strong volume is given validation when there is a pause or temporary move up (retracement) with lighter volume.

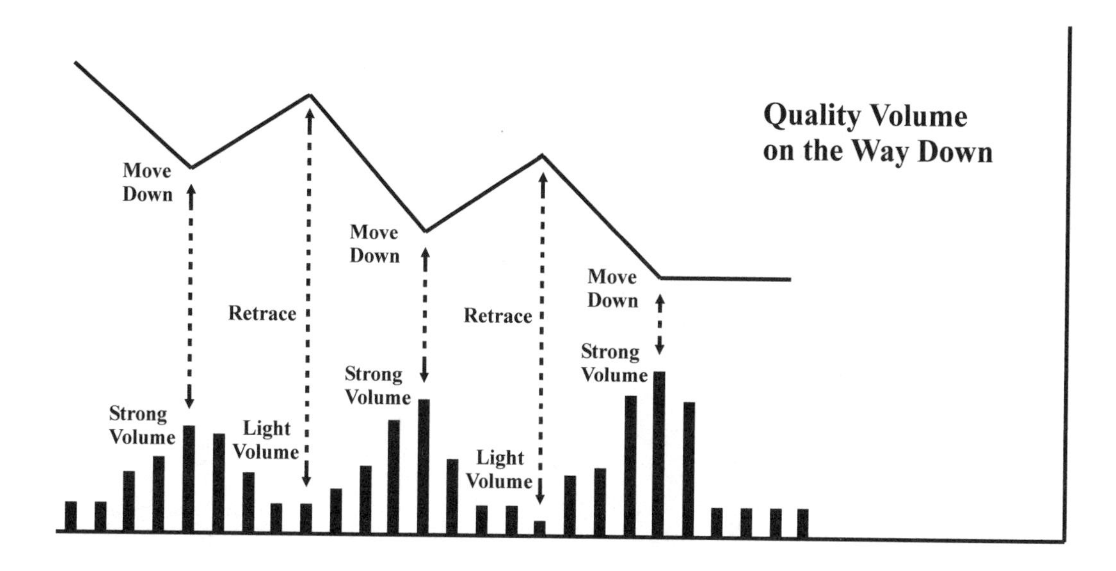

Figure 2-3: ***Quality Volume™ on the Way Down***

Let's take a look at an actual instance of quality volume in action; check out Figures 2-4 and 2-5.

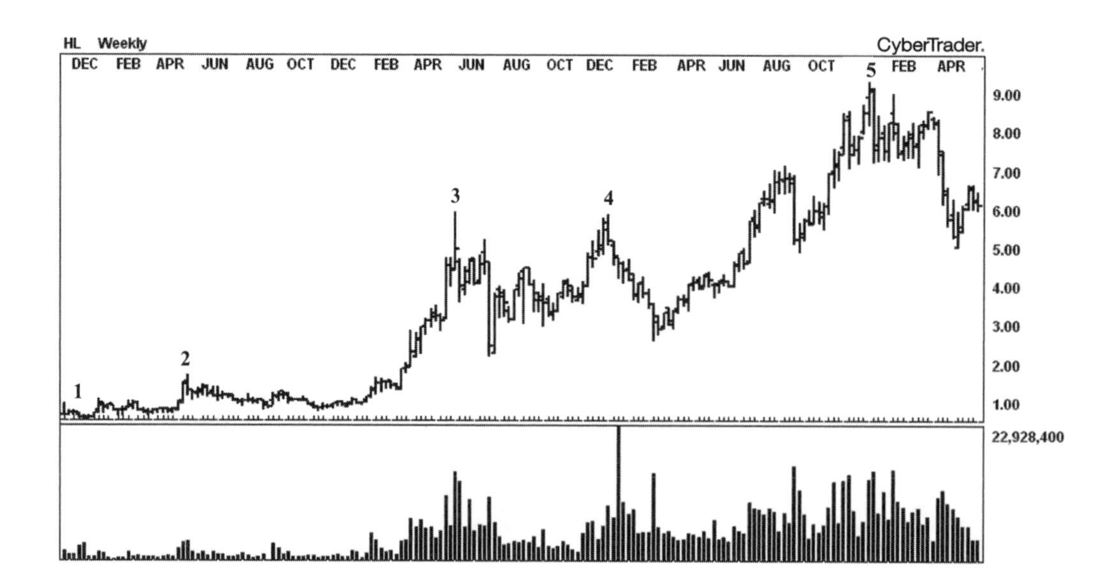

Figure 2-4: *Quality Volume™ – Hecla Mining Company (HL)*

(1) *December of 2000 – HL starts pushing to highs with volume. It hits a price point of $.75 with volume of 7.9 million shares.*

(2) *May of 2001 – HL reaches $1.70 with volume expanding to the 10.6 million mark. You can also see on the following retracement that HL pulls back on lighter volume.*

(3) *June of 2002 – HL breaks to the upside hitting the $5.90 price point with volume of 45 million shares. We again retrace with lighter volume.*

(4) *January of 2003 – HL again heads topside hitting $5.86 just four cents under the high of June 2002* (3) *with volume of 53.5 million. Hecla is pushing the highs with volume telling us it should take them out.*

(5) *January 2004 – HL hits $9.31 with volume pushing 51.1 million shares.*

When looking at this equity you can see that HL comes off a bottom with volume as its price is expanding. When price pulls back, volume contracts – this is the hallmark trait of quality volume.

Through quality volume, we find harmony in the market, even in moments of chaos.

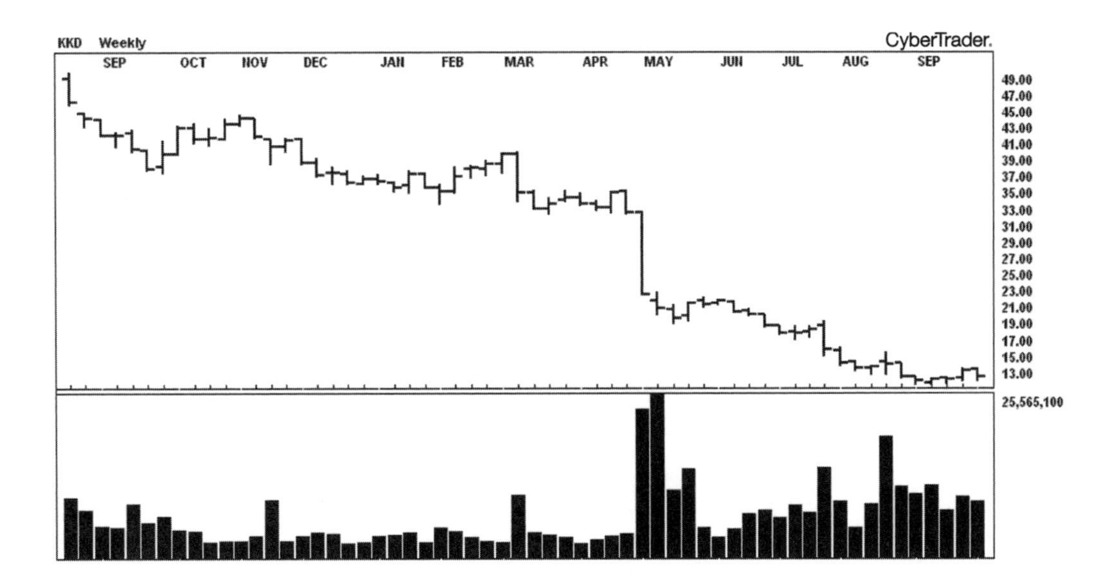

Figure 2-5: *Quality Volume™ on Way Down - Krispy Kreme Doughnuts, Inc. (KKD)*

If you take a ruler and vertically line up the high volume days with their respective price action, you'll see that they mostly occurred on downdrafting days. The weakening volume occurred during the retracements or up days. With quality volume, strong volume accompanies price action that moves with the overall trend.

The previous examples show you quality volume in its simplest sense. But what happens in a scenario where there is no quality volume? Check out the diagram in Figure 2-6 and note how volume disappears on upward moves in an uptrending stock.

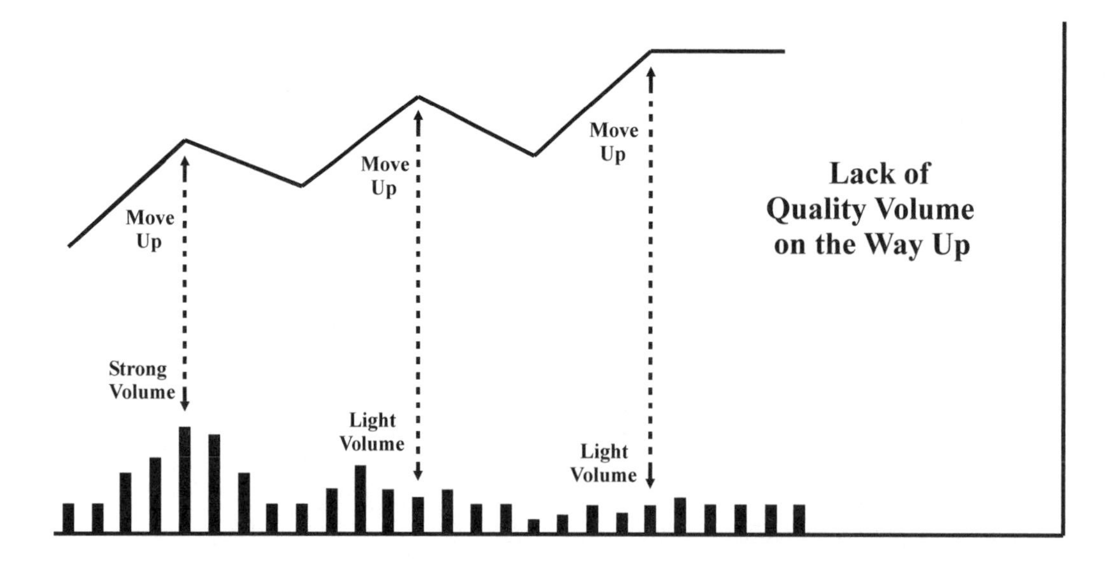

Figure 2-6: ***Lack of Quality Volume™ on the Way Up***

Picture that YES is moving through $25 and at that price point its trading volume is 1 million shares for that particular day. The following day it hits $27 and trades at 500,000 million shares and on the day after it hits $28 on 300,000 shares. What you have here is a road sign saying that the stock is going up in an unnatural sense and that a reversal may be just around the corner. This demonstrates a lack of quality volume since price is moving up (effect) without real volume (cause) - *the move is not real*. Figure 2-7 illustrates this example.

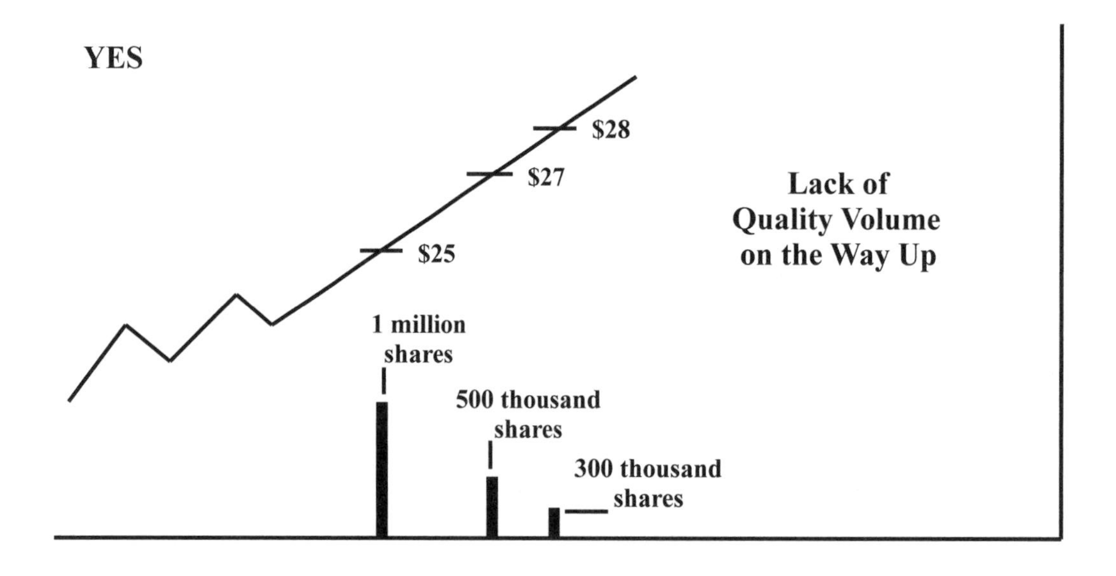

Figure 2-7: ***Lack of Quality Volume™ in an Uptrending Stock - (YES)***

Let's look at lack of quality volume in a downward sense. Say YES is in a downtrend with decent volume from $30 to $25, and all of a sudden volume begins to dry up and its price keeps moving down beyond $25, down to $20! Again, this reveals a lack of quality volume where price continues to move in an unnatural sense, i.e., an unreal move. These unnatural price moves should be road signs to you.

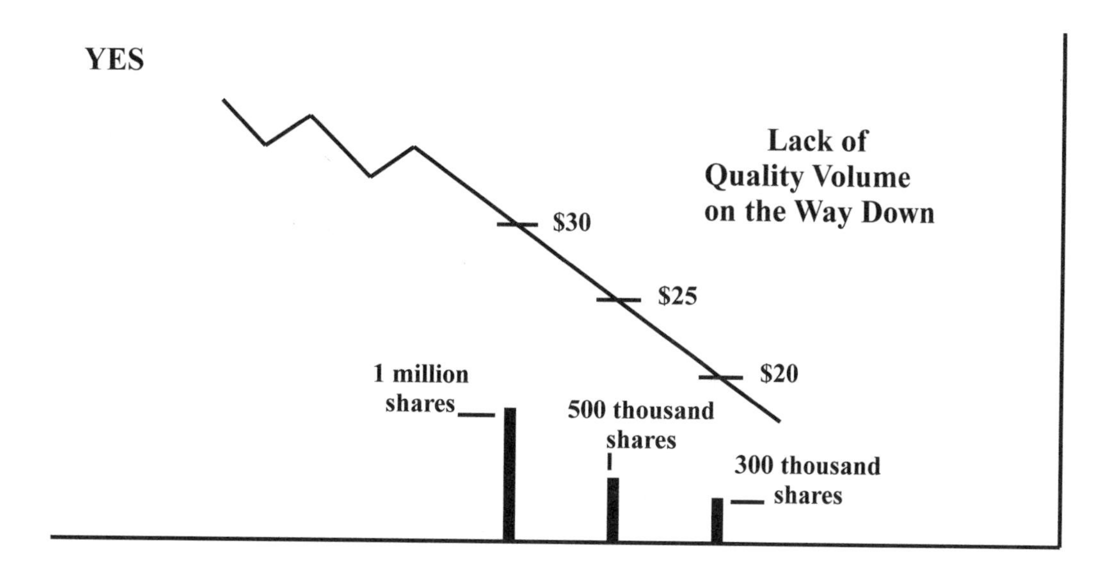

Figure 2-8: ***Lack of Quality Volume™ in a Downtrending Stock - (YES)***

Remember, the more consistent the correlation between volume and price (i.e., strong price moves with strong volume followed by retracements on lighter volume), the higher quality volume that exists. Accordingly, you should encounter more meaningful price moves. Always be on the lookout for price & volume consistency. . . . quality volume!

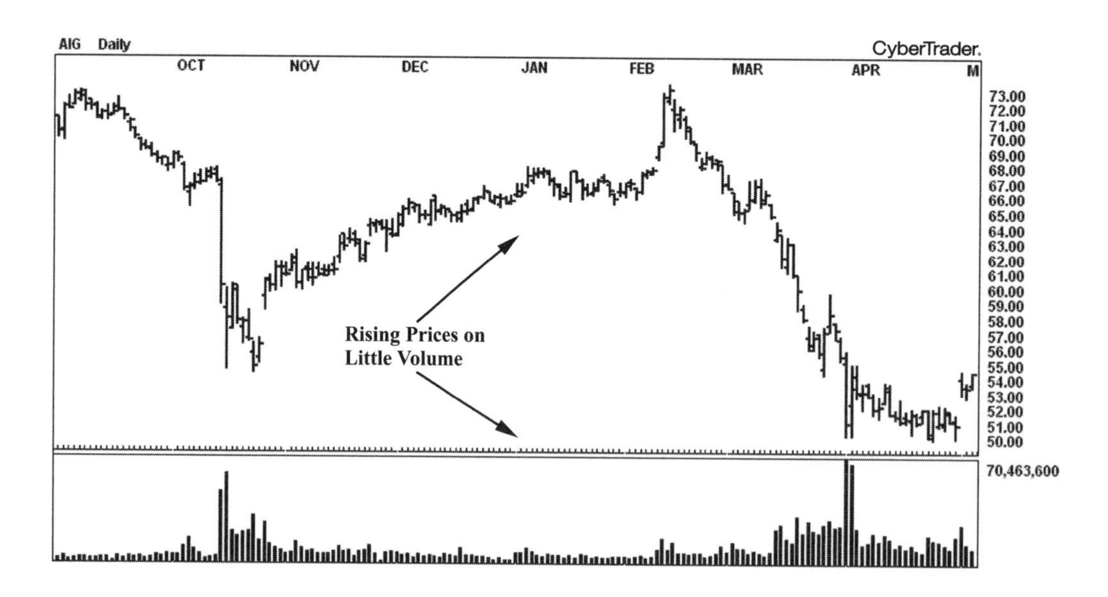

Figure 2-9: ***Lack of Quality Volume™ - American International Group, Inc. (AIG)***

Note how AIG's increasing price move occurs on incredibly little volume. This unnatural price extension can take place for only so long and in early February AIG begins a steady decline.

Real Price

Practically every time I look at a stock's chart, I first look for the last day of trading where there was an incredible spike in volume. On a normal chart with volume plotted in the form of vertical bars on the x-axis (the chart's baseline), a high volume day should stick out like a skyscraper. I refer to this day as "the last day with volume" or real price. The enormous activity of buying and selling emphasizes the point that this price is where *most* people are willing to buy or give up their shares.

> ***Definition:*** **real price** – The price point where there is an enormous amount of buying and selling activity.

Imagine YES is trading from $20 to $26 and at $24 it experiences an incredible volume day. Certainly for the near term, $24 should be regarded as its real price (Figure 2-10 provides an illustration). In this case there was an enormous amount of buyers; and I say buyers because YES was trending up. If YES had been trending down, then there would have been a great amount of sellers. Of course, there cannot be a buyer without a seller, but the trend pretty much tells you who for the most part had the initial impetus to complete the transaction, buyer or seller; this is also telling you who's in control, the bulls or the bears. This real price also signals where the stock's true supply and demand are, in essence where its supply and demand curves intersect, at least for the time being.

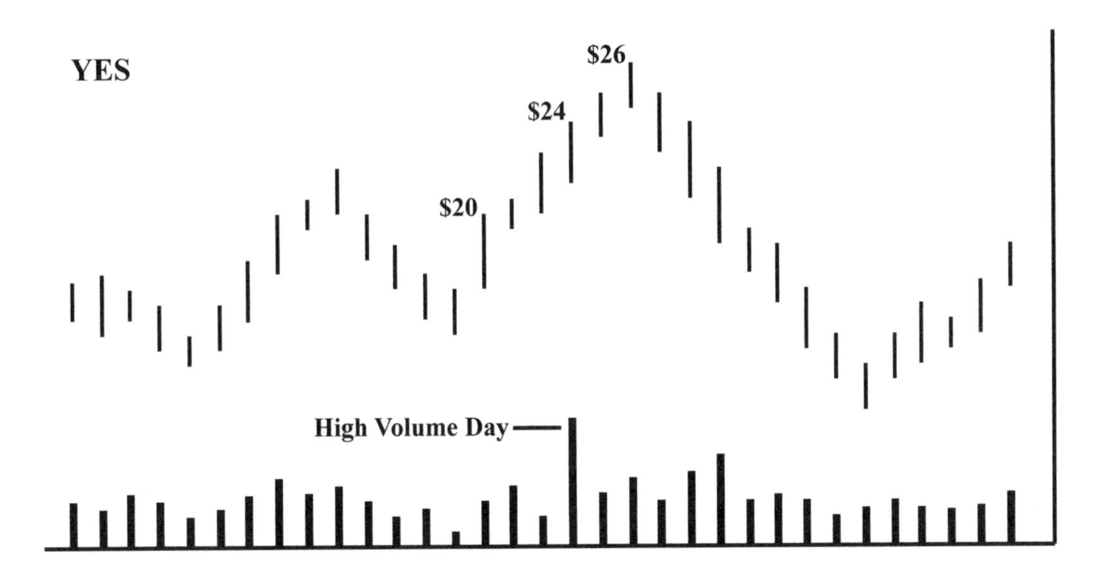

Figure 2-10: ***Real Price***

What happens after a real price has been established? Simple, the real price point becomes a gravitational point (until the next high volume day occurs) where prices, when extended beyond this point, will invariably want to head back to. Try to think of what happened that very day when there was so much activity. In an upward scenario, there were many buyers looking to get into the stock. They thought that that particular price was the real deal. After the high volume day, the stock goes up and subsequently begins to retrace.

Why does it retrace? Well, some of those that got in at the real price may be taking some money off the table and selling shares. The stock may in fact dip below its real price and this is where it can get exciting: people who missed out on the real price day and will want to take advantage and get in at the real price or even lower. What happens with the stock after that? It goes up. The same would work for a stock on its way down. The most important thing to remember is that real price helps you grasp the lay of the land and with real price, you have a sense of a price center point from which any movement beyond real price is merely an extension with prices bound to head back sooner or later. One way to think of it would be to imagine nailing one end of a rubber band to real price and stretching it as the stock's price moves away from it. The more you stretch the rubber band, i.e., the further price gets away from real price, the greater its tendency to "snap" back. One of the keys here is to have patience; try to "be the market" and get in as close as possible to real price.

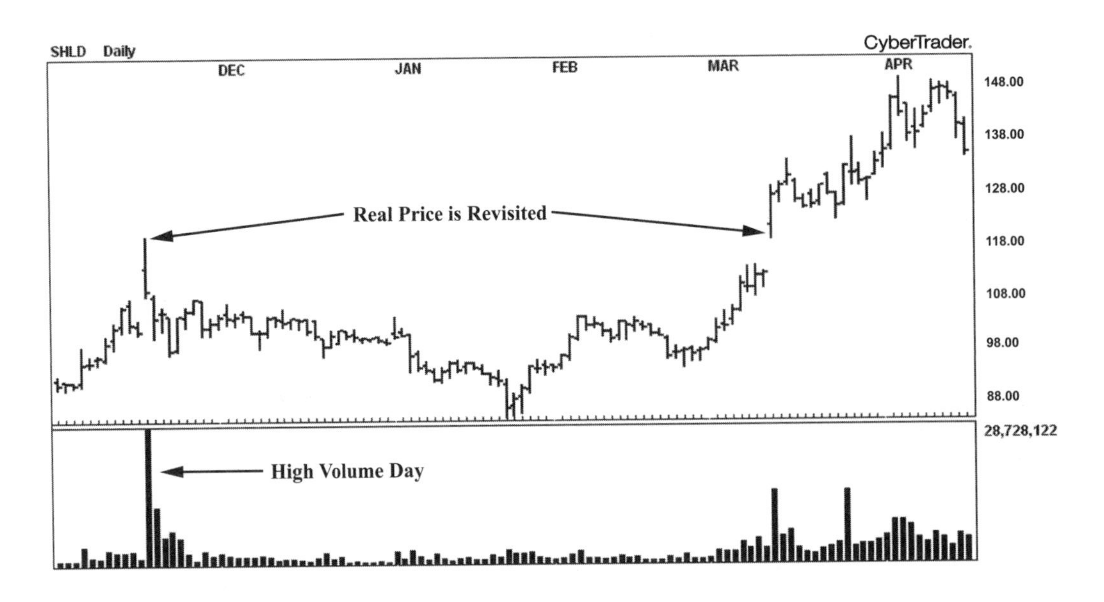

Figure 2-11: ***Real Price - Sears Holding Corp. (SHLD)***
On November 17, 2004, SHLD had a high volume day with 28.7 million shares traded and a high of $119.69 being established (real price). This price point was revisited on March 11, 2005 with SHLD blasting through the real price point on a relatively strong volume day (15.4 million shares).

You might wonder what real price might be on a high volume day if you have a wide price spread; that is, if there is a wide difference between the high and low for that particular day. Answer: simply look at the trend. If the stock is in an uptrend, your real price is the high for the day; downtrend, the low for the day.

Volume off the Top

When you have high volume occurring after the top of a prolonged uptrend it's important to note the price destruction that may follow. A price decline on high volume, coupled with wide price spreads spells trouble in paradise as it indicates that large operators are quickly getting out of the equity (in technical terms, it's regarded as "volume off the top").

> ***Definition:*** **price spread** – the difference between an equity's high and low trading price for a given time period, usually expressed in a daily amount with a vertical bar.

The reaction after the sell–off will give you the confirmation: if the equity goes up on anemic volume, count on seeing a change of the current trend that will take this equity down deep. Take a look at Figure 2-12. Notice how volume lightens during retracement after the "volume off the top" downdraft.

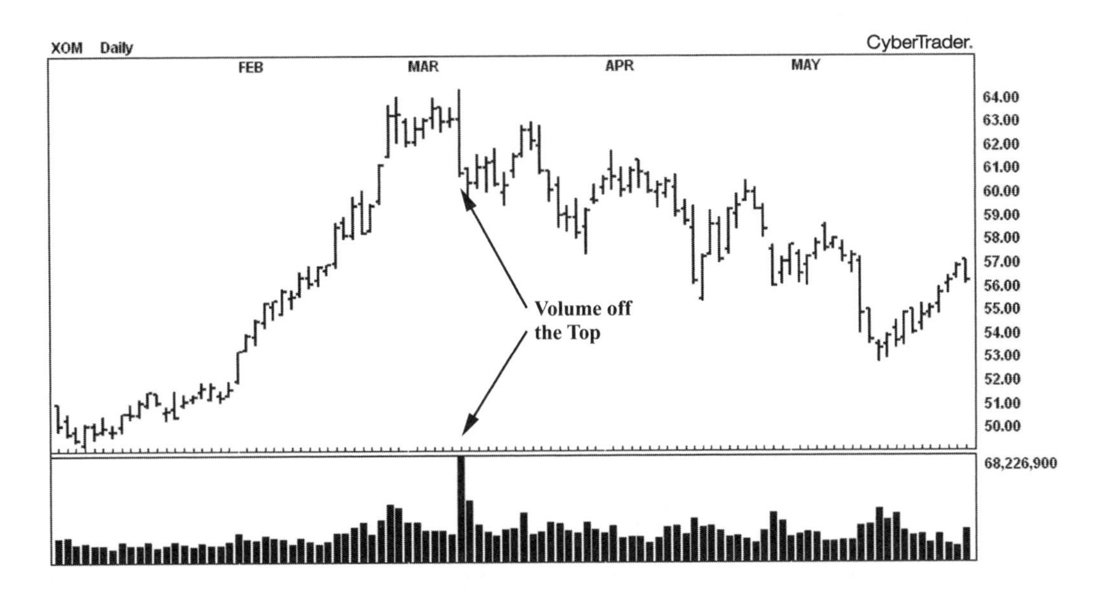

Figure 2-12: ***Volume off the Top - Exxon Mobil Corp. (XOM)***

Intraday Volume

Occasionally, you might catch yourself watching a stock midday and want to compare its volume to a previous day's volume, the only hitch is that the trading day is not yet over and waiting until the market close at 4 pm might not be the right answer. Your best bet is to estimate or project what volume will be at the end of the day by simply extrapolating the current volume to what it should end up as using the hours that have elapsed in the trading day. The only downside to using this approach is that you're presuming that volume throughout the remainder of the trading day will behave just as is did through the hours that have already elapsed.

An example (assuming your equity trades in an American market): you're watching YES and at noon YES's trading volume totals 3 million shares. From here the calculation is simple. Take volume of 3 million and multiply it by the amount of hours in the trading day (6.5 hours) and then divide by the hours that have elapsed so far (at noon, 2.5 hours would have elapsed). In short, 3 million times 6.5 divided by 2.5 equals 7.8 million shares. With this calculation, you are estimating that volume will total 7.8 million shares by the end of the day.

Remember:

Volume x 6.5 (hours in trading day) / Hours that have elapsed = Projected Volume.

Accumulation, Mark-up, Distribution and Mark-down

There are four phases to every stock or market move. You must remember that someone always has more information than you. When an operator (mutual fund, hedge fund etc.) draws up a battle plan, he will have a starting point and a set of parameters to guide him to a finish point.

Below are the four phases and their respective impacts on volume.

Accumulation phase - Accumulation always takes place at bottoms over a longer period of time. Operators build up their holdings during this phase in anticipation of selling at higher prices. An operator may want to buy 2 million shares (his "line") and that can take anywhere from six weeks to two years. The operator will do his best to accumulate the stock quietly and also keep its price down until he's satisfied with his inventory level. This commences the start of the mark-up phase.

Volume: Expect trading activity during accumulation to be very quiet; it almost seems as if the stock were dead. You may on occasion see a small spike in volume and price here or there, but price quickly settles down and so does volume. These occasional spikes are usually operators buying sizeable blocks but doing their best to keep their accumulation *quiet*.

Mark-up phase - The operator first makes sure there are plenty of positive press releases coming out, like the stock and/or company is doing great and that super money managers like Warren Buffet have been buying the equity (do you really think that information comes out by mistake when Warren is buying? No way. It comes out when Warren wants it to come out). This starts the mark-up phase in the equity. There are many folks that will charge right into those equities and push them higher. The operator may then buy more stock to push the equity beyond breakout levels to create buying frenzies pushing prices even higher. When there is a correction in the market, the operator will sit at certain price levels and support his equity by buying up shares. When the correction is over, the operator will continue to mark his equity up until his plan is fulfilled or until there is a development that alters his strategy.

The mark-up phase can go on from a few months to years. During this period, it's important to realize that the amount of cause that was built up before the move into the mark-up phase will give you a heads-up whether to look for a fast move through the mark-up and into the subsequent distribution or a more prolonged move where cause has been built up for years as in the gold market from 1999 to 2002.

Volume: Trading activity escalates and stays relatively strong throughout a stock's mark-up phase. The escalation starts with operators (after having decided they've accumulated enough) picking up their efforts to start a commotion to create interest from the public with the stock through press releases and stock flipping. Volume begins to wane around the time the crowd is finished responding and further attempts to excite buying have minimal effect.

Distribution phase - The distribution phase typically starts before the equity sees a top. Operators know they can't get out of large positions quickly. If you look at any of the large funds, they may have at any one time millions of shares in certain equities. They start working their way out of their positions when their price goal has been met, they have new information that they don't like or the equity's position is too large in relationship to the rest of their portfolio. This phase has stock moving from strong to weak hands.

Volume: Just as with the accumulation phase, volume here is very quiet. Operators unload their shares, do it quietly and do their best to unload while prices are still high. When operators reach the end of their load and see prices begin to slip, they may have a quick sale where they drop or dump what's left of their position; you'll see this in a serious downdraft day (also a seriously heavy volume day, i.e., *"volume off the top"*) which typically begins the mark-down phase.

Mark-down phase - The end of the distribution phase leads to the mark-down phase. Mark-downs are accomplished not by mutual funds (because many of them are precluded from selling short) but by hedge funds and other large operators such as private equity funds. What precipitates mark-downs? The need for an equity to have a new line of ownership support. With the largest holders having gotten out, operators understand that new ownership for an equity will start at a much lower price (almost seems like natural physics) and to that end will help drive the price down by shorting and selling into rallies and essentially make good $$ along the way. Just as operators have a plan for the way up, they also have a plan for the way down. Imagine how a hedge fund could enjoy the best of both worlds by driving the equity up, unloading, then driving the equity down . . . and then doing it all over again!

Volume: Both volume and price activity are much more intense during mark-down as opposed to mark-up. They're more intense because there really isn't a solid line of ownership for stabilization. But you can bet on this: once volume quiets down and price stabilizes, you can expect the accumulation to crank up and commence the price cycle once again.

The diagram in Figure 2-13 illustrates the four phases in action.

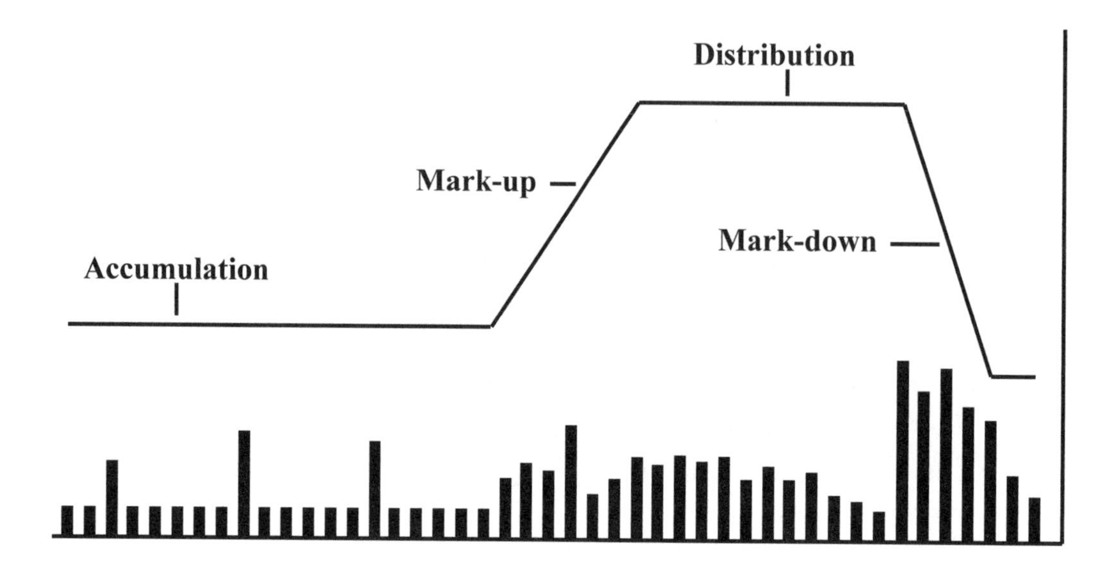

Figure 2-13: ***Accumulation, Mark-up, Distribution and Mark-down***

Something else to keep in mind: the more time a stock spends in the accumulation phase, the more protracted the mark-up phase will be – the longer the cause, the longer the effect! What a great segue to our next chapter!

3

Cause & Effect

Shallow men believe in luck.
Strong men believe in cause and effect.
~ Ralph Waldo Emerson

Cause & effect is a term you'll often hear me use on my broadcasts. Typically I'll say something like, ". .where cause equals volume and effect equals price, . . .". I'll get into this phrase shortly but right now I want to hone in on the power and meaning behind "cause & effect".

Paradigm with Power

Many people have a tough time grasping the concept; at times I'll even fail to notice evidence of cause and then suddenly, effect will come out of nowhere and thrust its trump card right in my face. One thing's for sure, you can't have one without the other. When you have cause, you have effect that follows and if you notice effect (or some result) invariably there was some form of cause that made it be. To fundamentally grasp the truth behind cause & effect, it helps to split the phrase into its individual terms.

Cause

> ***Definition***: **cause** – that which produces an effect or result; that from which anything proceeds, and without which would not exist.

What creates cause? The answer depends on what you are talking about. If you wish to address our very existence and what causes it, well that just may entail a very lengthy and esoteric discussion and more than likely, we might never arrive upon a concise answer. If you want to address a more pedestrian topic such as, "what creates lightning", cause in this case is much simpler to determine. For our purposes here in *Timing the Trade* though, we'll do our best to stick to cause as it relates to stock trading.

The English philosopher John Locke put it best, "cause is a substance exerting its power to act, to make a thing begin to be."

The "substance" insofar as we're concerned with *Timing the Trade* is the force that makes prices move. That force is primarily trading volume. What causes trading volume? Fluctuations in supply and demand. What causes fluctuations in supply and demand? Fear and greed. Yes, fear and greed, the primordial elements that have bolstered the upward surge of mankind. These elements, inasmuch as they constitute "cause", propel the world's capital markets and create shifts in supply and demand which in turn create surges in trading volume, invariably causing prices to move.

Effect

Definition: **effect** – a result or consequence.

Simply put, effect is what comes around or arises from cause. In the case of negative and positive ions crashing into each other in our earth's atmosphere, the resulting effect of this action is lightning. Where there is strong or surging volume in trading activity, the effect should be a definite increase or decrease in price (direction of price will depend on the direction(s) of supply and demand forces).

A Perfect Union

Let me use a simple real life example to bring meaning to cause & effect. Let's say that you begin training for a swimming competition that's basically a three-mile race. You begin training however only two weeks prior to the race. During this time frame you essentially build two weeks of cause. Now think of how you might perform if you begin training two months before the competition. With two months of cause, your performance should be better compared to how you might perform with only two weeks of training. Well, let's imagine that you train for an entire year, swimming three miles, practically every day. Your performance should be explosive! Well, it is these types of real life relationships that you should be looking for in the markets. If you note exploding volume, you should then expect a wide price spread as prices move with volume. Figure 3-1 includes an example of volume and price moving in a cause & effect like manner.

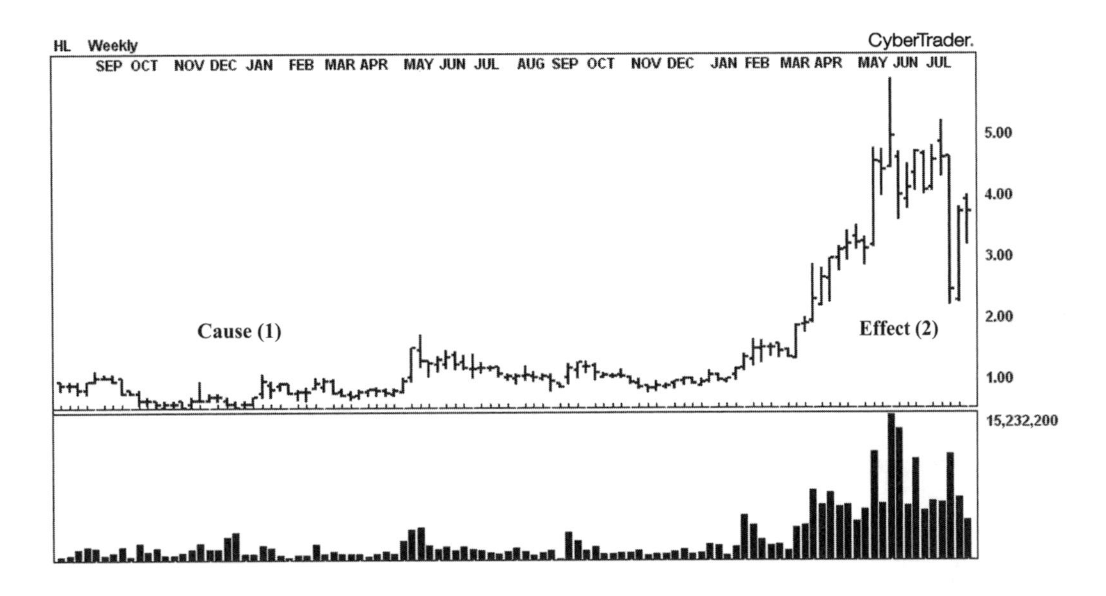

Figure 3-1*: Building Cause – Hecla Mining Company (HL)*
(1) *You can see this huge area where we have built cause for a larger move.*
(2) *And here is where effect rolls in and rolls in with force. See how strong volume accompanies the strong move in price.*

Notice how price stays relatively the same for a number of years and then there is a sudden surge in volume and subsequently a move in price. This "waiting" period is basically where cause has been building up, building steam, accumulating angst. An important thing to note here in this example and others where cause & effect come into play: with greater cause should come greater effect.

Road Signs

In the previous chapter, I touched on the importance of price moving in a certain lockstep with volume. Do you remember strong volume accompanying strong movements in price with retracements being accompanied by lighter volume? That principle applies here too with cause & effect. If you have effect but do not have sufficient cause, i.e., price moving on little or no volume, the road sign should be more than obvious: *the move isn't real.*

If you notice "one without the other" or in other words, effect with little or no cause, there is simply something wrong with the genuineness of the price move.

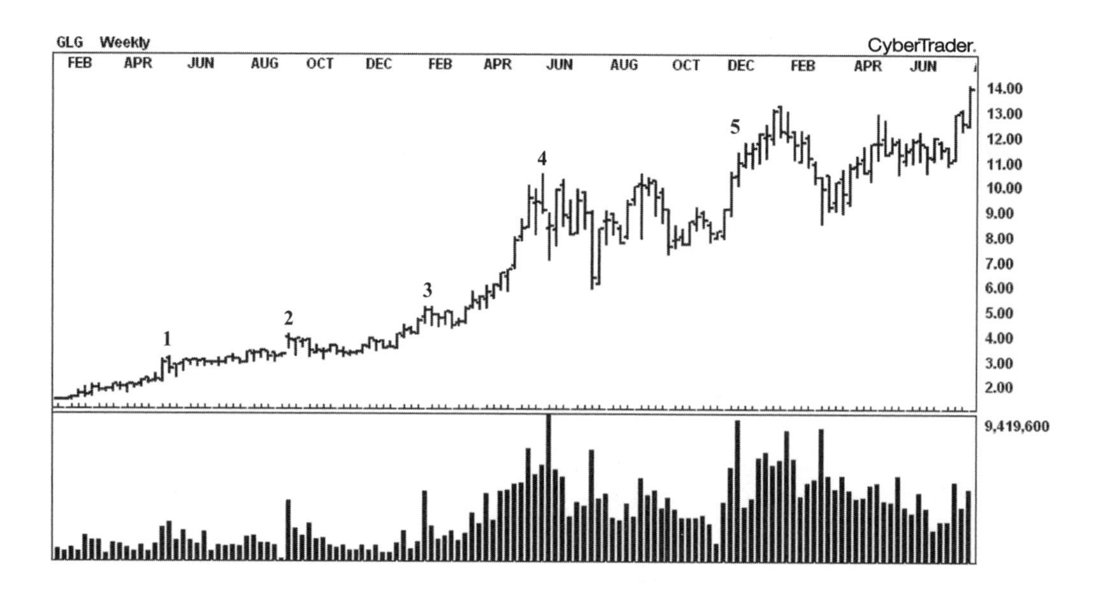

Figure 3-2: ***Cause & Effect – Glamis Gold Ltd. (GLG)***

(1) *The week of May 18th – we get a high of $3.00 with volume of 2.1 million shares; this is just after the gold market made its March 2001 bottom.*

(2) *We build four months of cause then expand on price and volume the week of September 21st, hitting the $4.00 mark with volume moving up to the 3.8 million share level.*

(3) *We build three months of cause then expand on price and volume once again going to the $5.12 price point with volume of 4.4 million shares the week of February 8th.*

(4) *May 24th – we reach the price point of $9.97 with volume of 7.3 million shares for the week. You can make the case that GLG had been building cause for a year to step up the price to a higher level.*

(5) *We build seven months of cause between May and December, then see its price take off the week of December 20th with volume totaling 9.1 million shares.*

Another Angle on Cause & Effect

Yet another way to look at cause & effect is to consider the element of time as being cause and then surges in volume and price movement being effect. Take a look at Figure 3-3 and note the cause that takes place prior to explosions in price and volume.

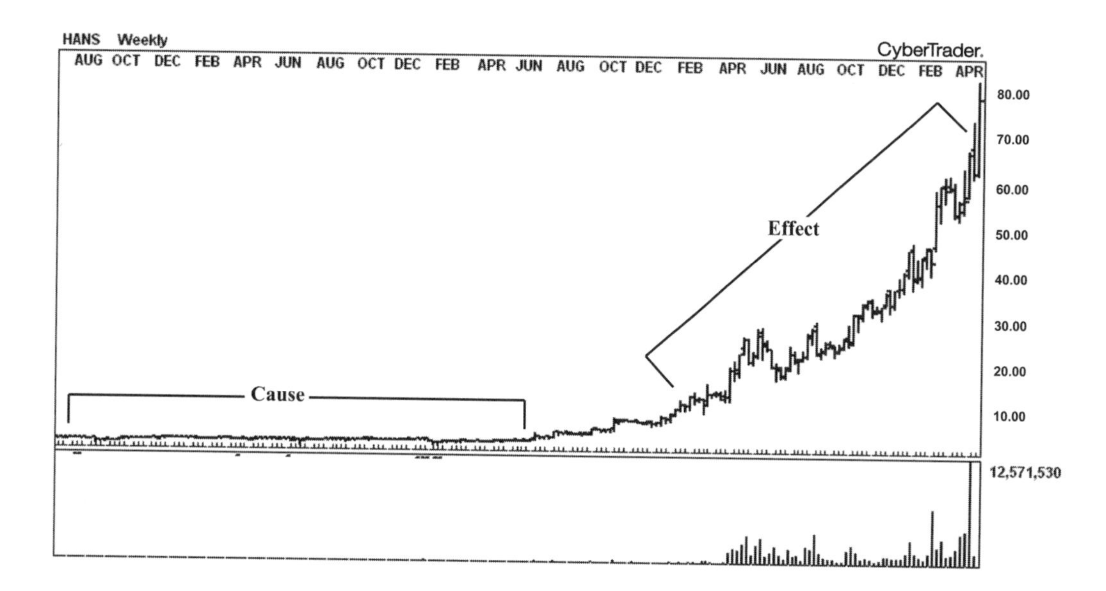

Figure 3-3: ***Time Equaling Cause – Hansen Natural Corp. (HANS)***

Interestingly enough, instances of time equaling cause can mark the accumulation phase of a stock with operators silently building their inventory followed by the mark-up phase (effect).

4

Candlestick Charting

Better to light a candle than to curse the darkness.
~ Chinese Proverb

Centuries ago, the Japanese created a visual aide to track historical prices of rice futures as they were traded in the local markets. Over time, the system became known as "candlestick charting" since some of the basic symbols used therein somewhat resembled candles in a graphic sense. The use of candlestick charting was pretty much confined to the Orient until the early 1990's when it was largely introduced to the Western world by Steven Nison in his excellent book entitled, *Japanese Candlestick Charting*. His book is still regarded as the premier go-to source on candlestick charting and I recommend it to anyone wanting to further his or her understanding on the topic. In this chapter, I will discuss some very basic candlestick shapes and formations.

The Basic Candle

You'll note in Figure 4-1, the basic candle is comprised of a body and possibly one or two shadows or wicks. What makes the basic candle so powerful is the amount of information it can convey. With one candle symbol, you can derive the opening, closing, high and low price for a given session or for that time frame that the candle is representing (a candle can be used to express activity in a minute, hour, day, week, etc.). For our purposes, we will be focusing on candles that represent a single day's activity.

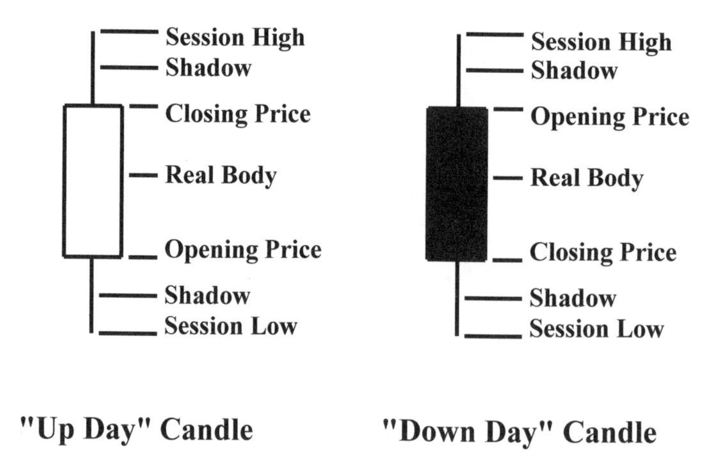

Figure 4-1: ***Basic Candle Structure***

Now let's break down the basic candle. As you can see in Figure 4-1, the opening and closing prices are first determined by the overall shading of the candle. On an up day or session, the candle's body will be white or clear and the closing price will obviously be above the opening price. Conversely, a down day is represented by a dark or black candle body and similarly the closing price will be below the opening price. Where the opening and closing prices are exactly located depends on the length of the body of the candle. Thus, a candle with a long body denotes a significant spread between the opening and closing prices.

Price movement beyond the opening and closing prices is denoted by the shadows on a given candle. Shadows represent price movement to the high and low points for the given session.

A point to remember is that not all candles have shadows. The trading price in a given session can fluctuate between the opening and closing prices and in those cases, the opening and closing prices become the highs and lows for the day.

Another point to remember is that not all candles have bodies. These candles without bodies are known as doji (pronounced dough-gee) and denote situations where the opening and closing price are virtually the same. We will discuss doji later in this chapter.

Finding Meaning in Candlesticks

Don't forget that there is a major battle that goes on everyday in the markets and the opposing forces are the bulls and the bears. Bulls fight to push the price up and bears fight to push the price down. The beauty of candlestick charting is that it can paint a fairly accurate picture of the day's fighting between the bulls and bears. A long white candle will tell you that the bulls have won the session where a black candle will demonstrate the bears as the victors. Situations where there is no clear winner (or a stalemate) between the bulls and the bears are represented by candles with virtually no bodies or doji, as mentioned earlier.

Candlestick charting was derived in an era where martial chaos reigned supreme, at least in relation to the current state of our society, where warring between Japanese feudal lords seemed to be practically an everyday occurrence. It's not terribly surprising that many formations in candlestick charting took on very colorful names with emotional and even militaristic overtones. Names as *hanging man*, *three soldiers advancing* and *dark cloud cover* are such examples. You can easily see how candlestick charting can be artfully entertaining upon mastery of its interpretations, but believe me, it can be a powerful weapon when used in conjunction with a sound trading plan.

Basic Formations

There are many possible formations in candlestick charting. What I'll be presenting here are formations known as reversal patterns. Why are reversal patterns important? They are crucial for the simple reason that they signal a change in direction and if you are aware of a change in price direction then you are in a better position to enter or exit a trade. It is important to note that reversal patterns or formations consist of two or more consecutive candles (typically, the candle which follows the reversal pattern provides verification of the move). Here are certain reversal patterns that are not only important to understand, but also relatively easy to spot.

Engulfing Patterns

There are three basic engulfing patterns and they are known as a bullish engulfing pattern, a bearish engulfing pattern and a last engulfing pattern. Before illustrating these patterns, you should note the following guidelines regarding engulfing patterns (these I have excerpted from Steve Nison's book):

(1) The market has to be in a clearly definable uptrend or downtrend,

(2) Two candlesticks comprise the engulfing pattern. The second real body must engulf the prior real body (it need not engulf the shadows), and

(3) The second real body of the engulfing pattern should be the opposite color of the first body.

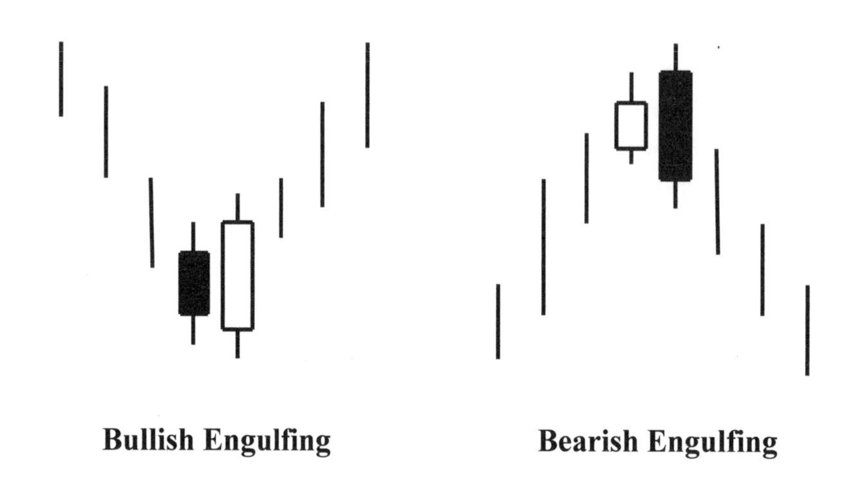

Figure 4-2: *Bullish and Bearish Engulfing Patterns*
A bullish engulfing pattern typically occurs near or at the end of a downward move and signals a change in direction to the upside. Its price movement is such that it "engulfs" the previous day's price spread (body) between the opening and closing prices (here we are using daily price moves), which in essence becomes the last move of the previous downtrend. This diagram includes a typical bullish engulfing pattern. Notice the upday (white candle) engulfing the previous down day (black candle).

The bearish engulfing pattern consists of a black candle engulfing a white candle after a significant uptrend.

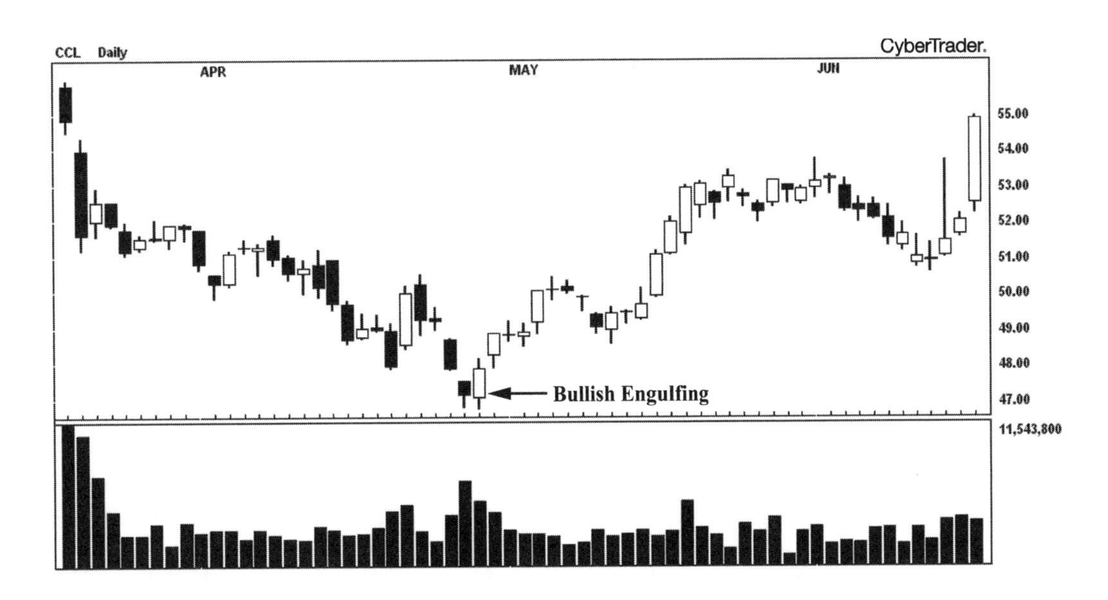

Figure 4-3: ***Bullish Engulfing Pattern - Carnival Corp. (CCL)***
This bullish engulfing candle occurs after a downtrend, engulfs the prior trading day's black candle and signals the start of a price move to the upside.

Conversely, a bearish engulfing pattern occurs near or at the top of an upward move and signals a change in direction to the downside. Check out Figure 4-4.

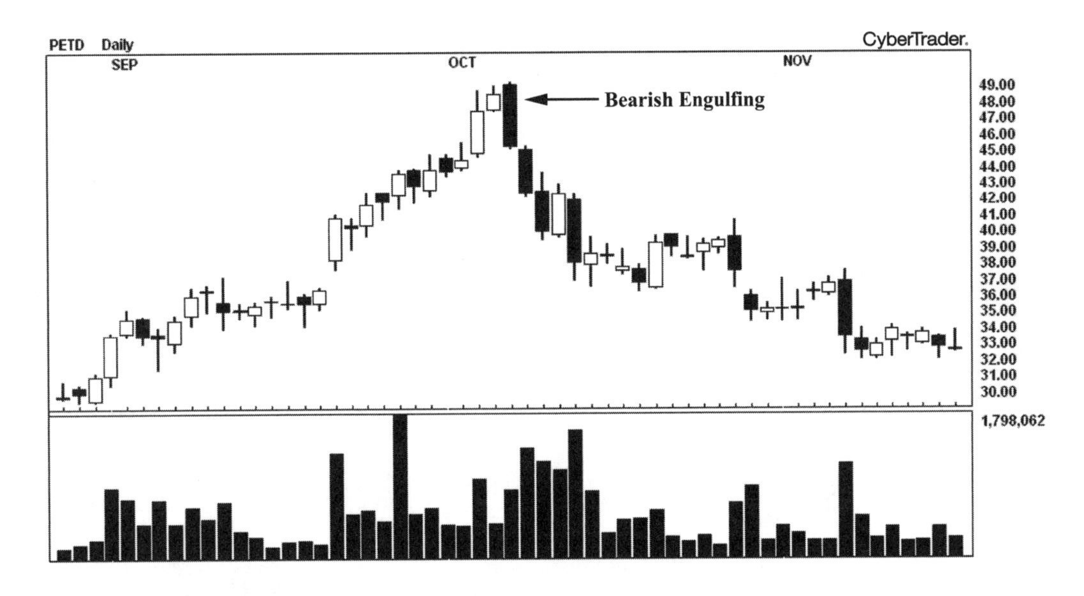

Figure 4-4: ***Bearish Engulfing Pattern – Petroleum Development Corp. (PETD)***
This bearish engulfing candle occurs after an uptrend, engulfs the prior trading day's white candle and signals the start of a price move to the downside.

You might be wondering what goes on in an engulfing situation. Well, essentially there is a strong turn in the tide of price direction. Let's say that in a protracted downtrend, for example, on one day the bears win out with the closing price being well below the opening price (i.e., a dark body), the following day begins with the opening price occurring below the previous day's close, but all of a sudden there is a change in the undercurrent with the bears suddenly being overtaken by bulls and the bulls win out the day by a landslide. The degree of the bulls' victory can be measured by the spread between the day's opening and closing prices. Compare that upward spread to the previous day's downward spread and you have a bullish engulfing pattern.

The last engulfing pattern we will discuss is named just that: *last engulfing*. It is very similar to the bearish and bullish engulfing patterns, the only difference is that the candle's color is similar to the trend: a white candle (up day) for an uptrending stock, a black candle (down day) for a downtrending stock. It's important to note that the candle being engulfed is the opposite color of the engulfling candle.

Imagine an uptrending stock experiencing a down day (dark candle). The bears begin the next day with an opening that's below the previous day's close - the bears are really happy. The bulls however won't give in just yet and end up having relatively a monster day with the close exceeding the previous day's opening price. Unfortunately for the bulls, the glorious day turns out to be their "last hurrah" (at least for the time being) as they watch the bears convincingly take over on the following day and continue to rip the bulls apart. Check out Figure 4-5 for examples.

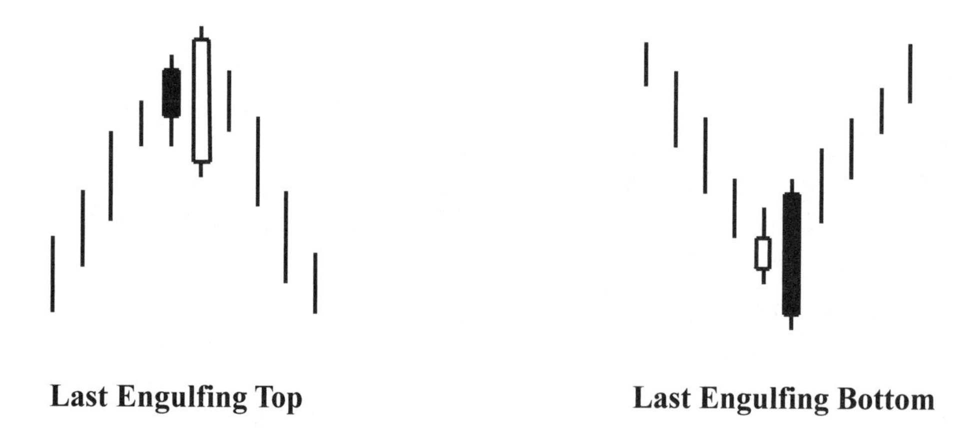

Figure 4-5: ***Last Engulfing Patterns***

Hammers and Hanging Men

In candlestick charting, hammers are basically formations with small bodies and relatively larger or longer shadows. They typically occur at the bottom of a downtrend. Three rules that apply to hammers are:

(1) The real body is at the upper end of the trading range. The color of the real body is not important.

(2) A long lower shadow should be twice the height of the real body, if it's not twice the height, it's not a hammer.

(3) It should have no, or a very short, upper shadow.

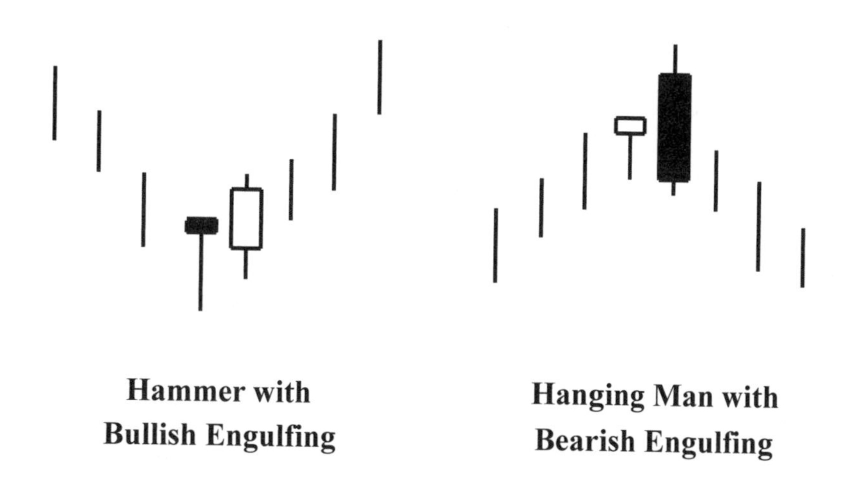

Figure 4-6: ***Hammer and Hanging Man***

Figure 4-7 includes an example of a hammer occurring at the bottom of a downtrend. Notice how the price activity seems to be "hammering" out a bottom.

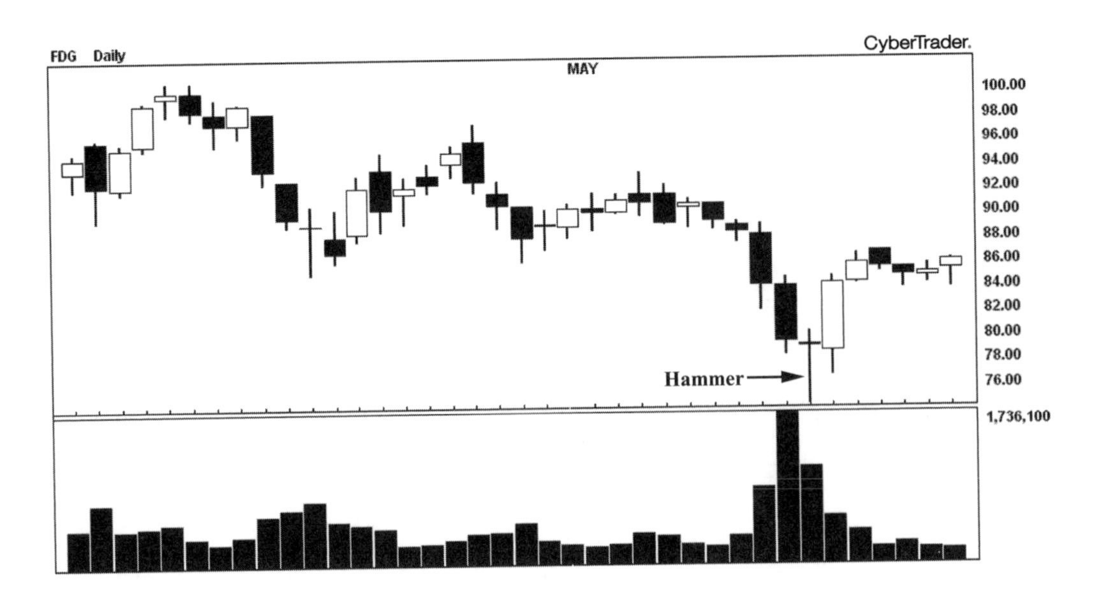

Figure 4-7: ***Hammer - Fording Canadian Coal Trust (FDG)***

In simple terms, a hammer is brought on by the battle that results between bulls and bears. At the bottom of a downtrend, the bears are basically pushing prices down, but somehow midstream they seem to run out of breath, virtually exhausting themselves. Here the bulls take over, push the bears out of the way and drive prices back up, claiming victory; the bears meanwhile lick their wounds and regroup to fight another day.

The hanging man formation occurs at the very top of an uptrend. The rules applicable to hanging men are the same as those for hammers; by themselves, hanging men and hammers look very much alike (take a look at Figure 4-6). Their dynamics are somewhat similar but I'll get to those in a minute.

Note the hanging man candles in Figure 4-8.

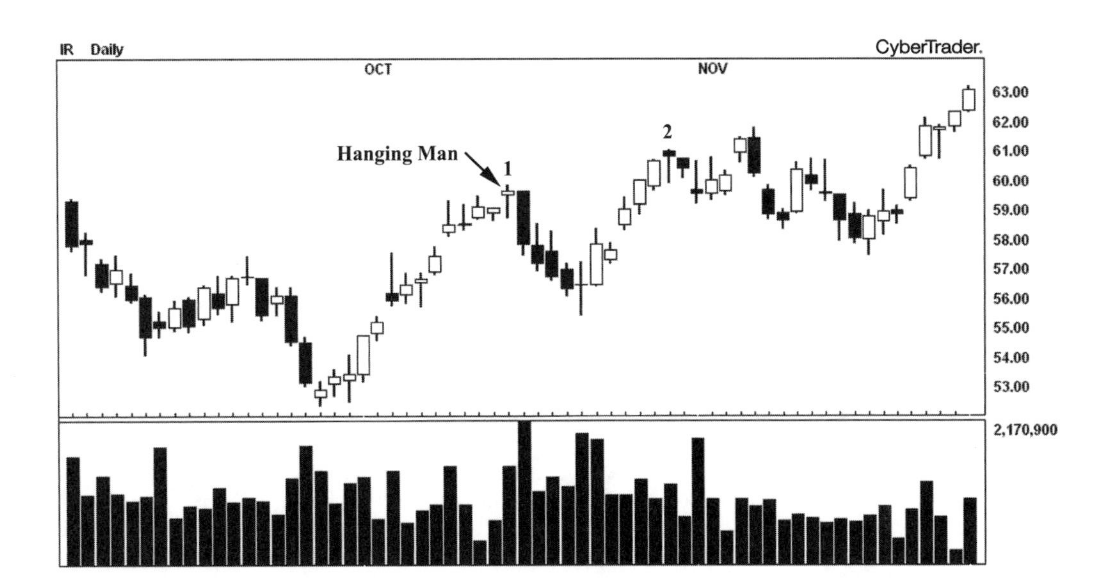

Figure 4-8: ***Hanging Man – Ingersoll-Rand Company Ltd. (IR)***
(1) *On October 15, 2003, a hanging man candle appears at the top of a trading range with volume totaling 1.5 million shares.*
(2) *On October 30th, we again have a hanging man but this time on lighter volume, 1.2 million shares.*

In a hanging man situation, prices open at or very near the high for the uptrend and suddenly there is a substantial sell-off with the bulls doing their best to push prices back up. Typically at the end of the day you'll see a hanging man formation. The sell-off that occurs during the day does however signal uncertainty in price which is usually followed by bearish success in trading sessions that follow.

Hammers and hanging man formations can be useful in spotting trend reversals. Although they look pretty much the same in appearance, their dynamics are a bit different but still powerful when interpreted correctly.

Shooting Stars

Another reversal formation to look out for is the shooting star. This particular candle represents an exhaustion move, much like a hammer, that comes at the end of an uptrend. With the bulls having won several battles on the way up, they have a final blowout and before the session is over, the bears come in and fight hard to win the day with the closing price coming in close or below the day's opening price. Figure 4-9 illustrates basic shooting star formations.

Shooting Stars

Figure 4-9: ***Shooting Stars***

Shooting stars do represent trading opportunities inasmuch as they signal a reversal of the current trend. The key here is to follow a truism regarding these formations: shooting stars usually get tested; this means that once prices have fallen after a shooting star, the shooting star's price level is revisited by the equity. On the revisit, volume becomes key. If volume is light (as compared to the volume on the day of the shooting star), expect the equity to turn around and the shooting star's validity to be confirmed. If volume is heavy, the impact of the shooting star may be negated with prices surpassing the shooting star's level.

> ***Definition***: **test** – the act or occurence of a stock reaching a particular price point.

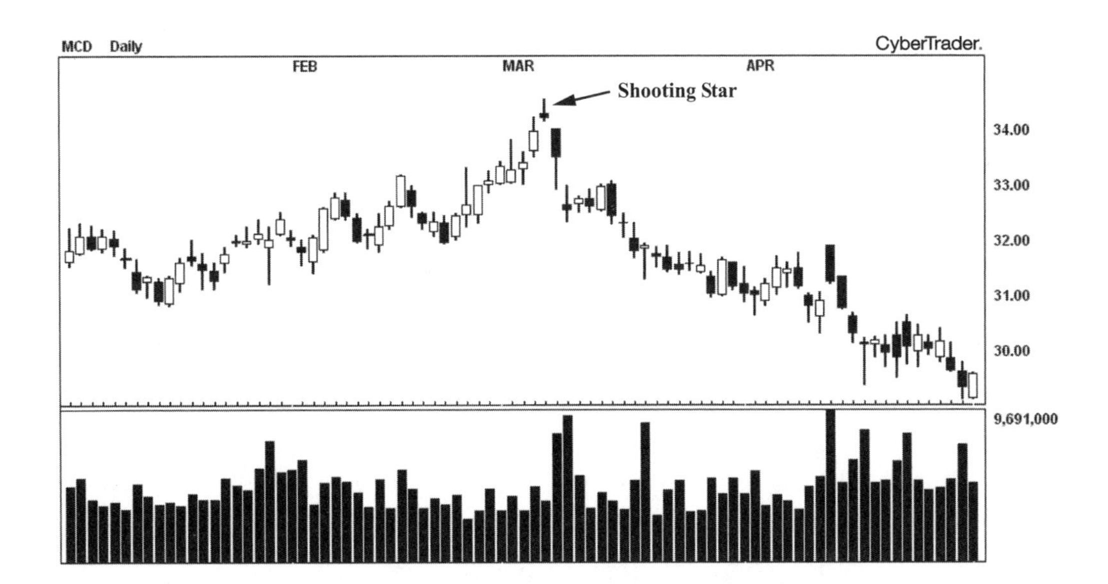

Figure 4-10: ***Shooting Star – McDonald's Corp. (MCD)***
On March 7, 2005, MCD gives us a shooting star signaling a change in the overall trend. The candle in this case comes very close to being an island top candle (similar to a shooting star); however, its low for the day is below the previous day's high.

Figure 4-11 below gives us a clean example of an island top. Note how the previous and subsequent days' trading highs do not meet or surpass the island top's low.

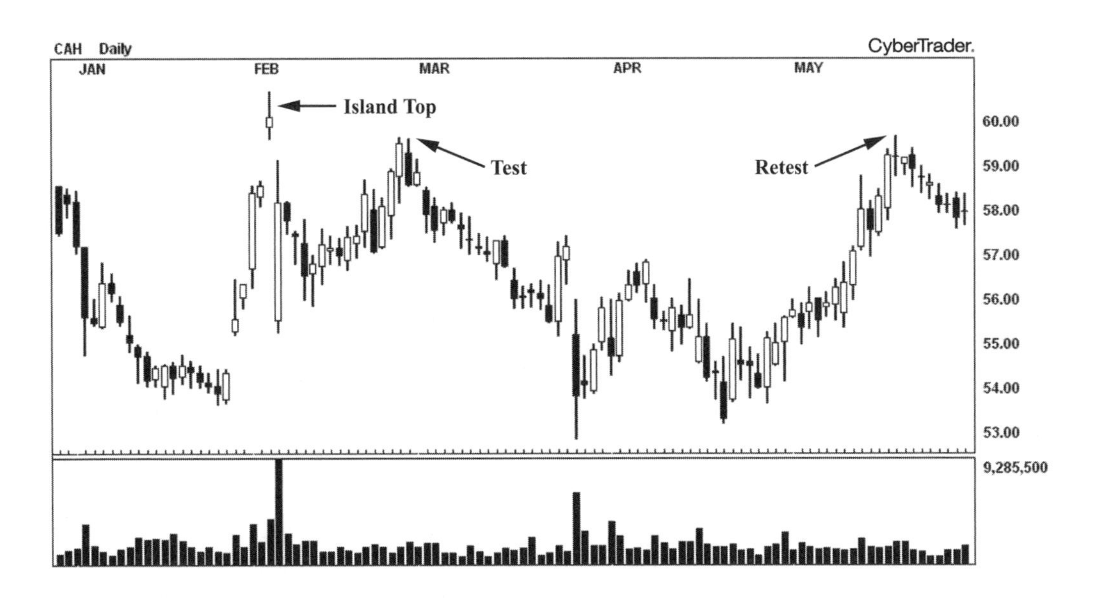

Figure 4-11: ***Island Top – Cardinal Health, Inc. (CAH)***

This is a classic example of an island top candle. Just as with shooting stars, island tops create resistance levels and usually get tested. In this example, the island top gets tested twice.

Doji

If you're a regular listener of my daily radio shows, you've often heard me use the term doji. A doji is merely a particular candlestick that is formed as a result of the opening and closing price occurring at or very close to one another. During the trading period, the price spread may be small or significant but regardless, the trading session ends with the closing price equaling or coming close to the opening price. Figure 4-12 includes examples of doji. Notice how the shadows may come in different lengths but the bodies are virtually nonexistent. One thing to remember: the longer the shadows, the more significant the doji. Why? Because there was more money lost during the session. The more powerful the doji, the more powerful the signal!

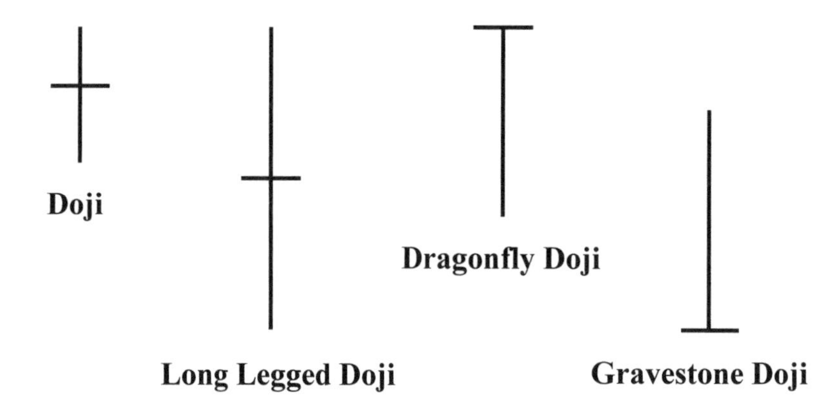

Figure 4-12: ***Examples of Doji***

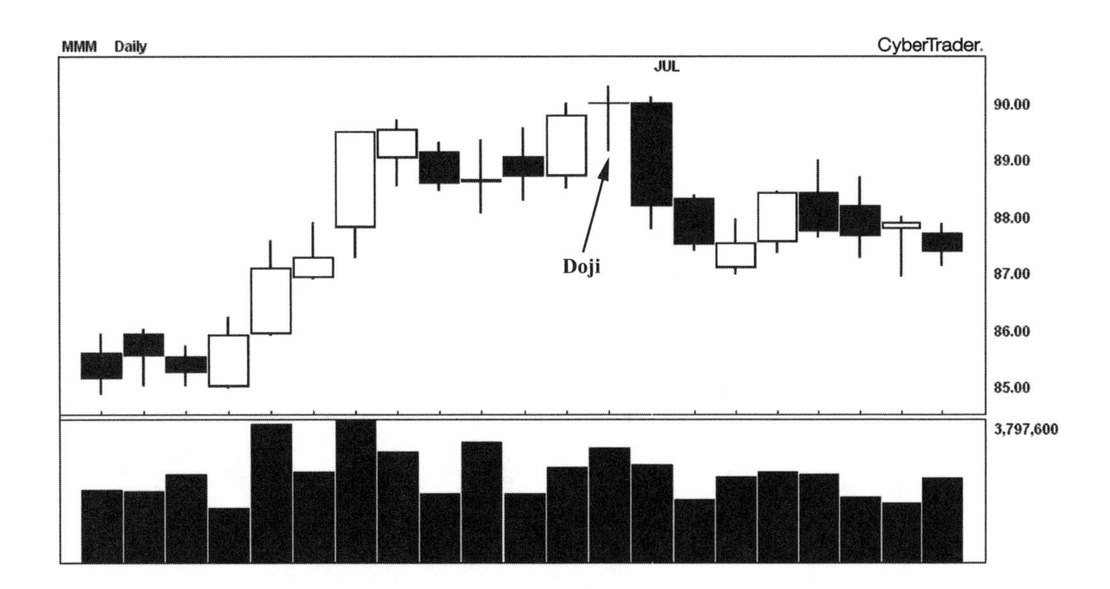

Figure 4-13: ***Doji – 3M Company (MMM)***
This beautiful doji signified a virtual stalemate between the bulls and the bears and marked a change in the tide.

Why are doji so important you might ask. Well, in real terms they represent the result of a battle that has ended up in a stalemate or a tie. What that potentially means is that the current trend, be it bullish or bearish, is running out of steam and that the opposing force is ready to take over. A doji can also mark a point of resistance or support where it will take a sudden surge to overcome the price point.

You will however run across, from time to time, doji that do not mark the end of a trend. In fact doji, particularly in downtrends, can mark the midpoint of the downward move. The midpoint is not exact, i.e., you don't count the number of trading days leading up to the doji and assume that there are a similar amount of days left in that particular trend. However, the doji does end up residing close to the middle of the trend's price range.

Since the doji doesn't precisely mark the end or midpoint of a trend, it is very important to supplement your identification of doji with other clues, such as a subsequent reversal formation and, of course, volume! If you note volume behaving in a manner indicative of a change in tide, i.e., drying up, then there is further validation that the doji is in fact signaling a change in tide or direction.

Keep these points in mind when encountering doji:

(1) If volume is heavy, prices should continue further into the trend, and

(2) If volume is light, prices should turn around, a true reversal.

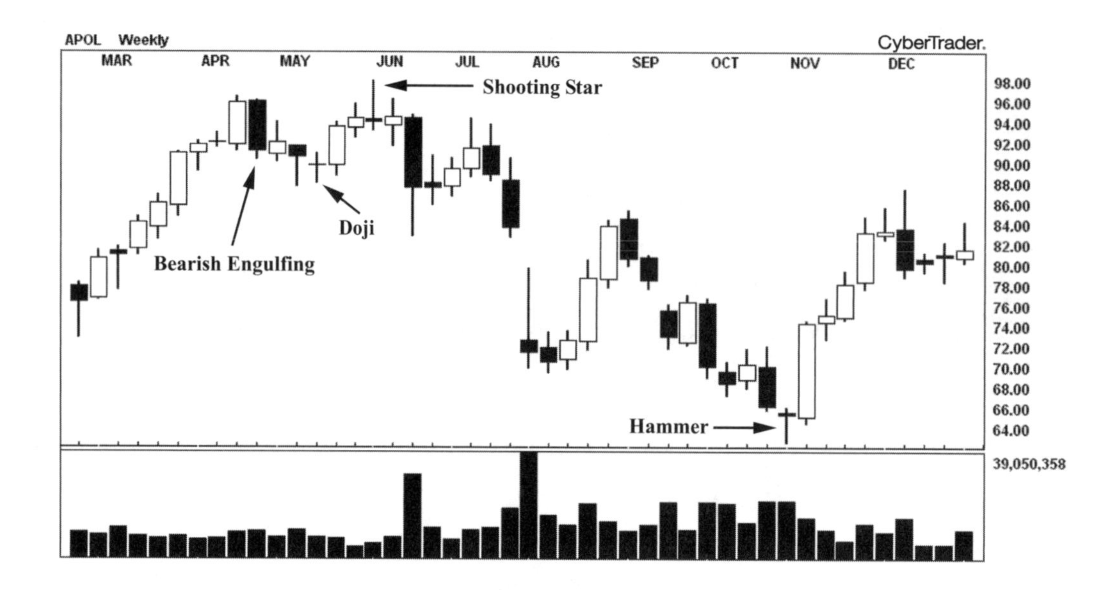

Figure 4-14: ***Various Reversal Formations – Apollo Group, Inc. (APOL)***

5

ABCs

Simplicity is the ultimate sophistication.
~ Leonardo DaVinci

In virtually all significant stock price movements, a recurring pattern emerges that consists of a strong move (thrust) followed by a retracement (breather). I use a simple designation to characterize these locomotion-like energy patterns. I call them ABC structures. An interesting thing however: once you understand ABC structures, you'll not only spot them in stock and market moves, you'll also see them everywhere in life. I can't stress enough the value of utilizing an ABC approach as your foundation to understanding how the market moves. Once you fully grasp this concept, you'll never look at the market or even life, for that matter, the same way again.

The Basic ABC Structure

What are ABC structures? Well, first of all ABC is a term I designate to a price formation as it moves in up or downward trends (on my radio show and in my seminars, you'll often hear me refer to these patterns as either ABC ups or ABC downs). We know that stock prices do not move in a straight line either up or down. In a defined trend, they expand (solid move), contract (retrace), and then continue their movement in the overall trend. I simply assign the letters A, B and C to points in these price movement patterns to assist in their identification. It's important to note that the ABC points are taken from the lowest lows and highest highs (i.e., extreme price points) and *not* the opening or closing prices; I'll get into this in greater detail in Chapter 6 - *Fibonacci*. Figures 5-1 and 5-2 include basic ABC structures for a move up and a move down, respectively.

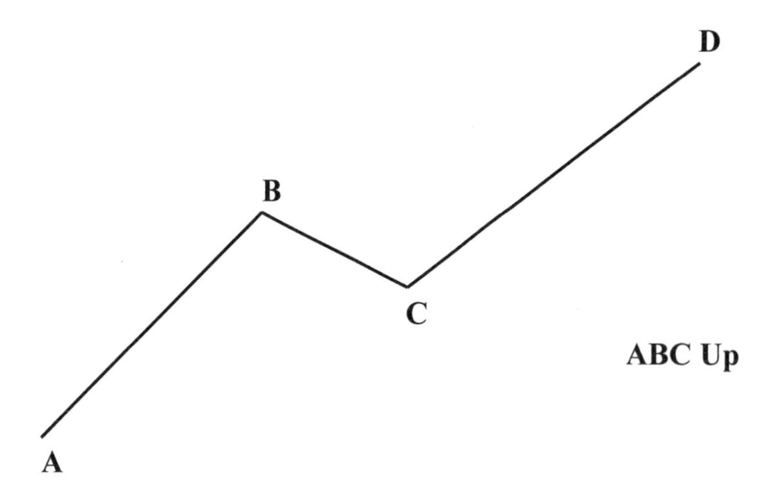

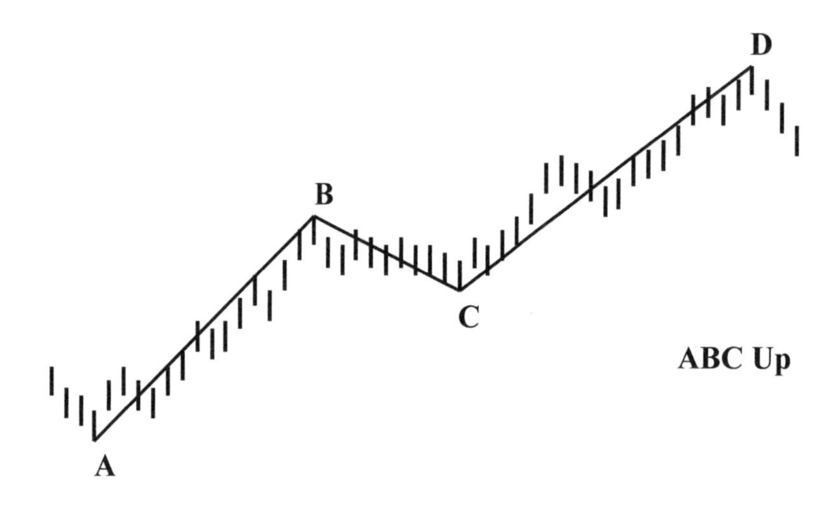

Figure 5-1: ***ABC Up Structures***
As you can see, A in these formations marks the beginning of the move and B represents the end of the first leg. The C point is the end of the retracement, essentially where the price stops, turns and continues in the general direction of A to B. The D point happens to mark the end of the continuation.

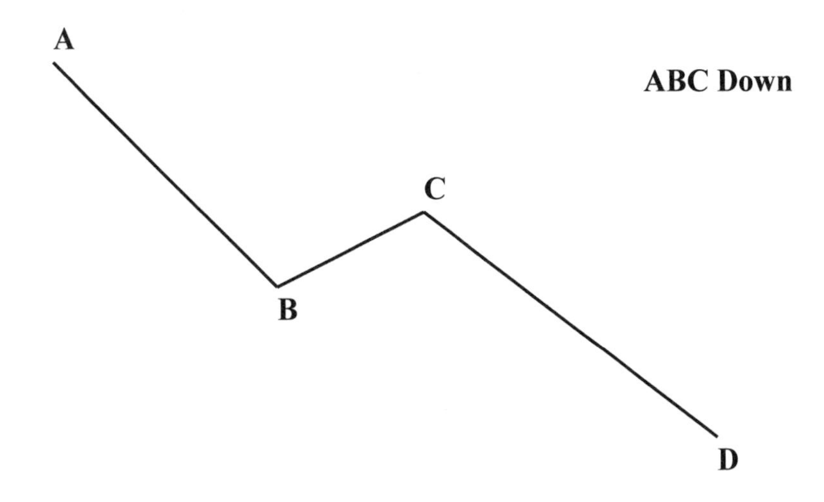

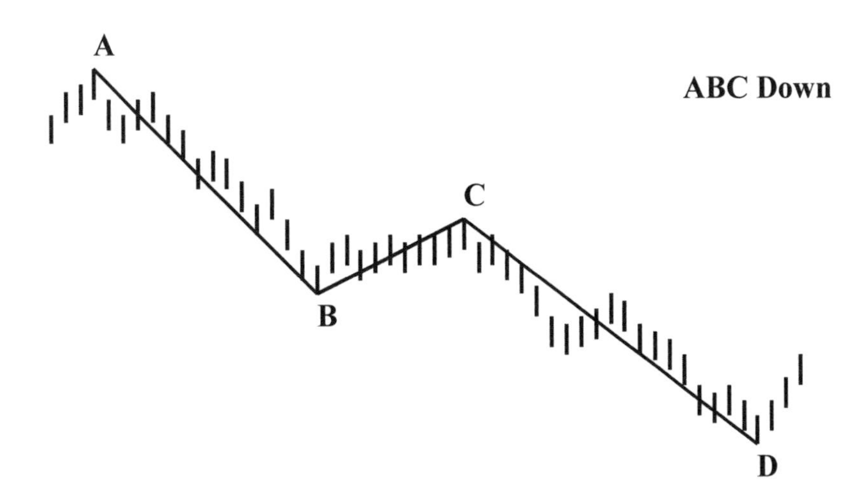

Figure 5-2: ***ABC Down Structures***

Once you understand the ABC structure, you will always be looking for it in the market and in life. Each and every one of us goes through ABC structures. So, the concept you are about to learn in the market will not be totally foreign to you; but once you understand the structure in the stock market, you'll be able to recognize where you may be in your own life, be it in an expanding, contracting, or consolidating phase.

The Importance of ABC Legs

Each leg of the ABC structure is critically important to the entire formation as a whole. What follows is a brief summary outlining each leg's contribution to our understanding of an ABC price move.

A to B

The A to B leg, as I mentioned before, marks the first move of an overall continuing move, either up or down. As it relates to A and B, the distance between the two, or spread in price, becomes important for two reasons: the distance helps us calculate a projection for a continuation (expansion theory) after the C point has been reached (i.e., the C to D leg), and the A to B distance also helps us calculate a retracement to the C point (contraction theory) using Fibonacci ratios (discussed later in a separate chapter). While addressing the first reason and before covering Fibonacci ratios, we will assume that the A to B leg will equal (in distance and price) the C to D leg.

To repeat: A to B = C to D.

So, if A to B = 10 points, then C to D should equal 10 points as well.

The expansion equation applies to ABC ups and ABC downs. Take a look at Figure 5-3 and Figure 5-4, respectively.

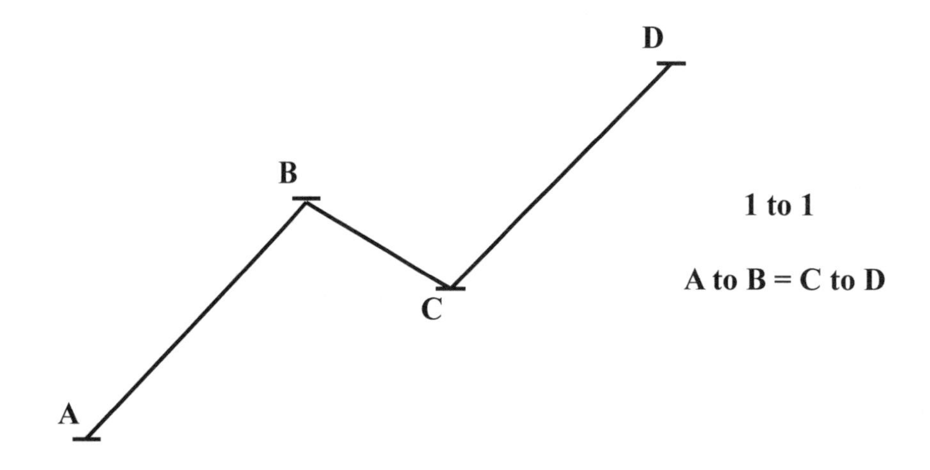

Figure 5-3: ***ABC Up Expansion***

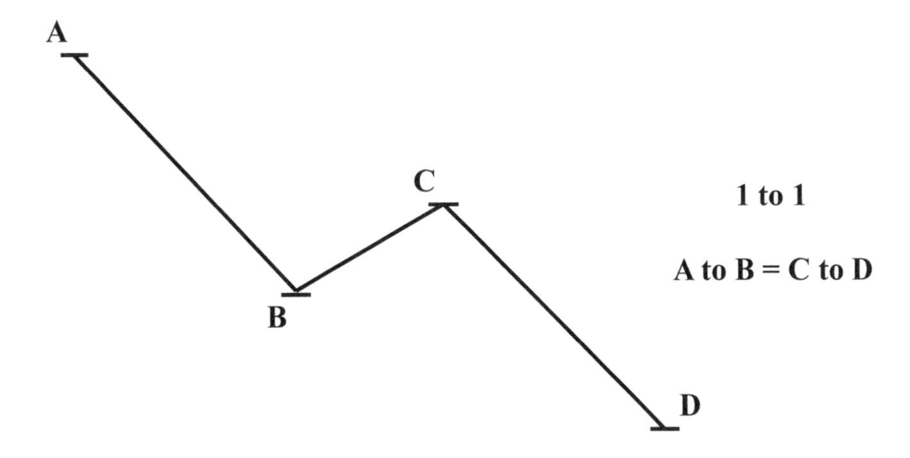

Figure 5-4: *ABC Down Expansion*

Does A to B always end up equaling C to D? No. It will depend primarily on the retracement of B to C, in particular, to what extent does the retracement occur? This will be further discussed in the Fibonacci chapter that follows.

The A to B leg is also important insofar as volume is concerned. Why? Because volume here will give you the first heads-up that the ABC structure is forming (through strong or accelerating volume). Going forward, the A to B volume will act as a benchmark for future volume fluctuations, particularly lighter volume during the B to C leg that will confirm the development of the ABC structure as well as the presence of quality volume.

B to C

The B to C leg is important inasmuch as it signals or predicts how much price will expand from C to D. The prediction element is very much tied into Fibonacci analyses and as such the relationships between the retracement levels and the potential price movement from C to D will be outlined in the upcoming chapter.

For now, however, we should note that in addition to the degree that price retraces from B to C, volume during this move is extremely important. Why? It is during this retracement that I look for lighter volume. Lighter volume during a retracement comprises quality volume and quality volume is paramount to *Timing the Trade*. Price action with this type of volume behavior represents genuine price movement. In simple terms, you have an initial price explosion with volume (or drop depending on direction) followed by a breather on lighter volume (retracement). The B to C leg is essentially the breather and it should be accompanied by lighter volume.

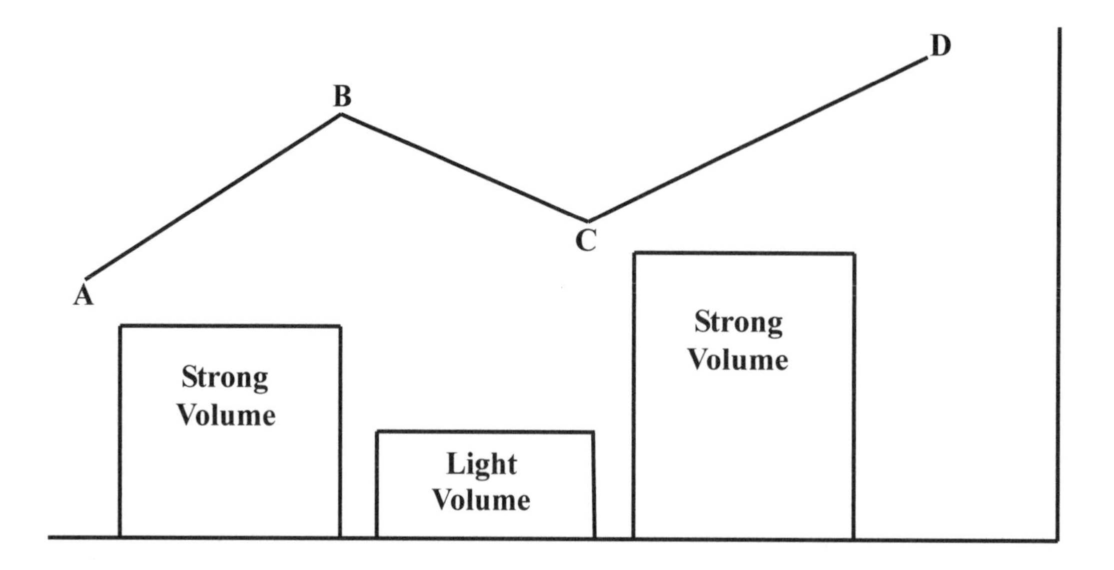

Figure 5-5: ***Light Volume on B to C Leg (ABC Up)***

The amount of the retracement, particularly in percentage terms, also gives you an idea as to how strong or weak the equity is. You can also see how the equity acted during its last ABC structure.

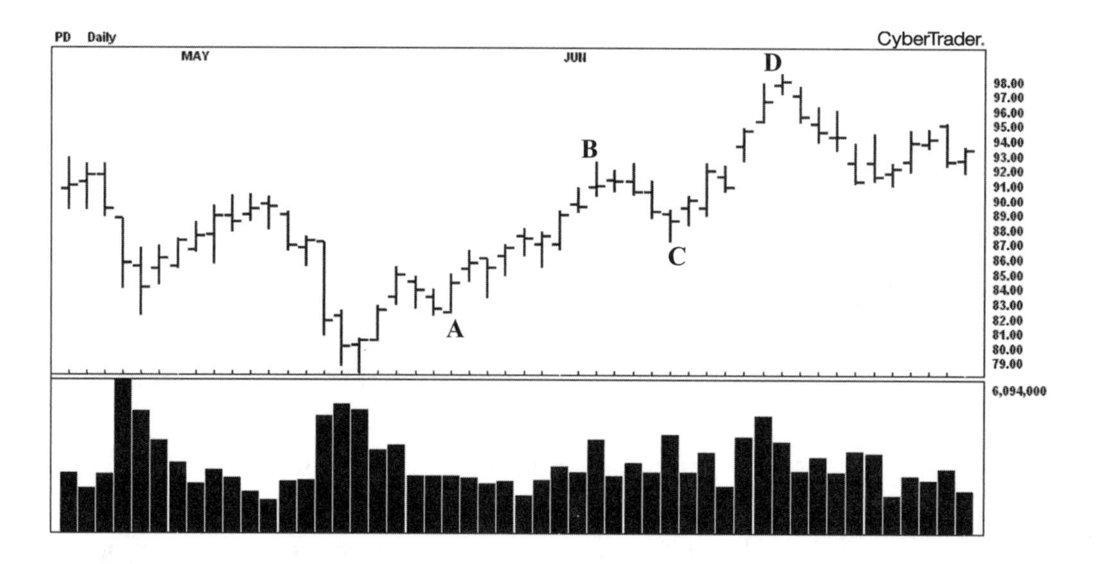

Figure 5-6: ***ABC Up – Phelps Dodge Corp. (PD)***

(A) *May 20th – the low for the day ($82.07) marks the A point of the ABC structure.*

(B) *June 3rd – the high of $92.46 marks the B point.*
(C) *June 9th – PD comes down to $87.11 and forms the C point.*
(D) *June 12th – PD expands to $98.42, its D point.*

If the B to C leg is not accompanied by lighter volume, then this should be a road sign to you that the overall move may not be genuine, quality volume is not present and you should probably stay away from this trade.

Figure 5-7 includes a diagram demonstrating light volume on a B to C leg in a downward move.

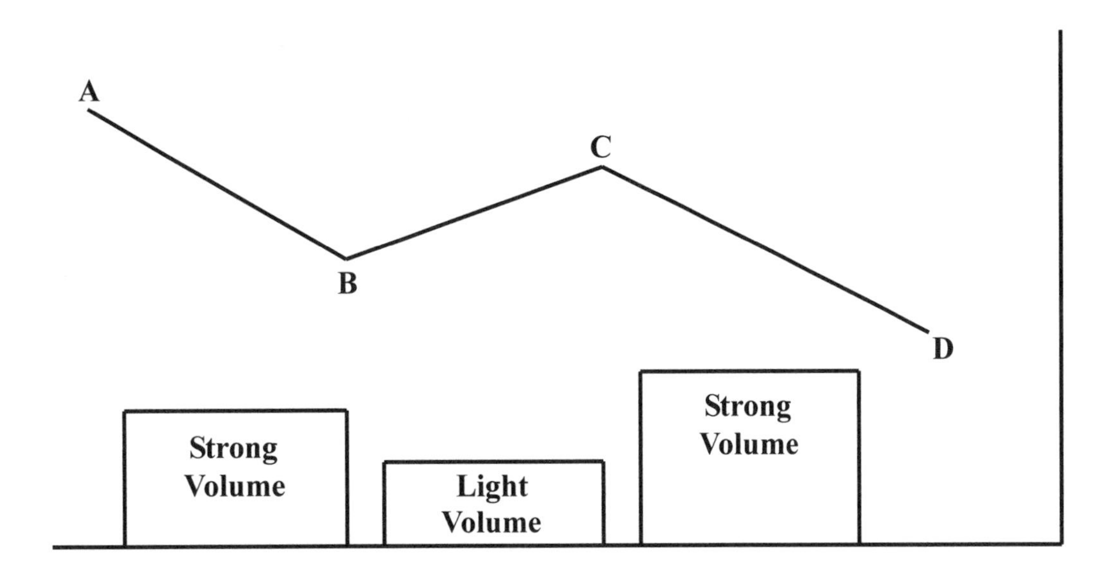

Figure 5-7: ***Light Volume on B to C Leg (ABC Down)***

Take a close look at the ABC Down in Figure 5-8, particularly the B to C leg and its light volume.

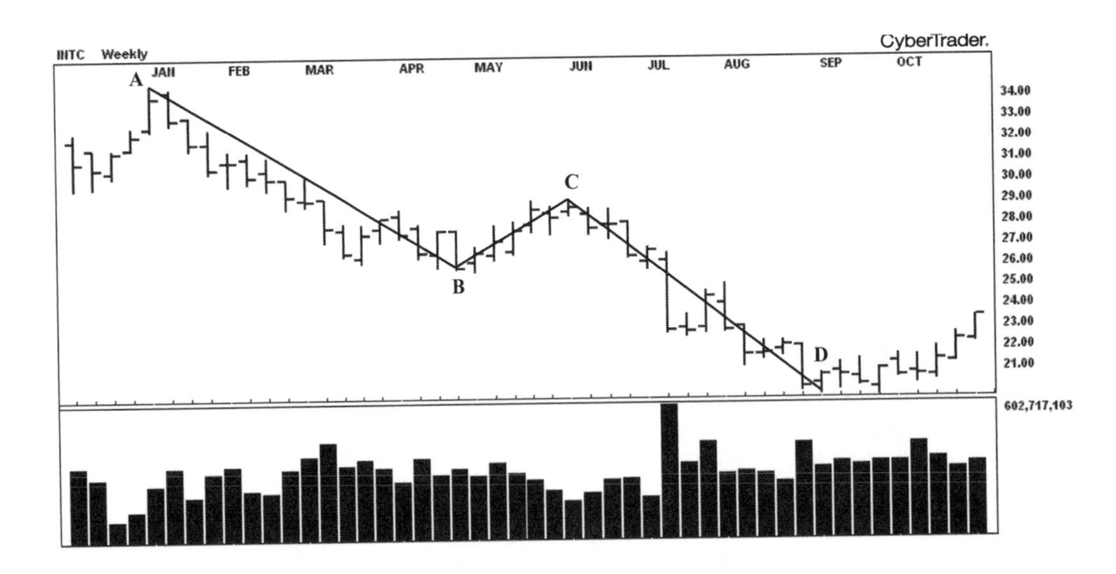

Figure 5-8: ***ABC Down – Intel Corp. (INTC)***
(A) *January 9th – the high of the day ($34.60) marks the A point.*
(B) *May 7th – the low of $25.61 marks the B point.*
(C) *June 11th – INTC moves up on much lighter volume to $29.01 and forms the C point.*
(D) *September 3rd – INTC expands to $19.85, its D point.*

C to D

The C to D leg is the final leg of the ABC structure. This segment is also referred to as the expansion leg. It is here where money is made, regardless if you are long or short. Throughout the C to D leg there is a continuation of price movement in the direction of the current trend.

During the C to D leg, it is important to take note of volume. If for whatever reason volume begins to dry up, you should become aware that the trend may soon be over.

Also, the C to D leg will pass the B point, a swing point (covered in a later chapter); in order for the equity to get its full price projection, it must pass the B point with volume.

Important: As an equity passes a B point, it must be on higher volume in order to potentially get a full price projection.

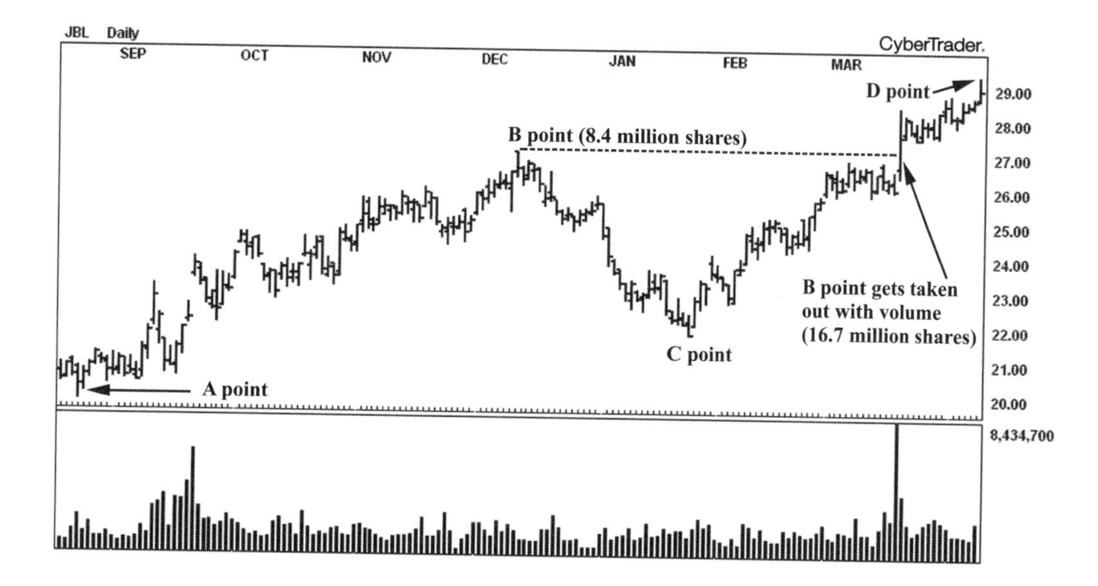

Figure 5-9: ***Passing a B Point with Volume - Jabil Circuit, Inc. (JBL)***
Here's a clean example of a B point being surpassed with stronger volume (i.e., B point taken out on volume). The B point in JBL's ABC structure is established the week of December 6, 2004 at a price point of $27.08 with 8.4 million shares being traded. After retracing to its C point on lighter volume (quality volume!), its B point is passed the week of March 14, 2005 on practically twice the amount of volume, 16.7 million shares.

Important: Throughout the book, I use *higher, stronger, lighter, lower,* etc. to qualify volume when comparing amounts. My rule-of-thumb minimum (or benchmark) for considering these terms is 10%, i.e., the difference between two amounts must be at least 10%, otherwise the two are *relatively* the same.

6

Fibonacci

The laws of nature are but the mathematical thoughts of God.
~ Euclid

"Who is This Guy?" Leonardo Pisano Bonacci was born in 1170, in Pisa, Italy. "Fibonacci" was actually a nickname given to Leonardo since he was a member of the Bonacci family. Today, "Fibonacci" is typically used when referring to his mathematical discoveries, particularly the numerical sequence for which he is best remembered.

In his book titled *Liber Abaci*, published in 1202, Fibonacci creates a mathematical problem which is basically responsible for the discovery of his mathematical sequence. The sequence starts with 0, 1, 1, 2, 3, 5, 8, 13, 21 and 34 and continues into infinity. Each number, except for the first two, is the sum of the two preceding numbers.

This sequence creates ratios that are incredibly powerful and insightful. The primary ratio is 1.618 which is essentially the number you approach as you take each number in the sequence and divide it by its preceding number. By taking .618 and subtracting it from 1, we get its inverse or .382. The .618 and .382 ratios drawn from this sequence occur in many aspects of nature, not to mention the evolution of mankind as well, including mathematics and science; even the great pyramids of Egypt are flooded with Fibonacci ratios in their designs and measurements. The reason I'm covering Fibonacci in this book is because his discovery is very important to what we are endeavoring to learn. If you grasp these principles now, you will later see their importance when you combine them with another important principle to *Timing the Trade* . . . . volume!

Now back to Fibonacci's mathematical problem. You'll be amazed at what was running through Fibonacci's head for him to stumble on his sequence. The translated excerpt below is taken from his book:

> *A certain man put a pair of rabbits in a place surrounded on all sides by a wall. How many pairs of rabbits can be produced from that pair in a year if it is supposed that every month each pair begets a new pair which from the second month on becomes productive?*

Rabbits!! Would you believe that rabbits are somewhat responsible for this tremendous discovery?!? Amazing!

Well of course we know that all the credit is due to Fibonacci, and as I've mentioned before, there are ratios that are derived from his sequence. Those that we are primarily concerned with are .382, .50 and .618 for price contractions (also referred to here as retracement levels) and price expansions. (Note: in my radio broadcasts and seminars, you'll hear me refer to these as "point three-eight-two", "point five-o", etc.).

Importance

How many times have you seen a stock start to take off? Were you tempted to buy it even though it had gone up considerably and it seemed as if it did not want to stop? How many times did you buy such a stock only to see it decline right away? Did you get out of it during its drop and then watch it creep back up? Frustrating, right?

Well, I have mentioned this before and I will mention it again: stocks do not go up in a straight line for the long term. They take breaks, breathers . . . they retrace. People in winning positions take money off the table (investors turn trader) and sell their shares. Before I get into the importance of Fibonacci ratios, you should understand what a retracement is.

Imagine a stock rising from $15 to $25 in a straight swoop. Will the stock continue going up? It could, but remember, never chase stocks! More than likely, the stock will take a brief dip. This we refer to as a retracement or a contraction. Basically the stock is "retracing" its price movement in a backward sense. A retracement can occur in a "long" or upward move as well as a "short" or downward move. What I like to see is a retracement on volume that is lighter than that of its previous move or the move that it is "retracing" (i.e., quality volume).

Fibonacci ratios, as I mentioned before, occur everywhere including nature, the universe, etc. but they also occur in retracements! Why? Well, humans beings are responsible for price movements in the stock markets. Humans are infinitely affected by elements in nature and the universe and these elements contribute to fear and greed in the marketplace! Fibonacci levels offer "targets" for stock retracements.

Another thing to take note of is that Fibonacci targets become leading indicators in that they are not entirely historical like the moving average convergence/divergence (MACD) or stochastics. You can take a move that has already occurred, look for the retracement and then your targets become predictors insofar as what the stock may do.

The universe is constantly expanding; however, this immense bubble does not expand in a progressively linear sense. What I'm saying is that the universe does not grow without stopping or contracting. Fibonacci attempts to offer some clarity to the contraction and expansion that goes on, and he has come closer to anyone through his ratios! I would love to get into a greater discussion regarding our universe and its endless expansion, karma and spirituality, but for now let's go over Fibonacci contraction and expansion theories as they apply to stock price movements and how you can benefit from them.

Contraction Theory

Upward Move

Using our rising stock example, let's say that YES, stops rising at $25. The last trend took YES from $15 to $25, basically 10 points. If we apply Fibonacci's contraction ratios to our 10 point trend, we come up with three amounts which when subtracted from $25, yield three different contraction levels.

A to B	Ratio	(1) Contraction Amount	B Point	(2) Retracement Level
$10	.382	$3.82	$25	$21.18
10	.50	5.00	25	20.00
10	.618	6.18	25	18.82

Figure 6-1: ***Fibonacci Retracement Calculations (Upward Move)***

(1) *The A to B amount of $10 is applied to the Fibonacci ratios to arrive at contraction amounts. In the first line of the table, $10 is multiplied by .382 to arrive at $3.82.*

(2) *Next, the contraction amount is subtracted from the B point to arrive at the retracement level. Continuing with the example above, the contraction amount of $3.82 is subtracted from $25 (B point) to arrive at the retracement level of $21.18.*

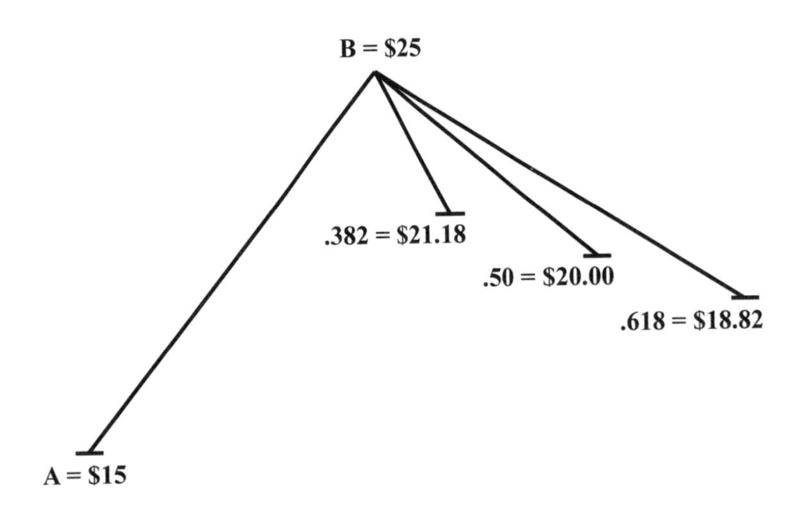

Figure 6-2: ***Fibonacci Retracement Levels (Upward Move)***

Here you can see that the three Fibonacci ratios, when applied to the initial 10 *point gain, yield three amounts. When these amounts are subtracted from the peak of the move (the "Focus" or B point), $25, three Fibonacci retracement levels are generated. In trading lingo, the levels are referred to as the .382 retracement, .50 retracement and the .618 retracement. Using our example where the last move was $10 and our stock reached $25, the .382 retracement would yield a $3.82 move which would make $21.18 our .382 target. The targets for the .50 and .618 retracements would be $20.00 and $18.82, respectively.*

Downward Move

It is important to note that the same method and application would hold true to a stock in a downward move; the only difference is that the amounts yielded from applying the Fibonacci ratios to the last move down are *added* to the bottom of the last move. Let's suppose YES has made a downward move from $25 to $15. Figure 6-3 below outlines the retracement calculations.

A to B	Ratio	(1) Contraction Amount	B Point	(2) Retracement Level
$10	**.382**	**$3.82**	**$15**	**$18.82**
10	**.50**	**5.00**	**15**	**20.00**
10	**.618**	**6.18**	**15**	**21.18**

Figure 6-3: ***Fibonacci Retracement Calculations (Downward Move)***

(1) *The A to B amount of $10 is applied to the Fibonacci ratios to arrive at the contraction amounts. In the case of the first line in the above chart, $10 is multiplied by .382 to arrive at $3.82.*

(2) *Next, the contraction amount is added (different from an upward move where the contraction amount is subtracted) from the B point to arrive at the retracement level. Continuing with example above, the contraction amount of $3.82 is added to $15 (B point) to arrive at the retracement level of $18.82. The targets for the .50 and .618 retracements would be $20.00 and $21.18, respectively.*

Figure 6-4 demonstrates the application of the Fibonacci retracement levels to a downward move and the resulting Fibonacci retracement levels.

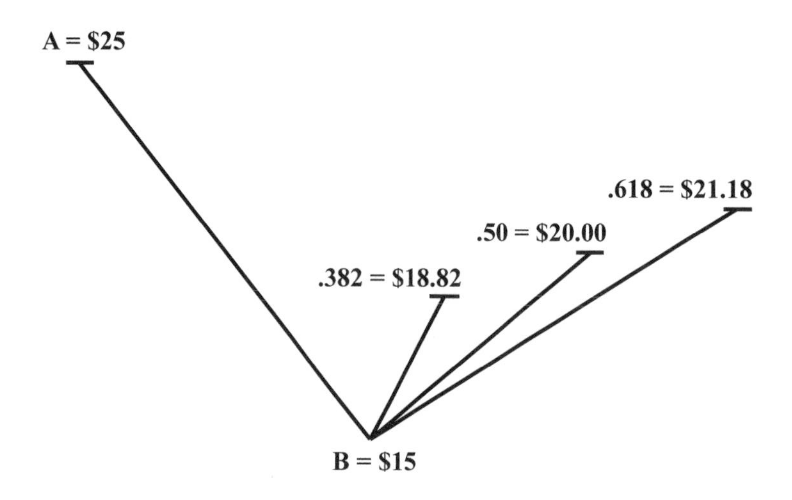

Figure 6-4: ***Fibonacci Retracement Levels (Downward Move)***
Note here that the retracement occurs in the opposite direction of the last move down. Keep in mind that ideally, you want to see lighter volume occurring during these retracement moves assuming you are short the stock or want to go short.

Price Axis Theory

Many times in my seminars, I'm asked, "Tom, which price point do you use to compute your Fibonacci levels? Do you use the open, close, high or low?" The answer is pretty simple: I use the intraday high or low, depending on which side of the trend I'm looking at. If I am looking at the end of an upward trend, I will definitely look to the last day of the trend and take its intraday high. If I'm looking at the beginning of the upward trend, I'll look to the first day of the trend and take its intraday low.

If I'm looking at a downward trend, I'll use the intraday high of the beginning of the trend and the intraday low of the end of the trend.

Figures 6-5 and 6-6 include an upward and a downward move, respectively. Note how we use the extreme ends of the moves to draw numbers for our Fibonacci calculations.

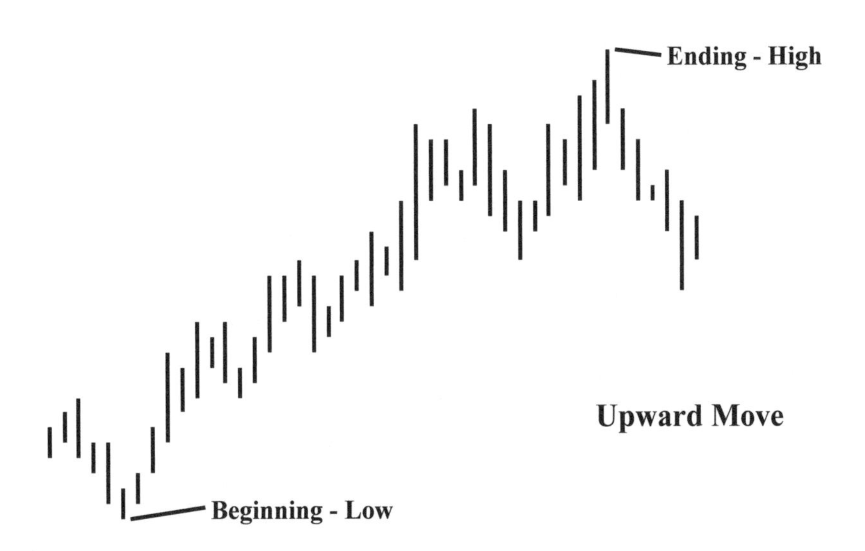

Figure 6-5: ***Price Axis Theory (Upward Move)***

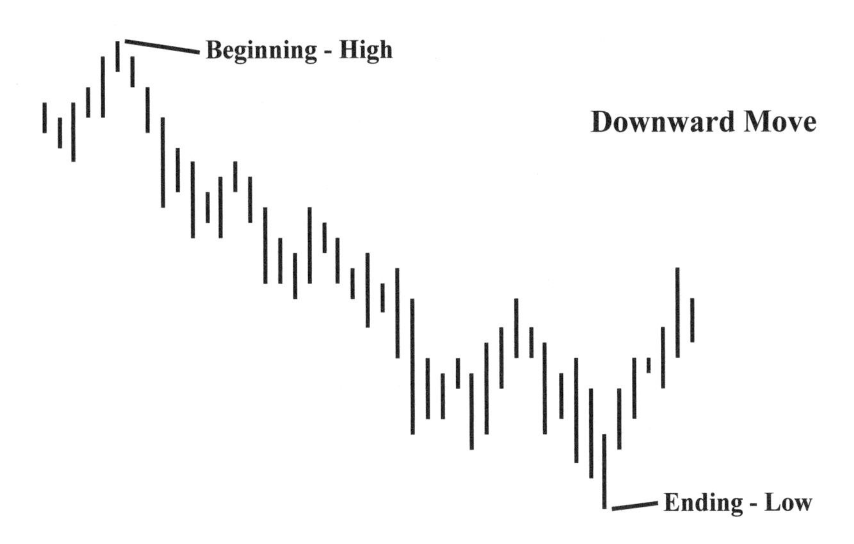

Figure 6-6: ***Price Axis Theory (Downward Move)***

Remember, we're not dealing with the open or closing prices when calculating Fibonacci, we're using the extreme price points which are the highest highs and the lowest lows.

Contraction Theory Matters

Question: Do stocks always retrace to the Fibonacci levels? Not always, but they generally do retrace to amounts that are very close to these levels. To this day, I am still amazed at how predictive Fibonacci levels can be. It almost seems as if these levels are magnets, drawing the retracements closer to them. The levels seem to act as support levels with prices virtually "bouncing" off of them. When a Fibonacci number is hit, it is truly amazing.

The general order of Fibonacci retracements is as follows: .382, .50 and .618. Question: What happens if a .382 retracement is broken?

(1) A .382 level that is substantially broken usually provides an indication that the retracement will have a tendency to continue to the .50 level. However, stocks that reverse at this level often continue along the established trend.

(2) If a .50 Fibonacci level is substantially broken on a retracement, the retracement will have a tendency to continue to the .618 level.

(3) If a .618 Fibonacci level is substantially broken on a retracement, the stock will have a tendency to continue its retracement to 100% of the last move up. If a stock reverses at this level, typically the most it will move (at least for the short term) will be to the top of the last move up.

Important: The smaller or tighter a stock's retracement is, the stronger its subsequent price move will be, either up or down.

Figure 6-7 includes a diagram outlining the general retracement tendencies.

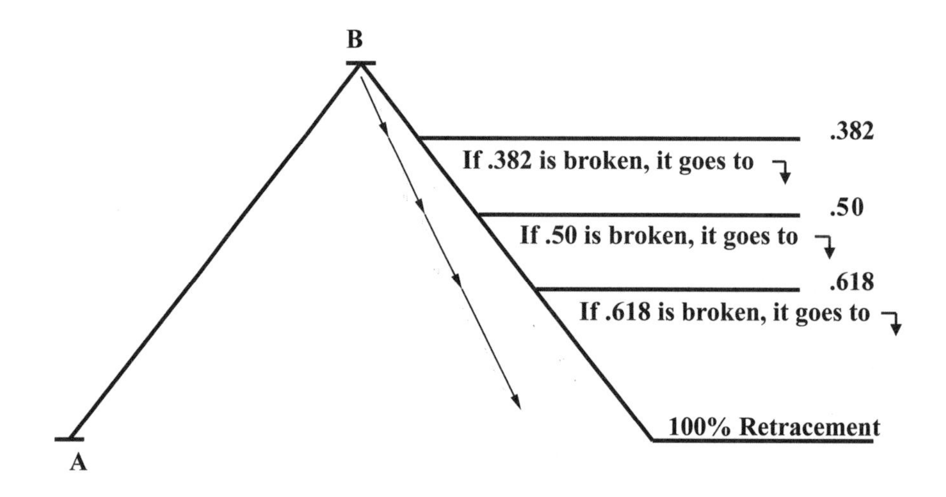

Figure 6-7: ***Broken Retracements***

These guidelines are not *absolute* - sometimes a stock will turn around just after breaking a Fibonacci support level. Again, an important element to keep your eye on is volume.

Expansion Theory

What happens after a stock finishes its retracement and begins to pick up steam for its next move? Does the application and importance of Fibonacci finish at the end of the retracement? No.

After a stock in an uptrend has finished its contraction or retracement and is gearing for its next move up, i.e., volume is starting to pick up, we say that the stock is ready to "expand". Just as with the retracement, the magical Fibonacci ratios do offer targets for the stock's expansion and those come in the form of 1 to 1, 1 to 1.382, 1 to 1.50 and 1 to 1.618 (also, 1:1, 1:1.382, 1:1.50, 1:1.618, respectively). How do we apply the Fibonacci ratios to arrive at the expansion targets? Easy. Just as we did with the contraction targets! We simply multiply the ratios to the last move, either up or down, and then add the resulting figures to the end of the retracement. In ABC speak, we just multiply the ratios to the A to B portion and then add them to C once C has proven itself to be the end of the retracement.

Figure 6-8 below demonstrates a simple 1 to 1 expansion.

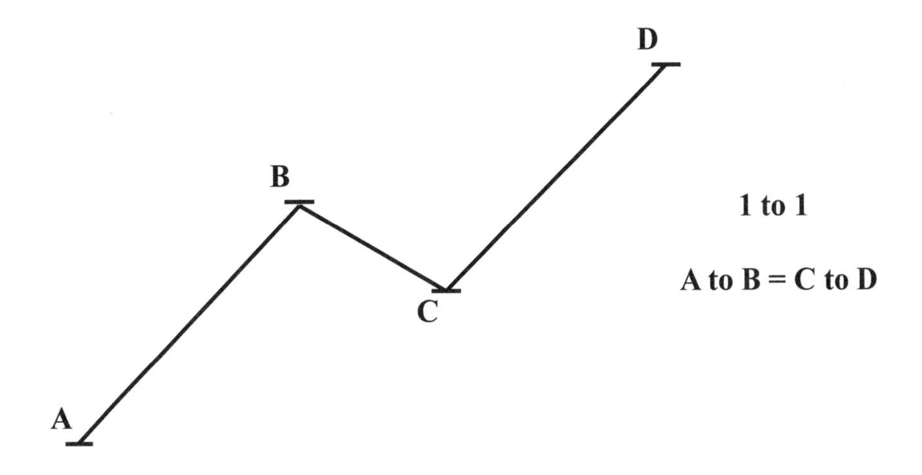

Figure 6-8: ***Expansion Theory (ABC Up)***
This example demonstrates a 1 to 1 expansion which is merely the distance from A to B applied to C once C has established itself. A "1 to 1.382" expansion

would be the A to B segment multiplied by 1.382 with the result being added to the C point. The same mechanics are performed for 1.50 and 1.618 expansions.

Utilizing our YES example in the *Upward Move* portion of the *Contraction Theory* section of this chapter, let's calculate YES's potential expansion levels. Figure 6-9 below provides the computations.

A to B	Ratio	Expansion Amount	C Point	Expansion Level (D)
$10	1.00	$10.00	$20	$30.00
10	1.382	13.82	20	33.82
10	1.50	15.00	20	35.00
10	1.618	16.18	20	36.18

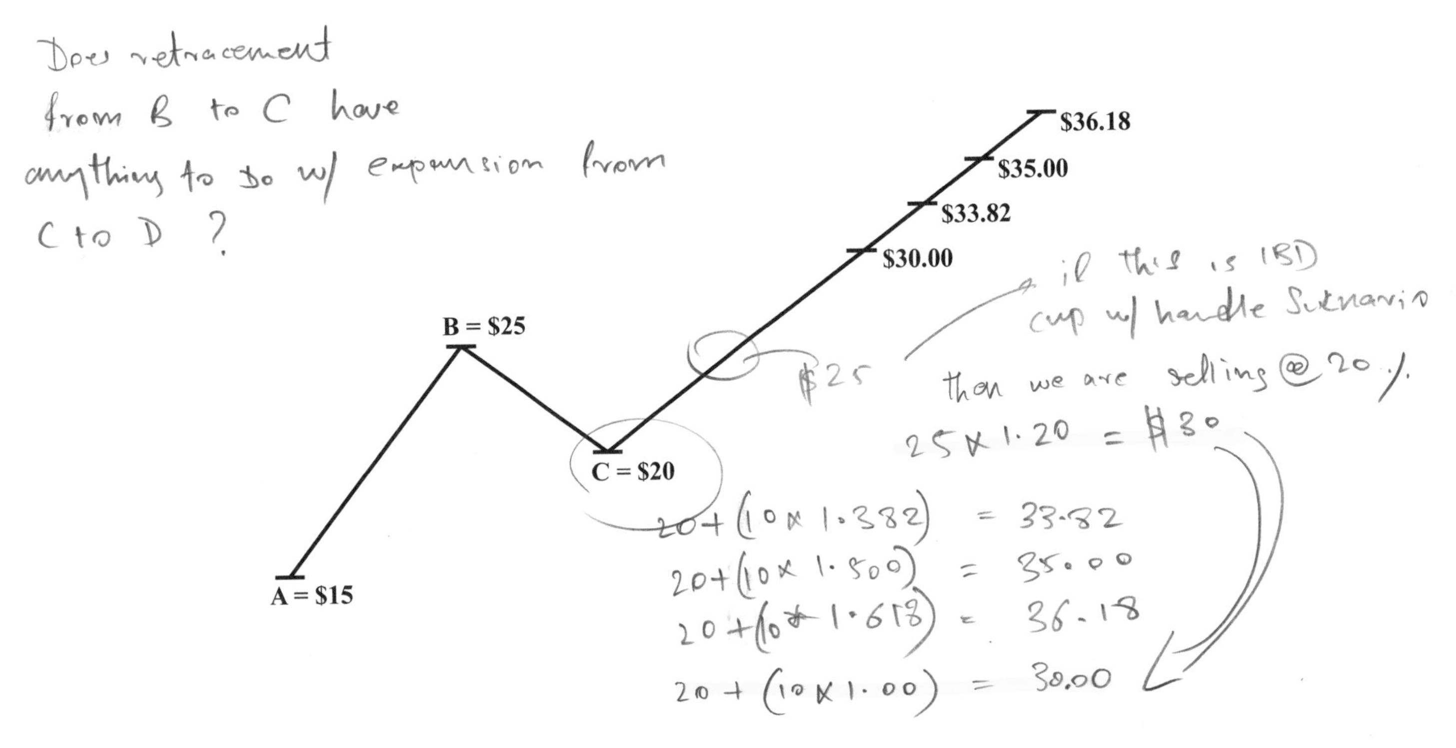

Figure 6-9: ***Expansion Targets (Upward Move)***
When calculating expansions, the Fibonacci ratios are applied (multiplied) to the A to B leg and the results are added to the C point to arrive at the expansion levels. This treatment differs from downward expansions where the results are subtracted from the C point.

Figure 6-10 demonstrates the effect of Fibonacci expansion on YES assuming that it is in a downtrend. The only difference is that the expansion amounts are subtracted from the C point.

A to B	Ratio	Expansion Amount	C Point	Expansion Level (D)
$10	1.00	$10.00	$20	$10.00
10	1.382	13.82	20	6.18
10	1.50	15.00	20	5.00
10	1.618	16.18	20	3.82

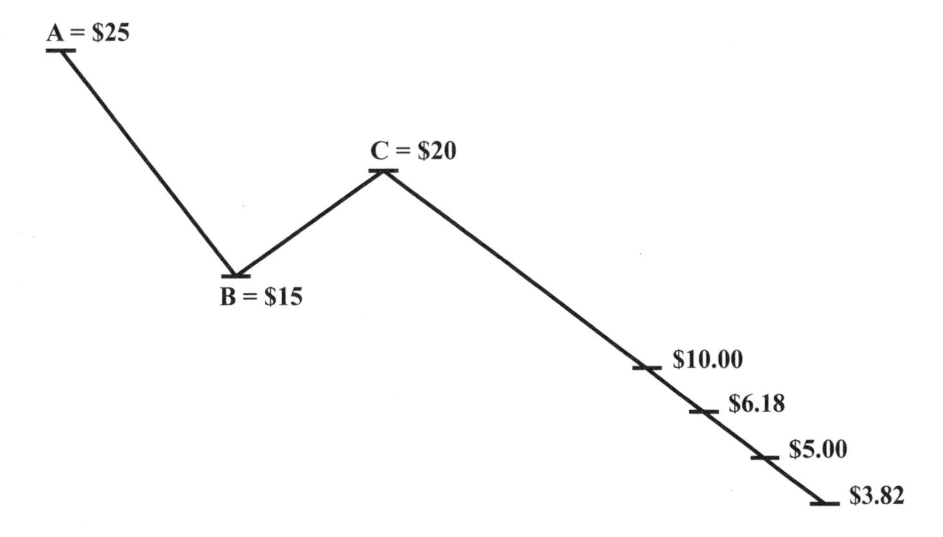

Figure 6-10: ***Expansion Targets (Downward Move)***

Expansion Theory Matters

While I've included the mechanics for calculating the various expansion levels I want to point out that I exit my trades at a 1:1 expansion point. Beyond that, I use the 1:1.382, 1:1.50 and 1:1.618 expansion points to gauge the strength of the stock or market. Here are some simple expansion theory guidelines:

(1) The easiest expansion to witness is the 1:1. If you are in a trade and you see it, this would be a good time to close your trade and take money off the table. As we go over risk/reward and money management in a later chapter, you'll notice that virtually all of our computations are based on the simple assumption that the stock will perform a 1:1 expansion. Beyond this point, I use the remaining levels to gauge the stock's and/or market's strength.

(2) A 1:1.382 expansion represents a strong move and indicates the presence of a strong market.

(3) Likewise, a 1:1.50 expansion represents a strong move and indicates the presence of an even stronger market.

(4) A 1:1.618 expansion (or greater) represents a problematic move. On the surface it looks amazing, but what it's saying is that price movement got out of control and more than likely without quality volume (also potentially an exhaustion move with capitulation just around the corner). A 1:1.618 expansion carries with it the most importance since it signals an overbought or oversold condition and the beginning of a major turnaround.

(5) Remember, the greater the expansion, the higher the probability that the stock will pull back.

These guidelines are applicable to stocks in both uptrends and downtrends.

7

Confluence

And see the confluence of dreams
That clashed together in our night,
One river born of many streams
Roll in one blaze of blinding light!
~ George William Russell

Confluence, as it's defined in Merriam-Webster's Collegiate Dictionary means a coming or flowing together, meeting, or gathering at one point.

Confluence, as I will be covering here in this chapter and in conjunction with Fibonacci ratios is:

> ***Definition***: **confluence** – the price range sandwiched between the .382 retracement level of a trend and the .618 retracement of a related subtrend; confluence reveals powerful support & resistance levels.

In the previous chapter I mentioned that Fibonacci levels tend to become support and resistance levels (depending on which direction the price movement is heading, up or down). Suffice it to say, when you have two Fibonacci zones yielding a mutual price range, this range becomes a powerful level of support or resistance. Figure 7-1 includes a very basic display of confluence and where it may lie in an upward trend:

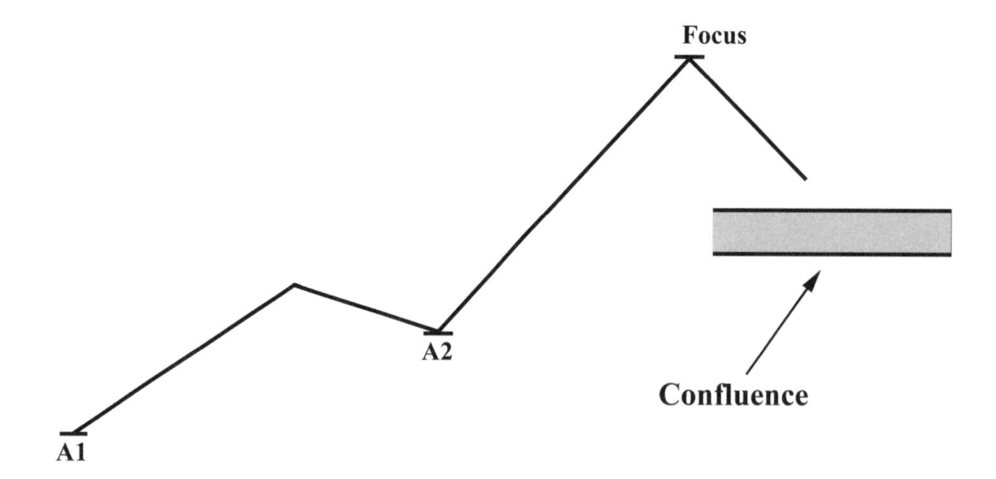

Figure 7-1: ***Basic Confluence***

My First Time

My first experience with confluence came at the hands of Joe DiNapoli in his excellent book titled *DiNapoli Levels*. In his book, Joe (also a good friend) does an incredible job at demonstrating the presence and effectiveness of areas of Fibonacci confluence. The first time I read his book, I felt as if I had been struck with an epiphany. I rifled through my old charts and computed different areas of confluence for each one only to find that in practically all cases, my confluence calculations uncovered incredible levels of support & resistance! The confluence numbers also revealed themselves as being uncanny predictors of price moves. It only made sense that if Fibonacci levels posed strong levels of support & resistance and also represented levels of price magnetism, confluence would do the same but in a much stronger sense since confluence is the mutual price range between the Fibonacci retracement levels belonging to a trend and a related subtrend.

With this monumental breakthrough in knowledge, I became a convert right away. Confluence became an integral part of my trading regimen and a very guiding principle in virtually all of my seminars and radio shows. Without question, confluence has been incredibly responsible for my successes in all my stock and commodities trading, up to this very day.

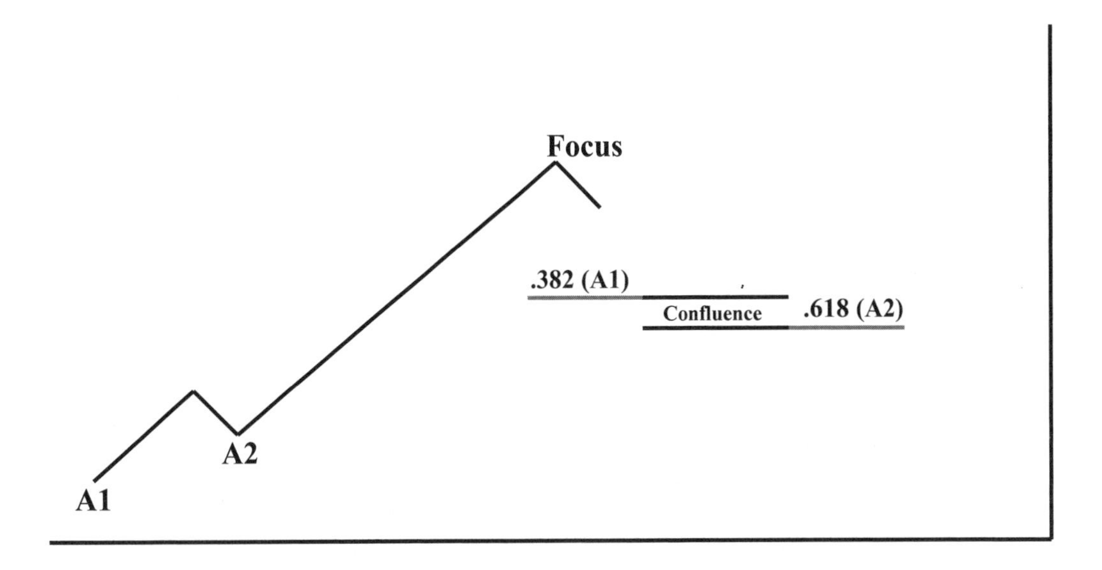

Figure 7-2: ***Confluence***

Calculation

First of all, it's important to fully understand to what we are applying the Fibonacci retracement ratios (.382 and .618).

Suppose that in an upward (or downward, depending on the movement) trend we spot a subtrend, that is a minor move up that is embedded in the overall move. If we take the beginning of that move and measure its distance to the top of the overall move, we have isolated a subtrend and with its measurement we can compute separate Fibonacci levels.

Up to this point, we have used "A" when calculating Fibonacci levels. The only twist (with confluence) is that by having a subtrend to contend with, we will use A1 and A2 to mark the beginning of the overall trend and subtrend respectively. That is, A1 will mark the beginning of the major, overall trend and A2 will correspond with the beginning of the subtrend. The end of both trends (which incidently is the same point for both), also known as the focus point, will be marked or denoted as "Focus" or "Focus point" in all calculations.

Oftentimes people will ask me how I spot the A1 and A2 points and the answer is pretty simple: they basically have to jump out at you – stick out like a sore thumb. (The more powerful points show up after large pullbacks in the markets and individual equities; this is where weak hands get cleaned out and new ownership is created). The A1 and A2 points are used to designate very pronounced moves. Figure 7-3 includes a very vivid example.

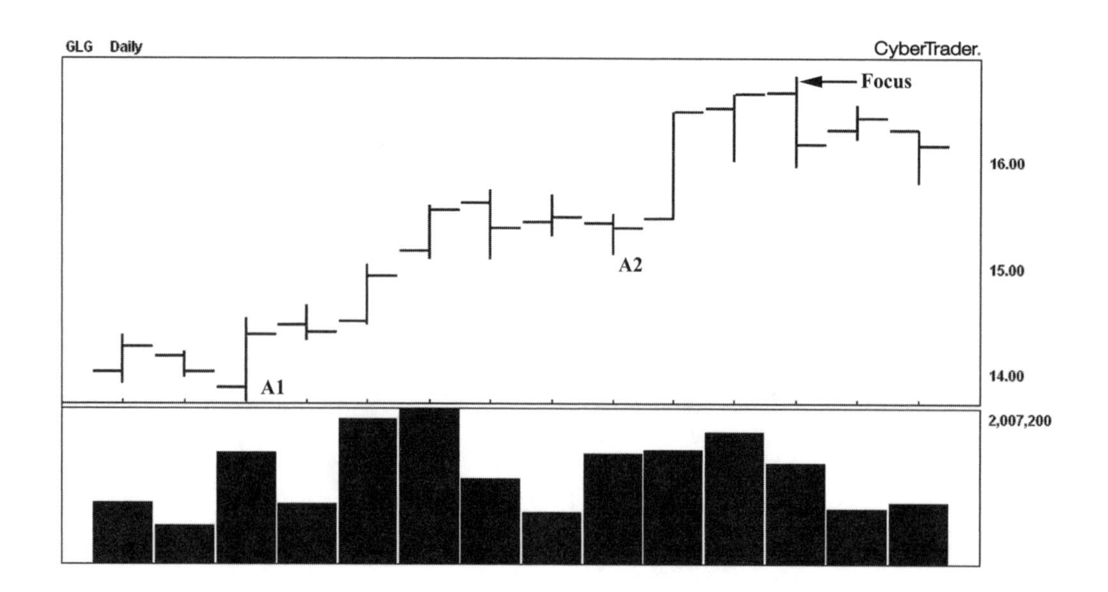

Figure 7-3: ***Identifying a Subtrend - Glamis Gold Ltd. (GLG)***
This chart shows us the basic set up for confluence. Note how you're taking two separate trends and combining them in order to get your confluence numbers.

So let's run through a simple confluence calculation! Suppose YES has had a major run up from $15 to $25. Right away it should be apparent to you that the overall trend, A1 to Focus, is from $15 to $25 and measures 10 points. Let's say that on its way, YES took a small breather at $20 and retraced to $18 before continuing on its way up. The subtrend, A2 to Focus, essentially begins at $18 and ends at $25 (Focus) and measures 7 points.

So! A1 to Focus is 10 points and A2 to Focus is 7 points. So far, so good.

Now for the A1 leg we apply the .382 ratio and for the A2 leg we apply the .618 ratio and subtract both of these from the Focus point. To simply spell it out: the A1 leg ($10) times .382 equals $3.82 and the A2 leg ($7) times .618 equals $4.33. Subtracting $3.82 from the Focus point, ($25) equals $21.18 and $4.33 from the same Focus point ($25) equals $20.67 yielding confluence of $21.18 to $20.67. Figure 7-4 highlights the computations.

Trend	Ratio	Retracement Amount	B Point	Retracement Level	
Overall (A1) - $10	.382	3.82	25	$21.18	Confluence
Subtrend (A2) - $7	.618	4.33	25	$20.67	

Figure 7-4: ***Calculating Confluence***
Note that the .382 and .618 retracement levels are calculated by subtracting the calculated amounts from the Focus point ($25). By looking at the retracement levels you can see the common area between the two levels is bordered by $21.18 on the top and $20.67 on the bottom.

As we plot these values on a chart (see Figure 7-5), we can see that confluence becomes the price area *between* the A1 leg .382 retracement level and the A2 leg .618 retracement level.

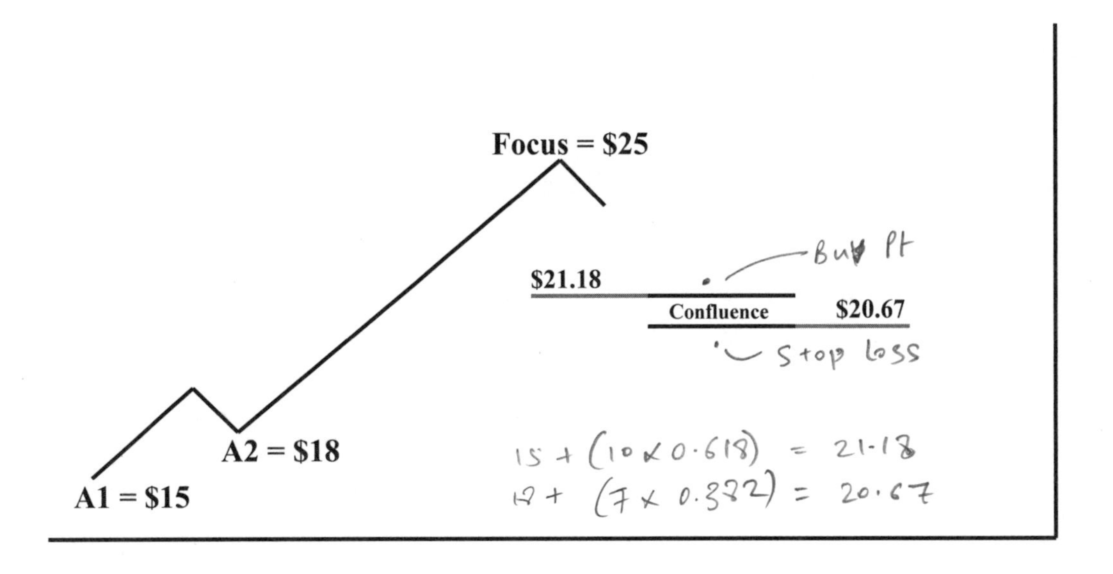

Figure 7-5: ***Plotting Confluence***

You don't even have to go through the trouble of plotting the points on a chart to figure out where confluence is, I've done it here only to further your understanding. By simply looking at the calculation table in Figure 7-4, you can tell what the upper and lower boundaries of YES's confluence zone are.

The Other Direction

We have just completed calculating confluence for YES and our stock was without question in an uptrend. What happens if YES is in a downtrend? Is the calculation different? Answer: not terribly different.

A downtrending stock will have an overall trend and related subtrend(s). The same principles apply; the only difference is that the retracement amounts are *added* to the Focus point (remember, retracements in downward trending stock occur in a northerly direction). The resulting values yield confluence on the way down. Figure 7-6 includes an example of confluence in a downtrending stock.

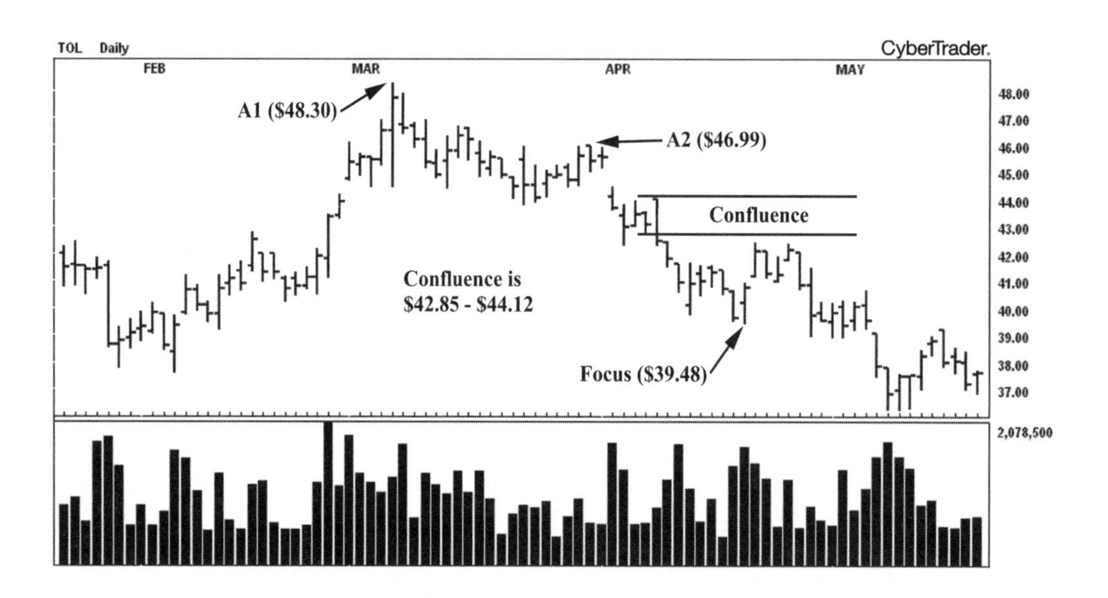

Figure 7-6: ***Confluence in Downtrending Stock – Toll Brothers, Inc. (TOL)***
TOL gives us an excellent example of confluence occurring in a downtrending stock. Confluence in this case comes up as $42.85 to $44.12. On its retracement, TOL reaches $42.45, just forty cents shy of the first layer of confluence.

The Brick Wall

Well, we've gone through an exercise on calculating confluence. What do we do next?

As I've mentioned before, confluence, when revealed, becomes a powerful level of support and resistance, something of a brick wall (I say "something of a brick wall" because confluence *can* be broken; otherwise it's a powerful level of support or resistance). How can we benefit from this brick wall? Easy. Of course only after you've determined that YES is a stock you want to trade, you would simply use the brick wall as protection between your entry into the stock and your stop or the point where you would get out!

In my seminars, discussions and teachings where I give the "brick wall" analogy to describe the strength of confluence, I stress that just like brick walls in real life, confluence (as I just mentioned) can be broken or violated. The key here (again) is volume. Strong volume: the move will continue further; weak volume: expect the stock to do a "180" and come back!

In our confluence exercise, we calculated confluence as being \$21.18 to \$20.67. Supposing that we have got the signal to enter (i.e., appropriate candlestick, etc.) we would place our entry right above \$21.18. Now we all know, or at least should know, that we should not enter a trade without identifying a point where we would get out in the event our trade starts moving against us (stops are discussed in Chapter 8 – *Stops*). In our example, we would use a point just below \$20.67 as our stop. Why? Because our stock will have to penetrate this "brick wall", and if it does, our stop will get us out of this losing trade.

Figures 7-7 and 7-8 include illustrations showing confluence and the appropriate sides to place entries and stops.

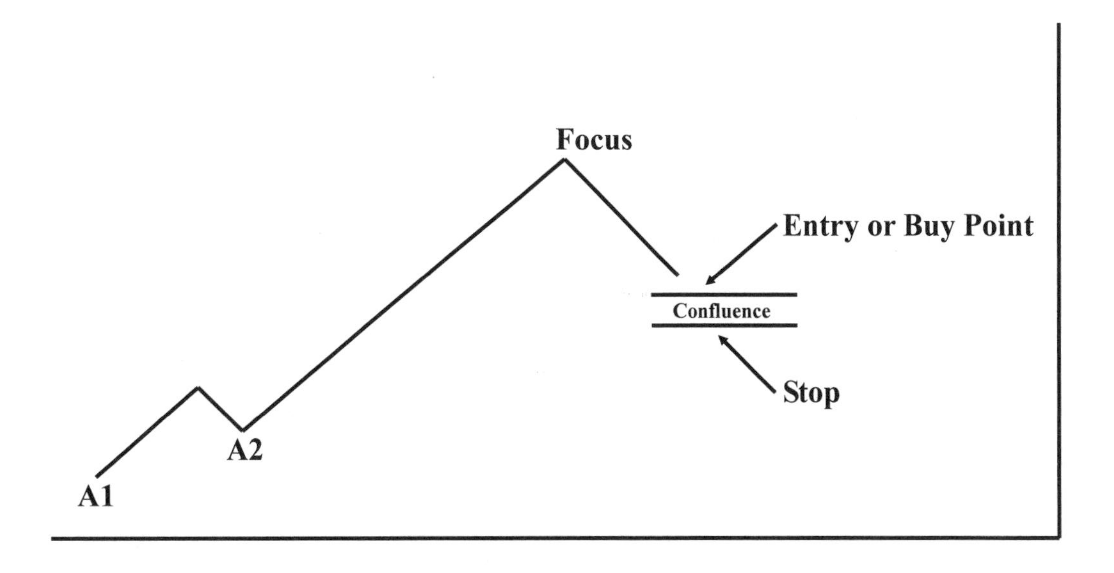

Figure 7-7: ***Entry and Stop for an Uptrending Stock***

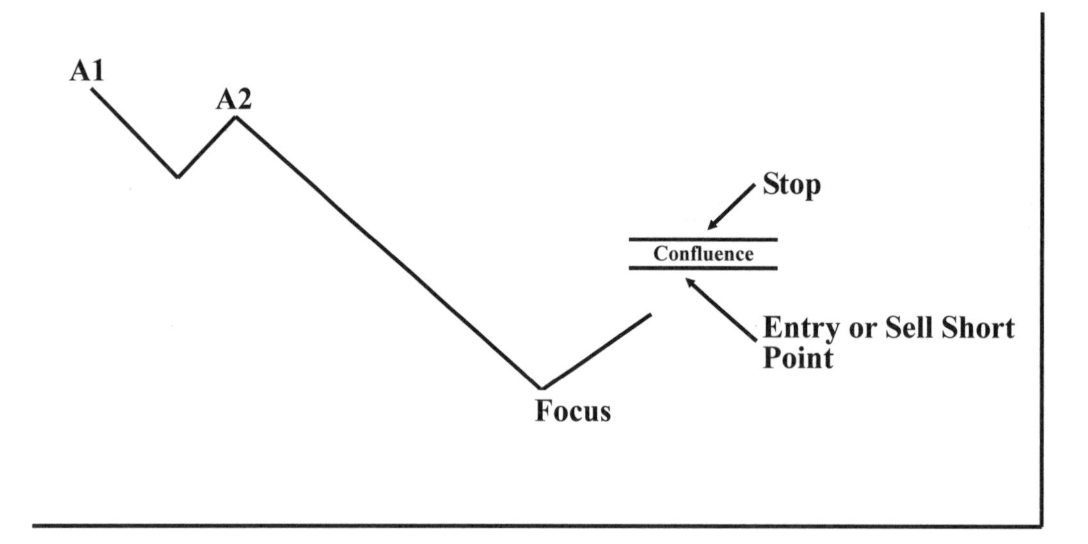

Figure 7-8: ***Entry and Stop for a Downtrending Stock***

Important Issues Regarding Confluence

True Confluence

Throughout this chapter, we have gone through exercises to calculate confluence numbers in order to determine where the "brick wall" is and to identify appropriate entry and exit points. You should however stay cognizant of the fact that your area of confluence might not be the "true" area of confluence. Now I'm not including this as a caveat but as a reminder that you should be aware of the importance of identifying the correct A1, A2 and focus points for your overall trend. With incorrect points, you may have calculated and identified an incorrect area of confluence.

Another thing to remember is that, while you are calculating confluence, you may still be in an overall trend. It's important to note that an upward trend will have more than just one B point but only one Focus point being the highest high of the overall move. The same applies in a downward move where the Focus point is the lowest low. The reason for this is because a protracted move will have several ABC patterns within it but there will be only one Focus point and that will be the highest high in an uptrend or the lowest low in a downtrend (Figure 7-3 demonstrates a good example of this). Remember, it's only after your stock has proven that it has commenced its retracement, will you be able to accurately calculate and identify its confluence.

A good point to keep in mind is the following: If you cannot with great certainty nail a stock's A1, A2 and Focus points, it makes great sense for you to look to another stock. It should be your goal to have as much clarity as possible!

Magnetism

I mentioned earlier that confluence, just like Fibonacci levels, represents a strong basis for price magnetism. What I'm saying is that prices tend to be drawn to confluence in their retracements, particularly with lighter volume. Whoa, remember volume? Yes, even with the topic of confluence, volume takes on great meaning.

As your stock is approaching its area of confluence, what is happening to volume? If volume is light, you can count on your stock to bounce right off of confluence, if it even goes as far as reaching it (as in Figure 7-9). If volume on a retracement is heavy . . . watch out! Your stock may in fact slam right through confluence.

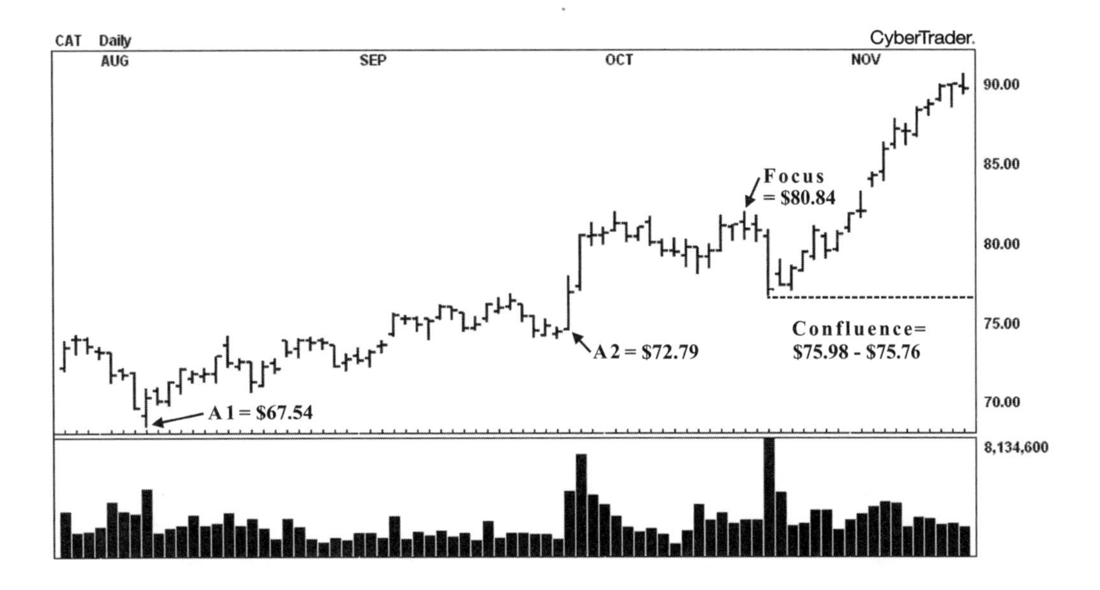

Figure 7-9: ***Confluence - Caterpillar Inc. (CAT)***
In this example, confluence is calculated as $75.98 to $75.76. The following table outlines the calculation:

	A Point	Focus	Leg	Ratio	Retracement Amount	Focus	Retracement Level	
Overall (A1)	$67.54	$80.84	$13.30	.382	$5.08	$80.84	$75.76	Confluence
Subtrend (A2)	$72.79	$80.84	$ 7.87	.618	$4.86	$80.84	$75.98	

Inversion

On many occasions I'll run across instances where A2 is well away from A1 and sometimes even beyond the halfway mark between A1 and the Focus point. What this creates in the context of calculating confluence is an A2 retracement level that comes in *above* the A1 retracement level – it looks as if the levels are inverted.

Does confluence still exist with A1 and A2 being inverted? Yes. The space or price distance between the two levels is your confluence zone.

Figures 7-10 and 7-11 illustrate examples of a normal and an inverted A1 and A2 retracement level, respectively.

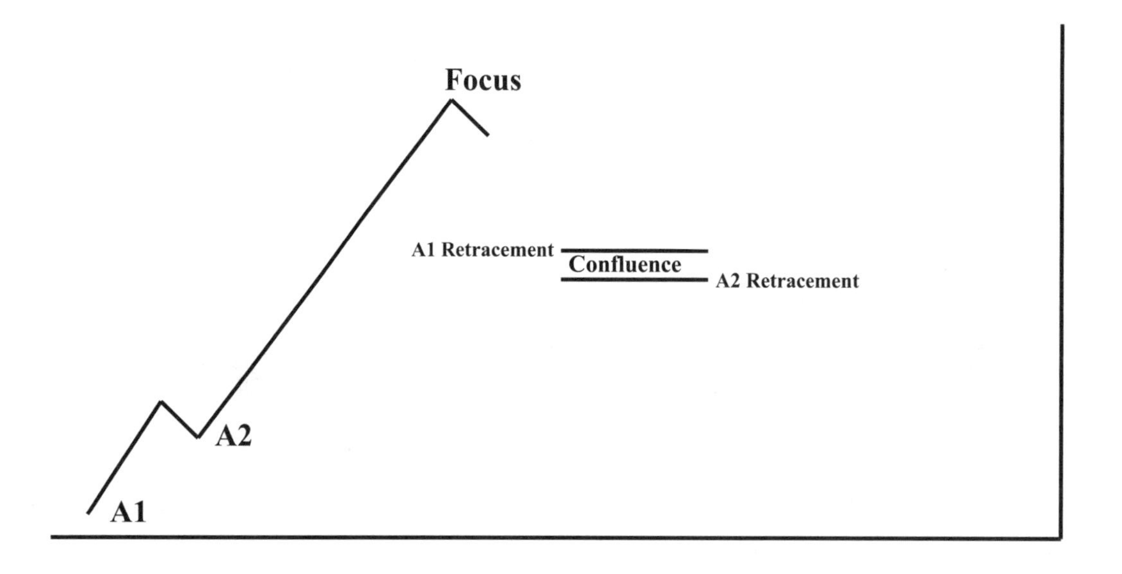

Figure 7-10: ***Normal Confluence Configuration***

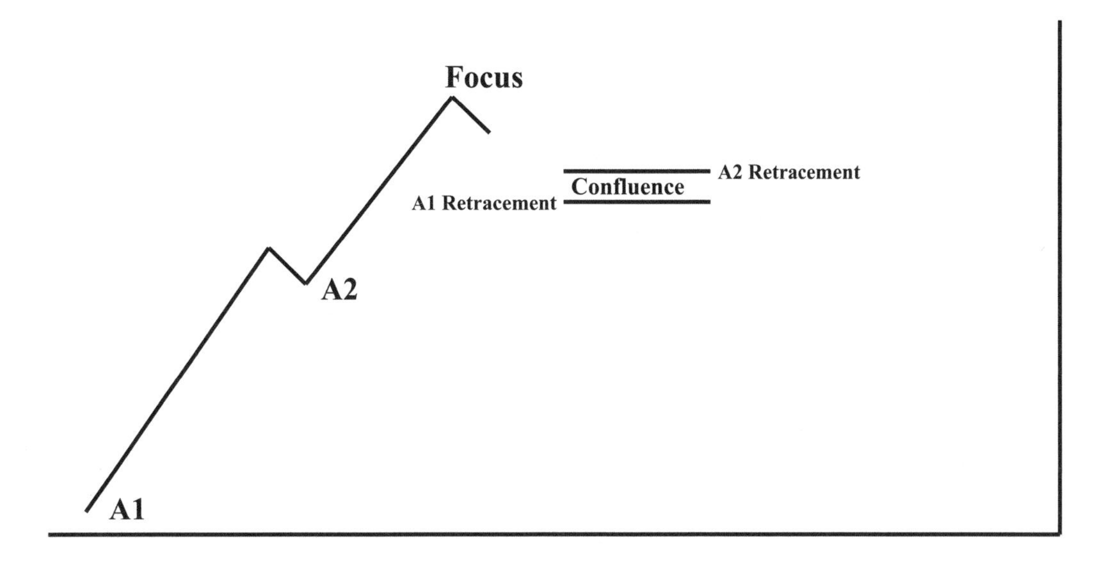

Figure 7-11: ***Inverted Confluence Configuration***
As compared to the normal confluence set-up in Figure 7-10, A2 in this case is further away from A1 yielding an inverted confluence set-up with the A2 retracement level coming in above the A1 retracement level.

Confluence Calculator

Throughout this chapter we have manually calculated confluence. It may seem somewhat tedious, especially at first, but computing something manually does help you grasp the individual components of a larger calculation or concept.

To make life easier, I've made a free confluence calculator available on my website, TFNN.com.

The confluence calculator is quick, accurate, easy to use and best of all, free. Check it out!!

8

Stops

Confidence comes not from always being right
but from not fearing to be wrong.
~ Peter T. McIntyre

A trading stop can be considered one of investing's most underappreciated gems and perhaps one of trading's least understood concepts. What is it? It is an out. It is an opportunity to live to fight another day – essentially a mechanism that confirms that you've made an incorrect trading decision (remember that we're in a game of probabilities – keep these in your favor) and keeps you from incurring further losses. It basically pulls you out of a bad trade. There are various types of stops, i.e., stop loss, trailing stops, etc., I'm going to cover stops that save you from disaster.

Let's use an everyday example to analogize the importance of a stop. Pretend you have taken your 1982 Oldsmobile to the mechanic's for a new a/c compressor and a tune up. The compressor will cost you about $500 installed and the tune up will run you $150, total tab $650. While it's in the shop, you get a call from Joe, the head mechanic. He calls to tell you that by opening the hood, he has basically opened a can of worms discovering that not only are you in need of a compressor, you need new belts, hoses, and by the looks of it you might be needing a new radiator soon!! This is going to cost a lot. Knowing that your car is already pretty old and that you definitely need a/c to get it sold, you decide to go ahead with the various other improvements including the tune-up but you give Joe explicit instructions to complete repairs to a point where the bill does not exceed $800.

What you've done is you have placed a "stop" where the repair bill will not get out of hand or go beyond $800. Stops in stock trading work much in the same way where they keep losses from getting out of hand.

Why Stops are Important

Stops are important for three primary reasons: 1) they help you measure and quantify the amount of risk you undertake with each trade, 2) they help preserve your capital (thus allowing you to "stay in the game"), and 3) they help you reach psychological peace of mind.

Measuring Risk

Let's say we own 100 shares of YES at $50 and we have identified a point in its chart where if it hits this amount, it's bound to go even lower or if it hits this point, we have a confirmation that we have entered this trade at the wrong price point and perhaps even at the wrong time (e.g., sudden turn in the market). Now let's say that this price point we have identified is $47 (this price point can be also based on confluence, where the stop should be placed on just the other side). The difference between our entry price ($50) and the point we have determined that we should be getting out ($47) is $3. This essentially means that we are willing to lose $3 on each share of YES. Considering that we purchased 100 shares, we are willing to lose $300. Here the importance of a stop becomes tantamount because without placing a stop at $47, it is very possible that our stock will hit $47 and keep going lower (more than likely when we're not at our screen or are not able to pay attention to YES's trading activity) thus widening our potential loss.

Figure 8-1 includes a simple diagram illustrating our YES example.

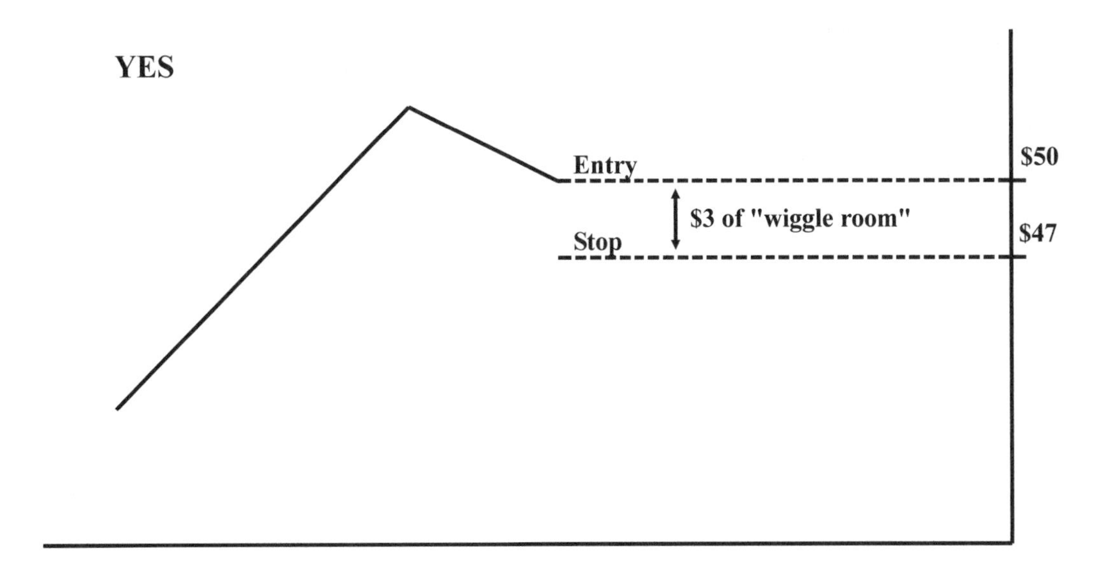

Figure 8-1: ***Placement of Stop (YES)***

Notice that the stop allows us $3 of *wiggle room* in case we got in at the wrong place. You can't expect a stock's price movement to go your way immediately once you enter a trade. If you believe YES will take off to the moon once you get your order in, you're in the wrong business.

The determination of risk is important especially when combined with projected price appreciation (reward). We will go into more detail regarding risk/reward and money management in a later chapter, but for now remember that stops help you quantify risk or *the amount of money you are willing to lose.*

Preserving Your Capital

Using our YES example, imagine that we are in at $50 and the stock hits $47. Well, if we had a stop loss in place (at $47), we would be out, but we don't and the stock continues its slide and drops down to $45. Now our $300 potential loss has turned into a $500 potential loss. What do we do now? Pray? Now, had we placed a stop loss at $47, our shares would have automatically been sold and we would have lost $300; that's it, end of story. By not having lost more, we have to a certain extent preserved our capital.

Let's say YES begins a long slide down to $25. The company's management is suddenly under SEC investigation for overstating revenues, i.e., they reported having sold more widgets than they actually did. Without the $47 stop you are now down $2,500. You're down roughly 50% on YES. Yes, ouch and guess what, you have to make 100% on your remaining money to get back to even (take a quick look at the loss recovery chart in Chapter 18 - *Risk and Money Management*, Figure 18-1). Will you be able to sleep at night? Say you used up your entire capital base on this trade, $5,000 and you decide to get out. Now you have half of what you started with. Want to get back into a trade? Fine, but what happens if you experience another substantial loss? Your capital will draw down closer to zero. Want to keep on trading? Well, in order to trade you have to have capital and there's no better way to preserve your capital than by employing stops!

Peace of Mind

We all need peace of mind. Whether it be at work, at home or on the road, peace of mind benefits us all. With stock trading, you need it like a plant needs sun and water. There are so many variables to trading, so many seen and unseen distractions. Do you think a cluttered, anxious mind is going to help you achieve trading nirvana? No way!

Do you think that placing your hard-earned money at risk is going to help you sleep easier at night? Not really, in fact the more you place at risk, in a relative sense, i.e., what the amount means to you, the harder it will be for you to think clearly, speak comfortably and even sleep restfully. What I'm trying to say here is that firm stops will help you get closer to achieving peace of mind while you are risking your money in a stock trade.

Let me stress the importance of practicing and maintaining *firmness* in your stops. With a trade in place, you may have a battle going on in your own head, take stop, move stop, etc. Bottom line, don't move your stops; for by doing so you'll not only wreck your trading plan, you'll lose more money.

Let's paint a picture. Suppose you had purchased Enron Energy at $90 a share and you placed a stop way down at $80. Well, by all accounts this does not look like a tight stop but, anyways, let's continue. Let's assume that the SEC announces that it will look into Enron's accounting practices. The stock starts sliding and rather than pushing your stop downward, you hold still. Enron trades below $80 thus triggering your stop – you are out. You have lost $10 a share. Not a pretty picture. Does this give you a good feeling? Probably not at first.

Enron however continues its slide and drops like a rock all the way down to ten cents a share upon news that Enron management has been indicted for fraudulent reporting. How do you feel now? Validated? You bet! You've been dealt a psychological high-five by having placed and maintained a firm stop. With your Enron trade you lost only $10 per share compared to other investors and traders who had no stops and lost *much* more. (Not to mention the many faithful long-term Enron employees who were precluded from selling their shares during the slide only to see their retirement nest eggs substantially disappear.)

The example I just used is a very traumatic and emotionally sensitive topic for many people. But losing a great amount of money is no fun. Bottom line, use firm stops!!

Types of Stops

There are two simple ways to set a stop. As for determining where to set a stop, I'll cover that soon. There are several types of stops but I will focus only on a **stop-loss limit** order and a simple **stop loss**.

A stop loss of the limit variety is basically an instruction by you to sell (or buy, if you are short) a stock at specific price once a stop price level has been reached. Say you have a stop to sell XYZ at $30 and it's currently trading at $31. If a trade goes off at $30, your shares are then introduced in the market to be sold at $30. The danger with this type of stop is that your order to sell your shares might not be executed. This would particularly be the case if the stock price is dropping quickly. When the first trade goes off at $30 and the next bidder in line wants to buy at $29.50, your shares just might be passed up. This is why a simple stop loss order is better.

The simple stop loss order simply executes your order at market. Using our XYZ example above, if XYZ hits $30 and triggers your stop, your order becomes a market order thus selling your shares to the highest bidder (in the case of a buy stop for a short sale, you would basically be buying shares from the highest seller). The downside to this approach is that you might not be filled at the stop price you have designated but rather at a slightly different price. Still, this is better than having no stop at all.

Stops, Where to Set Them

In determining where to set a stop, I'll first look to confluence. I'll next look to a recent swing point (if there is one) as a level for support or resistance. I won't however look to see how much money I'm willing to risk in order to determine my stop. Your stop should be primarily based on a technical aspect (confluence, swing point, support, resistance, etc.).

Before getting into *where* to set stops, maybe we should address *when* to set them. The quick answer: right away, once you enter a trade, end of story.

Confluence

Remember our discussion on confluence? Refer back to Chapter 7 – *Confluence* if you need to. Confluence is like a brick wall where prices meet major support (or resistance) when attempting to move further in their trends.

If you've calculated an area of confluence, you may have entered at any point just outside or even inside of confluence. Your stop should be placed just on the other side of confluence or the "brick wall". Check out Figure 8-2.

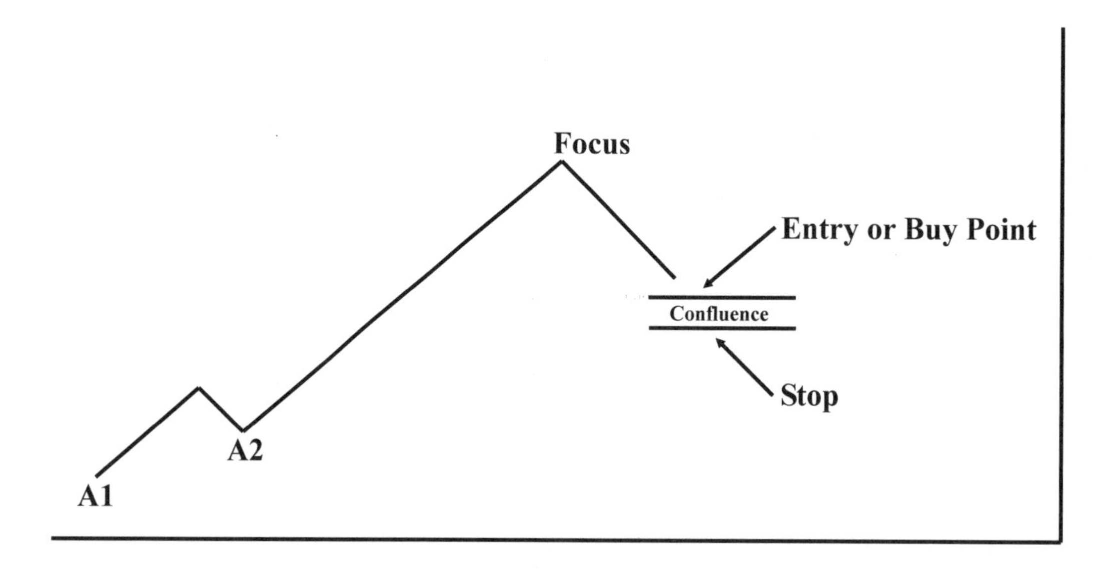

Figure 8-2: ***Placing Stop at Other Side of Confluence***

Note that here again you can give yourself *wiggle room* when setting your stop. Your placement does not have to be right on the opposite side of confluence but rather a few cents away. Keep in mind that I will be covering the dynamics involved in the width of your stops (compared to your entry point) in Chapter 18 – *Risk and Money Management* – the chapter will also address how the width between your stop and entry will dictate how many shares to buy.

Swing Points

Chapter 10 – *Swing Points* includes discussion analyzing the dynamics which underlie swing points. I may be getting a little ahead of myself here, but swing points offer optimal points to place your stops, particularly if they coincide with confluence. If you have a swing point price level that is at confluence, or at just the other side of it, you have greater strength in your "brick wall".

Note: When setting your stops, try not to place a stop at whole or rounded numbers, e.g., $45.00 or $45.50, etc. These numbers can represent psychological targets where they mostly (and I've seen this in my years of trading) get taken out. Ideally, you want to set your stops (as well as entries) in odd or nonrounded numbers. Please note though that throughout this book I use whole, rounded numbers to denote stops for the sake of simplicity. But please, don't forget to place your stops in unrounded, fractional amounts.

Trailing Stops

Here is where I'm forced to introduce an exception to the rule when it comes to maintaining firmness in your stops. Suppose you went long on IBM at $75. Your decision to enter the trade was correct, IBM has surpassed your price projection of $85 and is now currently trading at $87. Normally at this point I would take money off the table and take my beautiful wife and family out to a nice restaurant.

Now let's say IBM has not quite reached your price projection and is trading at $83. What will you do? What are you going to do when you initially had set your stop at $72? Well, here the name of the game is to protect your profit and you do so by setting a trailing stop.

A trailing stop is merely a stop that *trails* your stock that happens to be moving in your favor. When do you set a trailing stop? Where do you place it?

When: After the trade has moved in your favor and the stock has established new support or resistance, depending on your direction.

Where: At the new support or resistance level.

Check out Figure 8-3!

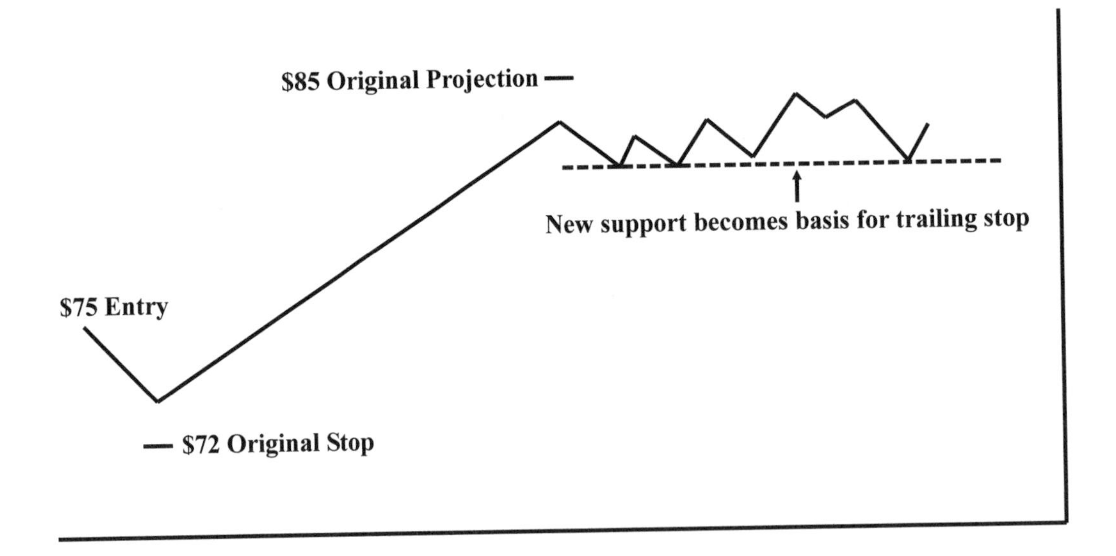

Figure 8-3: ***Trailing Stops***
This chart demonstrates the placement of a trailing stop on a stock that continues to move in favor of the trader. New support becomes the basis for placing a trailing stop (your new stop would be placed just on the other side of this support). Note how its placement protects the profits that have been earned so far.

If you've shorted a stock, then look to new resistance!

9

Support & Resistance

The reverse side also has a reverse side.
~ Japanese Proverb

Support & resistance. What are they? Before we get into it, let's take another look at the four stages of a stock's price cycle. They are its accumulation phase, mark-up phase, distribution phase and mark-down phase. These phases occur in the order I've listed them and they tend to repeat themselves over and over throughout the life of a stock.

The accumulation phase consists of a long period where operators will *quietly* accumulate a stock in anticipation of future price moves. Essentially there are heavy hands that are accumulating the stock in anticipation of it increasing in value in the short or long term. This phase typically establishes points of support in the stock's trading behavior.

The mark-up phase generally follows accumulation and it is during this stage that a stock's price will go up. The weaker hands are typically not aware of the accumulation phase (at least while it's going on) but nonetheless try to get in with the operators marking up the price.

The distribution phase is usually where the heavy hands unload and they typically do this inconspicuously. They either see no more appreciation in price to come or they simply want to take money off the table. Either way they are unloading their shares.

The mark-down phase includes periods of price destruction where once the weaker hands see that operators have gotten out and they no longer can take the heat, they get out in a fury. This typically will drive down the price. It's usually after this period that you'll see the "from weak hands to strong hands" trading taking place. This period will typically lead to an accumulation phase.

Figure 9-1 includes a chart of MSFT demonstrating the four stages in a particular trading period. Notice what is happening to price during each of the phases. Do you see any basic similarities with MSFT and other stocks whose charts you've run across?

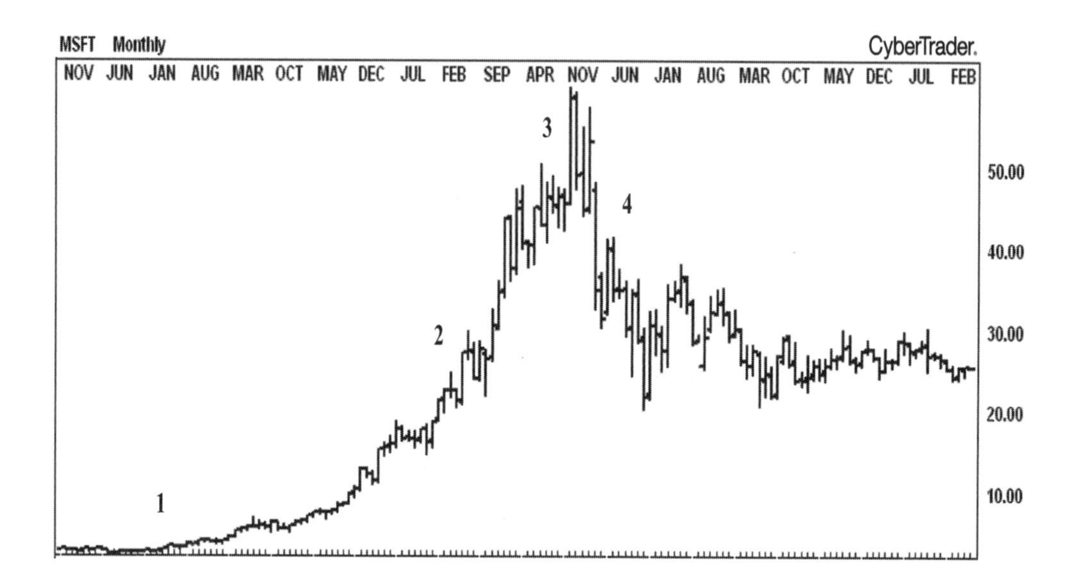

Figure 9-1: ***Four Stages of Price Cycle - Microsoft Corp. (MSFT)***
(1) *Accumulation*
(2) *Mark-up*
(3) *Distribution*
(4) *Mark-down*

Support Can Be Beautiful

O.K. Now that we've once again covered the basic stages of a stock price cycle, let's move on into support & resistance. First support. What is it? Support is where an operator will come into an equity and support his or her own position. Yes, you may have many operators in the same equity depending on the size of the float. If you took a Microsoft or GE you could have up to 30 or 40 different operators in that equity at any one time. If you look at a small-cap equity, you might have only four to six operators working the equity. These support levels are clearly marked on the charts whether they be horizontal or diagonal. When we pull back to these levels with lighter volume, it's telling us that there are no more sellers in the equity. At this point, operators go back to work accumulating their line of stock.

Using a real life analogy, let's assume the accumulation phase of a stock's price cycle as being the foundation of a house. The longer a stock is in an accumulation phase, i.e., the more shares that are traded, the stronger the foundation, and the stronger the foundation, the more floors that can be built on the house; therefore the harder it will be for this stock to go below this level.

Figures 9-2, 9-3 and 9-4 illustrate simple examples of support. It's important to note (as I mentioned previously) that a line of support doesn't necessarily have to be horizontal. It can be diagonal and hug the lows of an uptrending or downtrending stock.

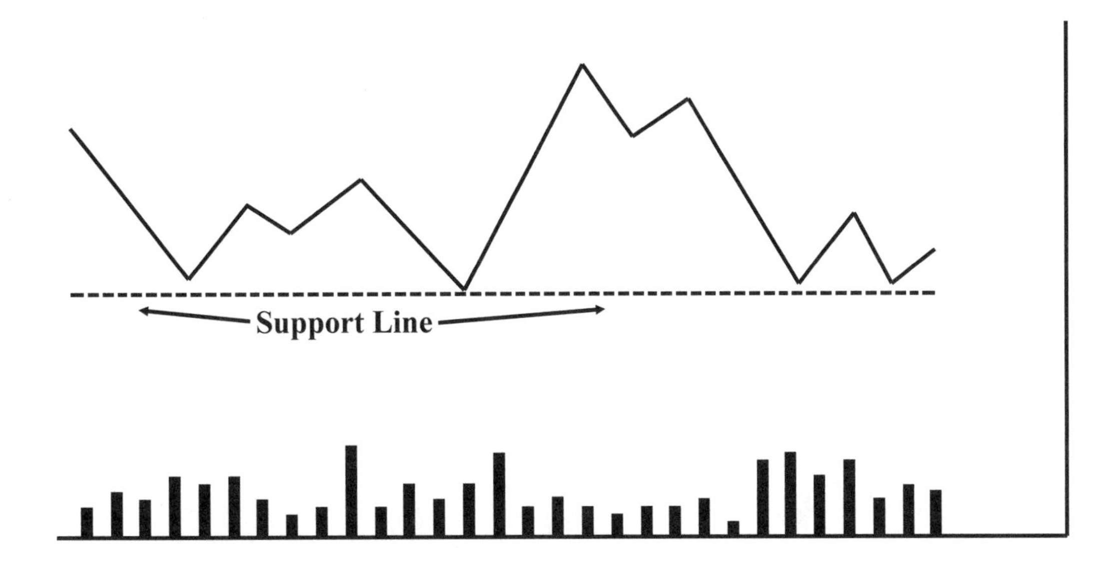

Figure 9-2: ***Flat Support Line***

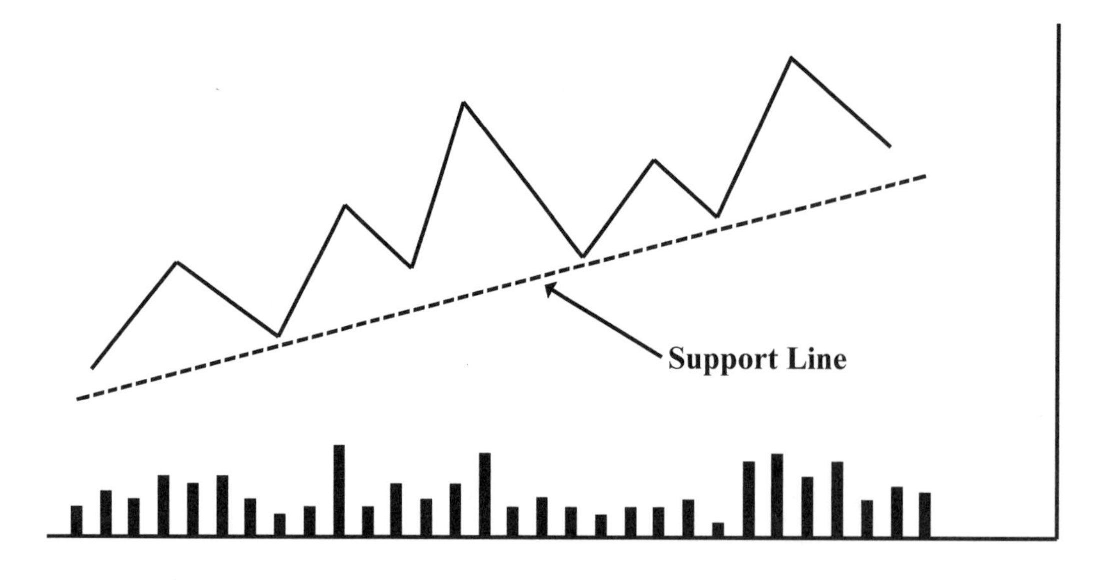

Figure 9-3: ***Diagonal Support***

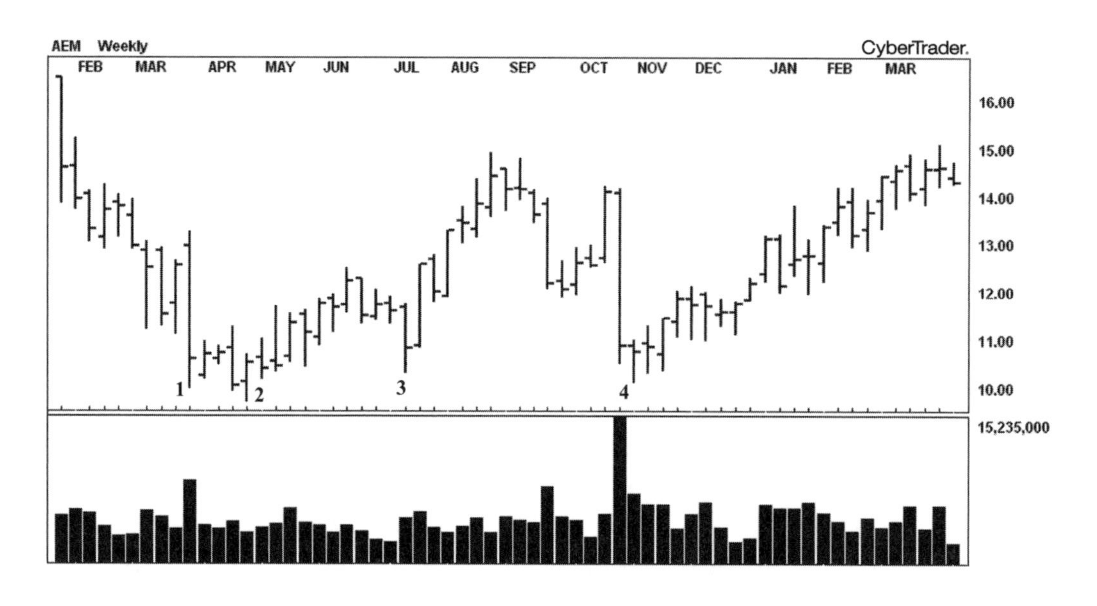

Figure 9-4: ***Support – Agnico Eagle Mines, Ltd. (AEM)***

(1) *AEM hits a low of $10.00 the week of April 4th, closing the week at $10.58 on volume of 8.7 million shares.*

(2) *The low of $10.00 is tested with AEM hitting $9.72 the week of May 5th; it closed the week at $10.52 with volume totaling 3.3 million shares.*

(3) *The equity hits $10.32 and closes the week out at $10.82 on volume of 4.7 million shares.*

(4) *AEM slams down hard the week of October 31st hitting $10.52 with monster volume of 15.2 million shares. The following week AEM hits a price point of $10.11 with volume coming in at 7.3 million shares.*

Notice how volume varies on each test of the $10.00 support level, ranging from 3.3 to 15.2 million shares, yet it isn't sufficient to blast through with conviction.

Break in Support

Once a stock has established a strong support level, it will take quite a bit of selling pressure to pierce that level of support in order for prices to break through and stay beneath it. As I said before, the longer a stock spends in its support-building phase, the more difficult it is for prices to pierce support. In the case of a house's foundation, more cement would require a stronger jackhammer for destruction. In the case of stock trading, the jackhammer is essentially downward volume.

Now let's say that YES's support level is perceived as being $15 and its price has just gone to $14.80. Well, the first thing you want to ask yourself is, "is this move for real?" Does this break in price have conviction, enough conviction to indicate that the price is going down for a good while? The answer to that depends on VOLUME!

Well, this is where it can get interesting. A break on support with little volume could be a road sign that this equity is not going to stay down for long. It is for this reason that I look for breaks in support on lighter volume to identify trading opportunities. I'm going to outline a system for identifying trading opportunities later on in this book, but for the purposes of this chapter, just be aware that a break of support can be very foretelling of a stock's future price inclinations just based on the trading volume during the break!

Support levels are much like swing lows (Chapter 10 - *Swing Points*) inasmuch as they represent critical moments of trading activity which in turn create critical points in a stock's price behavior.

Just as with swing low points, remember the following for support levels:

(1) A stock that breaks a support level with strong volume confirms that it will likely go lower,

(2) A stock that breaks a support level with lighter volume creates uncertainty in that it lacks conviction; keep an eye on it for a turn in direction,

(3) A stock approaching a support level over a longer period of time with its volume starting to dry up is basically saying that it will build a bit of cause here (accumulation) and then start moving higher.

Again, throughout this book I introduce guidelines that involve some fairly absolute qualifiers when referring to volume; these include higher, stronger, lighter, lower, etc. In my analyses of volume comparisons/fluctuations I personally use 10% as a benchmark to regard an amount as truly being "higher" or "lower", etc. Anything less than 10% is *relatively* the same.

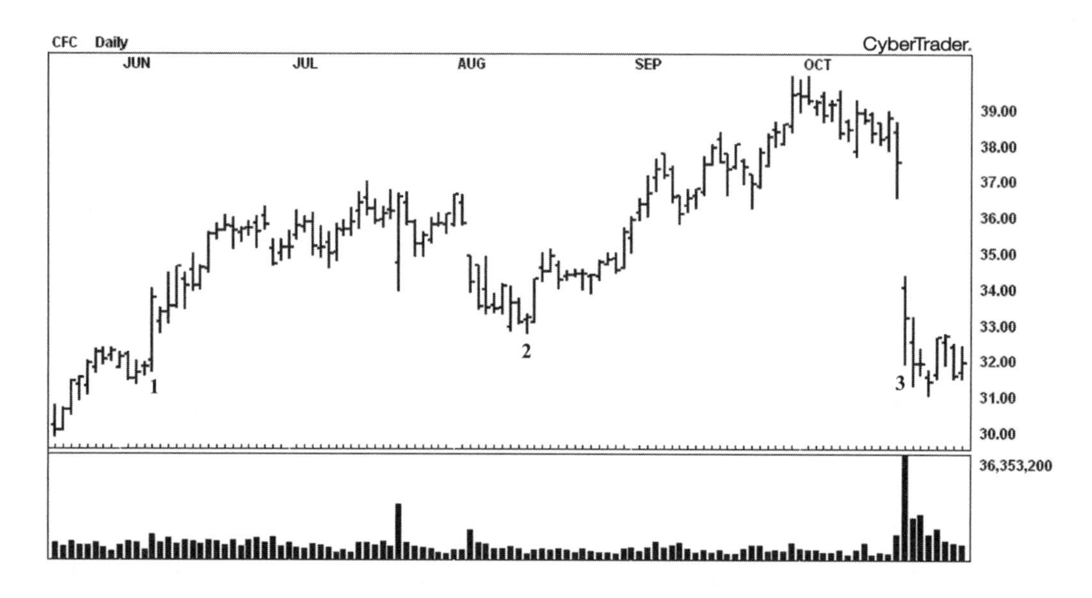

Figure 9-5: ***Break in Support – Countrywide Financial Corp. (CFC)***

(1) *June 7, 2004 – This was a breakout day and also the last day with volume on the way up running at 9 million shares. The low for the day was $31.67 establishing a support level.*

(2) *August 13th – CFC pulls back to the $32.74 mark with volume of 2.4 million shares. At this point, you can picture an upward sloping support level taking root.*

(3) *October 20th – CFC comes down on 36.3 million shares taking out the equity's support level.*

Support Becoming Resistance

What happens when you have a break in support that occurs with conviction, i.e., volume? Support all of a sudden becomes resistance. It becomes resistance because of overhead supply (owners at higher prices who failed to get out). Check out the diagram Figure 9-6 illustrating an example where a break in support *with* volume creates a resistance level where support was previously.

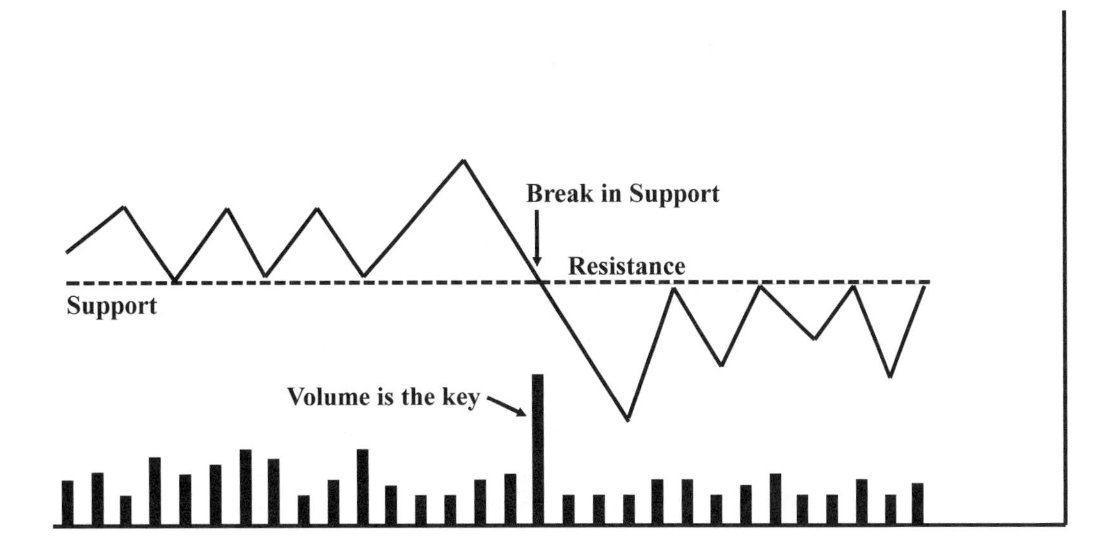

Figure 9-6: ***Broken Support Becoming Resistance***

Vive la Résistance

Resistance is formed as a result of a stock being overbought or in situations where there is overhead supply.

In an overbought scenario, everyone who wanted to own XYZ stock owns it. When there appears to be no more buyers, the distribution stage of the stock usually commences and it is here where a level of resistance is formed. Think of this level as a ceiling in our hypothetical house.

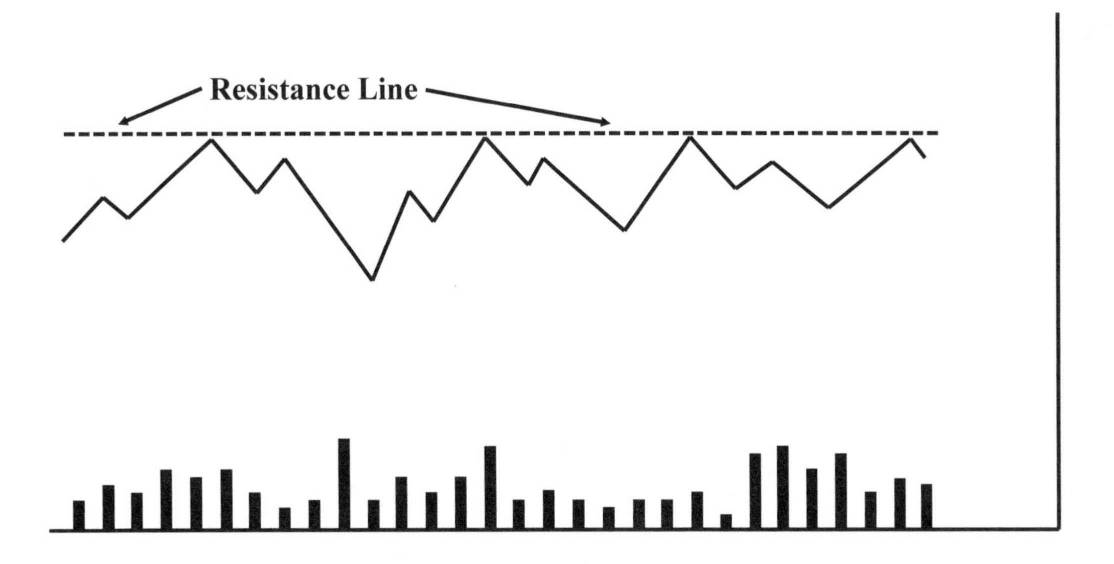

Figure 9-7: ***Resistance***

Overhead supply does not have to come at the absolute high but rather at different price points where there was significant trading activity. Let's say a stock had significantly high volume days at $35, $37 and $40. It is currently trading at $33 and is making a northerly charge with decent volume. Our stock is going to have to contend with those traders, investors, people, funds, etc., who own the stock at $35, $37 and $40. These owners may just want to get out at their cost basis just to save their portfolios. They may even get out at a lower amount because they feel that the stock will never reach their basis, or they just might need the cash. In whatever case, our stock will have to contend with those who own at a higher price level (overhead supply). Figure 9-8 gives us a simple example of resistance created by overhead supply.

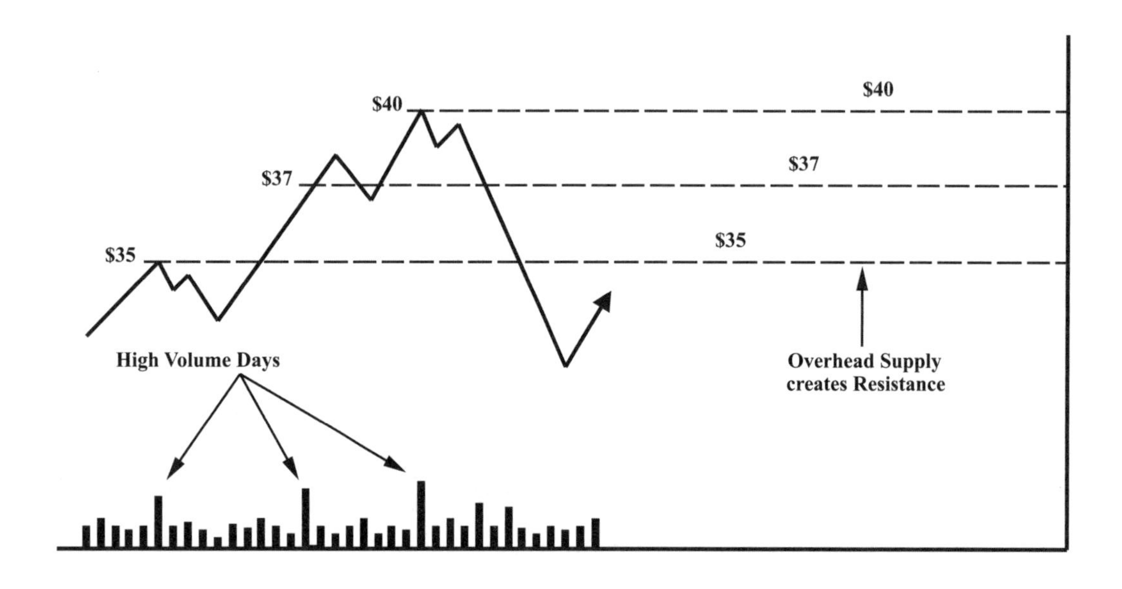

Figure 9-8: ***Overhead Supply Creates Resistance***

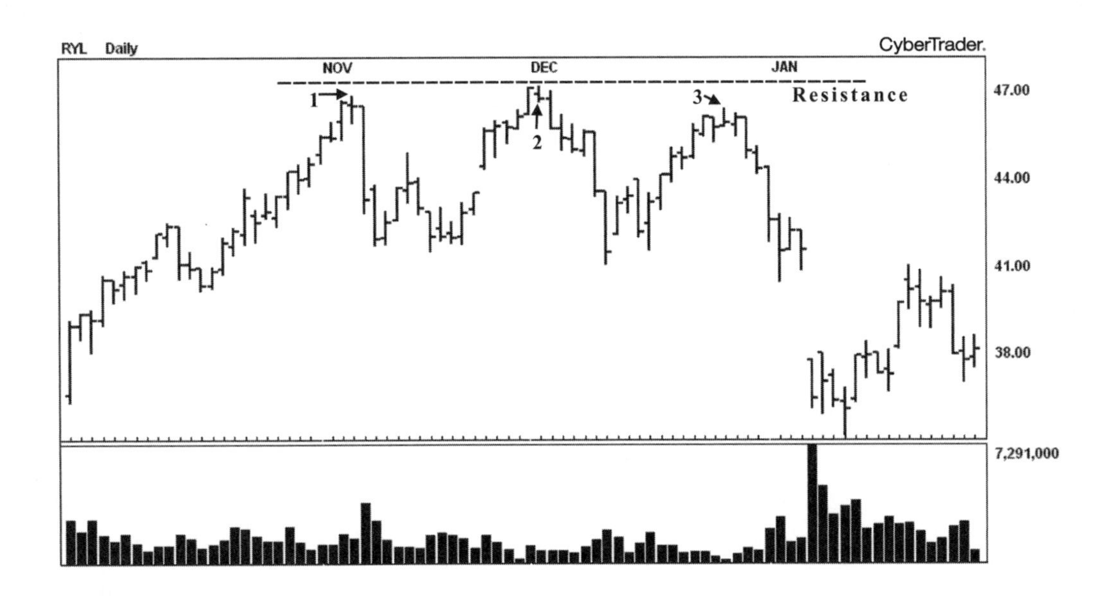

Figure 9-9: ***Resistance – The Ryland Group, Inc. (RYL)***

(1) *On November 6, 2003 – RYL reaches a high of $46.53 on volume of 1.6 million shares.*

(2) *December 2nd – RYL hits a high of $46.85 on volume of 837 thousand shares.*

(3) *On December 26th – RYL reaches $46.07 on anemic volume of 257 thousand shares.*

Note how with each drive to the top, volume drops off and so does price. Look to volume for an indication whether resistance will be meaningfully broken.

Resistance levels are much like swing highs in that they represent critical price points that a stock will have to contend with during its price appreciation. Just as with swing highs, the following are applicable to resistance levels:

(1) A stock that takes out a resistance level with volume confirms that it will likely go higher, and

(2) A stock that takes out a strong level of resistance with lighter volume is likely to turn around.

If our stock has surpassed the $35 and $37 levels of overhead supply with strong volume, then pierces $40 with scant volume and closes below $40, expect the stock to begin a countertrend move. The break through resistance is not real and the price should not hold.

Where Resistance Becomes Support

Back to our example. Let's say our stock has broken through $35 and $37 with decent volume and is approaching $40. With volume and conviction to boot, our stock smashes through the $40 ceiling and gets to $43 and takes a small breather. Therefore, since the $40 price level was broken with conviction and our stock has proven that it wants to stay higher, the $40 level that was previously a level of resistance now becomes a level of support. Why? Due to the amount of trading activity that took place at $40, there was a great amount of share exchanging going on. Where there once were holders at $40 just happy to get their basis back, there are now new holders at $40 who are anticipating making money with their new purchase. Think of our imaginary house again. If we pierce through the ceiling and make it to the next level, the ceiling becomes the floor for the next level. And the more amount of time that is spent in establishing that new floor, the more difficult it will be in the future to pierce that price level. Take a look at Figure 9-10 for an example of where resistance becomes support.

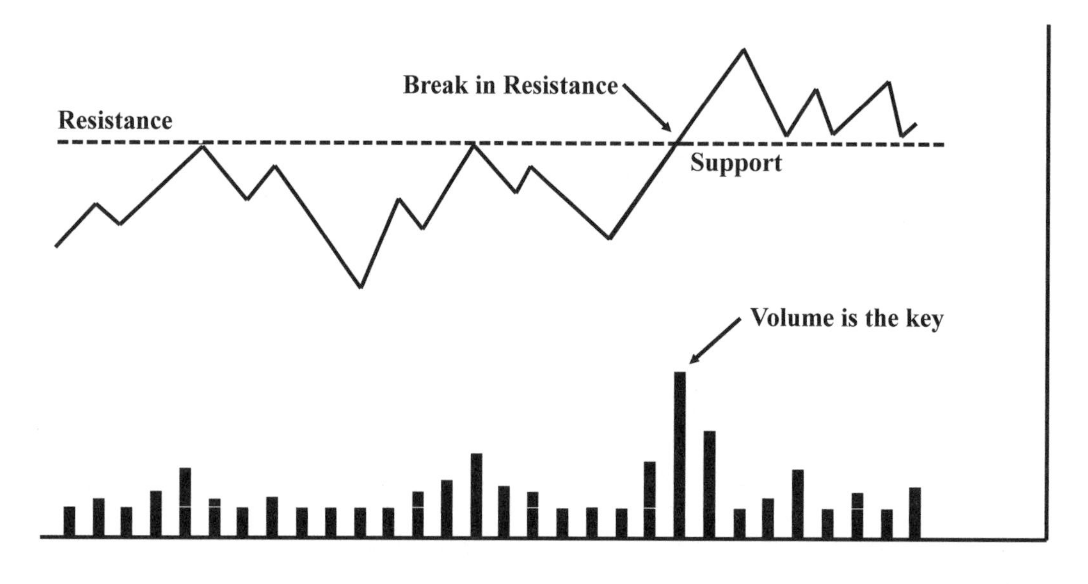

Figure 9-10: ***Broken Resistance Becoming Support***

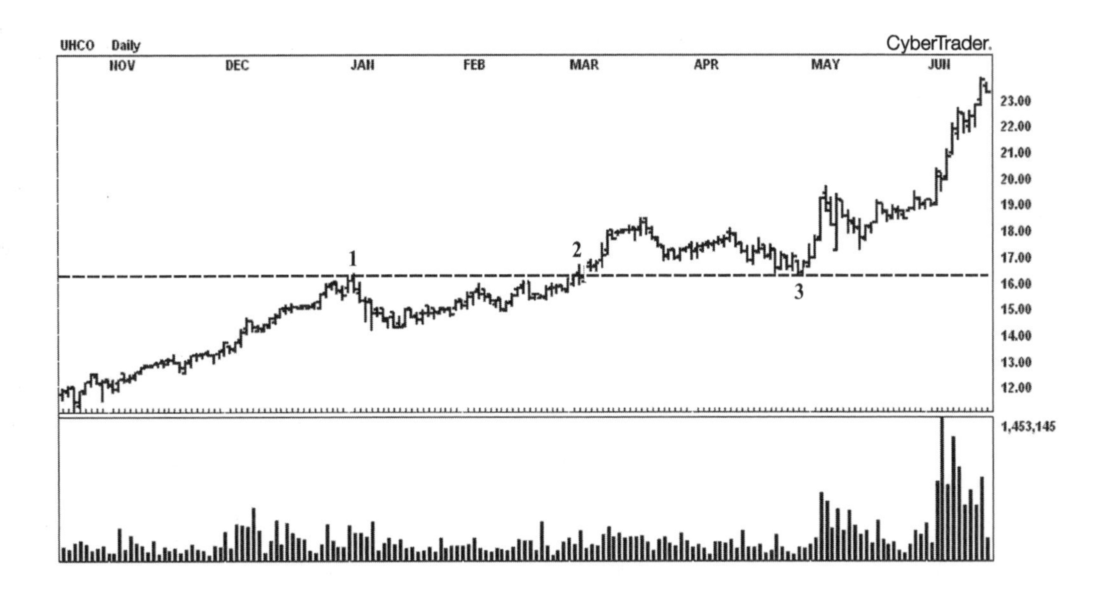

Figure 9-11: *Resistance Becoming Support - Universal American Financial Corp. (UHCO)*

(1) *On January 4, 2005, UHCO reaches a high of $16.35 on 294 thousand shares and turns around creating a swing high.*

(2) *The break of the January 4th swing high occurs on March 3rd.*

(3) *The swing high resistance point on January 4th* (1), *which has now become support, is tested on April 28th. The test is successful, support holds, and UHCO turns around and heads north.*

10

Swing Points

Without mountains one wouldn't see the plains.
~ Chinese Proverb

An important concept that will definitely reinforce your trading is that of swing points. What are they? Well, stocks as you very well know will not go up or down in a straight line; in fact they retrace (in essence turn around) for their next move, be it up or down.

Figure 10-1 shows simple examples of swing points. Notice how price movement halts at the swing points and begins to move in the opposite direction.

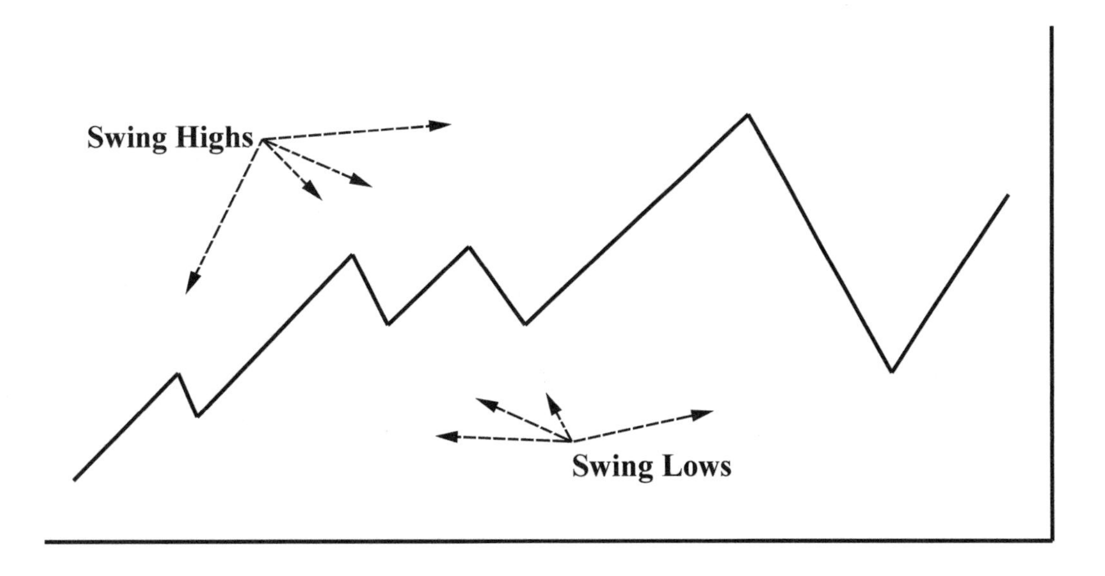

10-1: ***Swing Highs and Swing Lows***

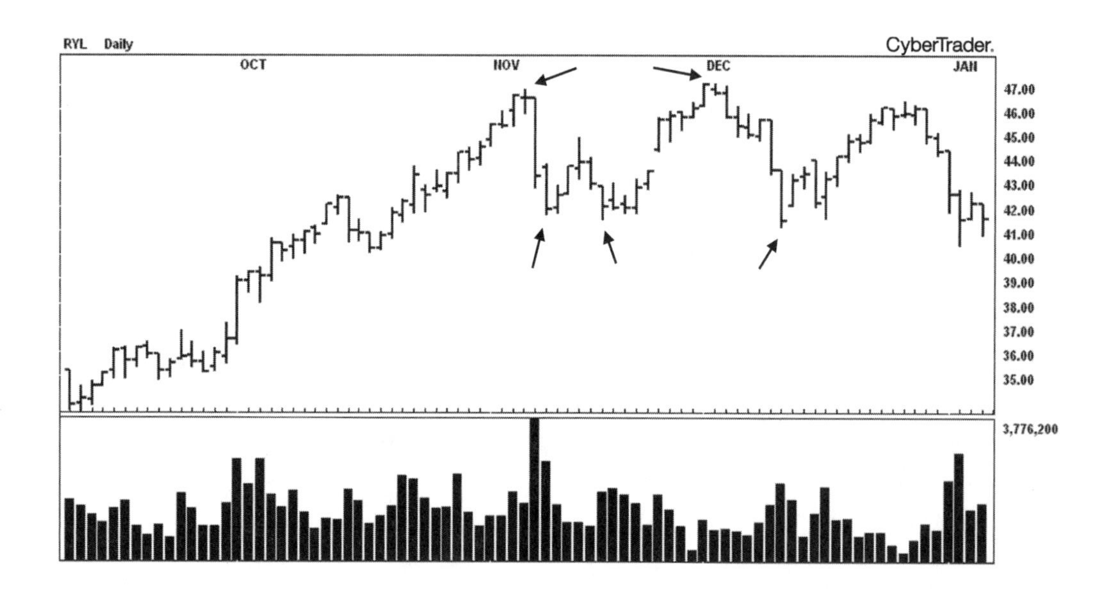

Figure 10-2: ***Swing Points on a Chart - The Ryland Group, Inc. (RYL)***

Swing points can be identified in different time periods. It is possible to note swings on an intraday basis as well as daily, monthly, yearly, etc. It's important for you to remember however, that swing points become more significant on a longer term basis. For example, if you pull up a chart of IBM for a month and compare that to IBM for an entire year, you'll see that both include swing points; however, the swing points on the yearly chart should be more pronounced and as a result become more significant in terms of identifying levels of support and resistance.

> ***Definition***: **swing point** – a point in a stock's price movement where there is a sudden, significant turn in direction; this point becomes an important level of support or resistance.

I should point out that swing points should not be confused with "swing trading" in which traders try to determine when and where swings are occurring in real time. Swing points, as I cover them in this chapter and throughout the book, involve changes in price direction that have occurred in the *past;* those price points act as price plateaus or thresholds to assist *present* and *future* trading decisions. Swing points will be introduced as a "mechanism" to supplement your trading rather than as a trading style by itself ("swing trading").

Swing points are where you'll be basing major trading decisions.

Swing Point Significance

Swing points are immensely critical and to comprehend their importance it is vital to understand exactly what they denote or represent in the form of trading activity. As you saw in Figure 10-1, price movement will often turn directions and these turns signal monumental shifts in supply and demand. Figure 10-3 includes a simple chart demonstrating a simple swing, in which the price movement of YES has turned after experiencing upward momentum. In fact the price turns at $30 in this example. This price becomes a very critical point because it is this price that will create a level of resistance, if and when YES turns back around and starts heading north. Why does it become resistance?

Try to picture what goes on at the swing point. Around this price, $30, you may have distribution or simply a significant shift in supply and demand. Basically people and operators are getting out of the stock by selling their shares to other investors. New investors have a cost basis of $30, but to their dismay their shares are losing value as the price starts heading down. The new investors may all have different mindsets in terms of how long they wish to hold on to the stock. Some may get out right away and some might just want to hold on to their shares for the long term. Regardless, those that stay in are in a losing position and being in a losing position is no fun. One thing for sure, the new investors' cost basis of $30 stays imprinted in their minds throughout the entire ordeal.

Let's say the stock hits $23 (at this point the new investors are down seven points or roughly 23%!). Suddenly, the stock turns around and starts heading north, fast approaching $30. As it gets close, the new investors are experiencing very interesting emotional and psychological dynamics. They may be thinking to themselves, "whew, this has been a rough ride, if it hits $30, I'm going to sell and get out even!" It's easy to see that this $30 mark becomes a serious bump in the road, virtually a level of resistance. Why? Because to move beyond $30, YES will have to contend with those owners who previously bought YES at that price and just might be itching to sell in order to save their portfolios (the existence of owners with a higher cost basis is regarded as "overhead supply"). There is one significant force that will help push YES past $30 and that is volume! Check out Figure 10-3.

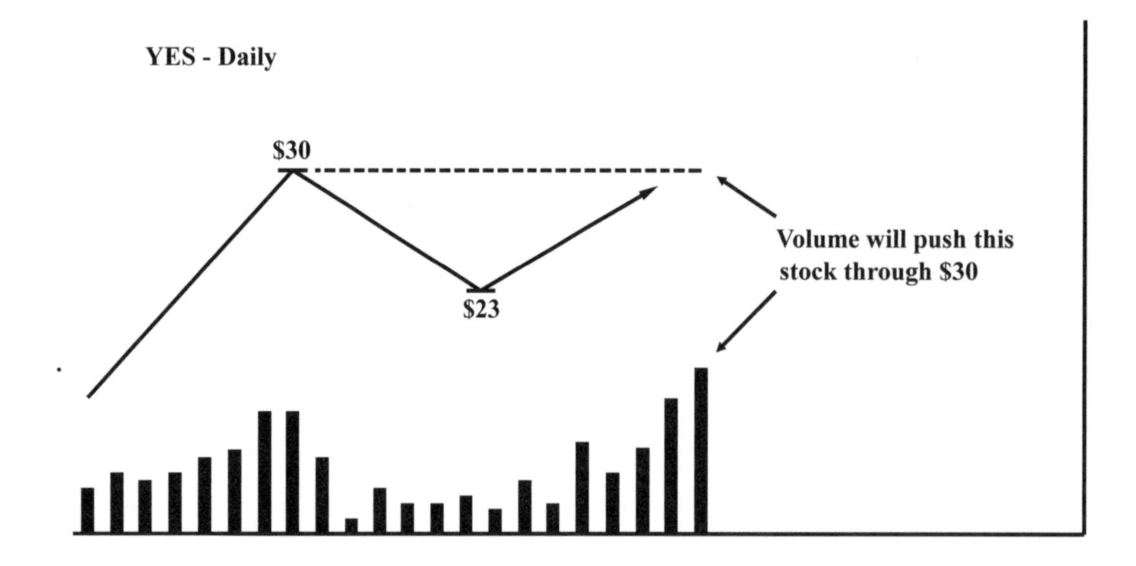

Figure 10-3: ***Approaching Swing Points with Volume***

Why not take a look at how a swing point can be a powerful level of support. Let's just go on with our example and suppose YES continues to $35. It settles and then starts to retrace. What was resistance (and a swing point) at $30 has now become a powerful level of support. Take a look at Figure 10-4. This is a classic example of broken resistance becoming support (previously covered in Chapter 9 – *Support & Resistance*).

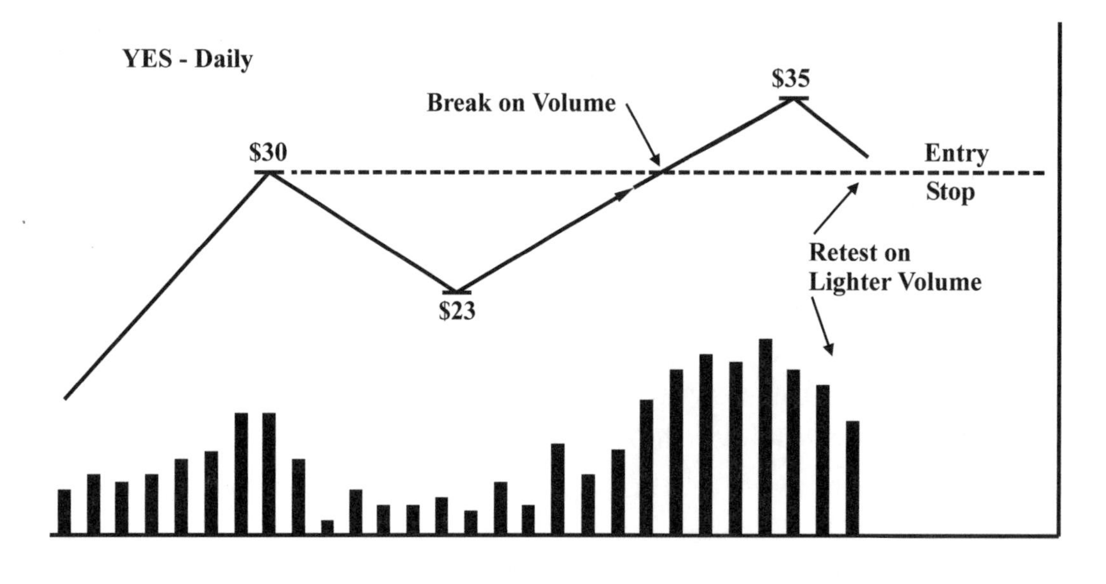

Figure 10-4: ***Passing Swing Point with Volume, Followed by a Retracement on Lighter Volume***

Continuing with our example and realizing that $30 is a great level of support, if you trade this stock, it's easy to see that a price above or at $30 would be your entry and a price just below $30 would be your stop.

Taking Out Swings with Volume

As I noted in Chapter 2, volume is crucial to all aspects of my trading repertoire, and when I couple it with swing points, the two become a powerful tool.

Once you have become comfortable with recognizing swing points, you should get in the practice of determining the volume associated with those points. This way you'll be able to tell if future price moves take out previous swing points, with or without volume. For example, if on March 1st, YES stock had a sudden turn and formed a swing point at $38, the fact that it traded 1 million shares on that day will become significant when that swing point becomes tested down the road.

Sticking to our example, let's say that YES goes down to $27 and then starts heading north again. As it approaches $38, volume is strong and YES in fact surpasses $38 on March 31st, with volume on that particular trading day totaling 1.3 million shares (don't forget that trading volume totaled 1 million shares on March 1st). So in my trading speak, I would say that on March 31st, YES "took out the March 1st swing high, *with* volume".

The amount of volume that occurs in tandem with any test is crucial. You might want to look at the difference in terms of a percentage; the higher the percentage difference, the greater the significance.

Figure 10-5 illustrates our example.

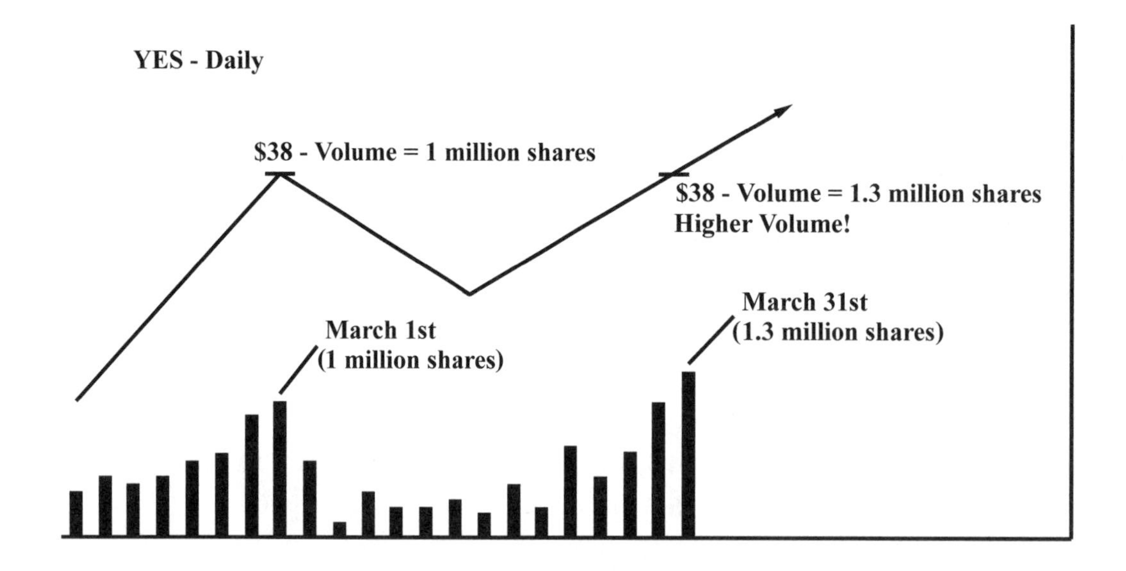

Figure 10-5: ***Taking out a Swing High with Volume***
Notice how YES's volume as it approaches its recent high of $38, strengthens and takes out the swing high with volume (1.3 million shares on March 31st).

Figure 10-6 includes a real example of a swing high being taken out *with* volume. Note the subsequent move up, due in part to the conviction of strong volume.

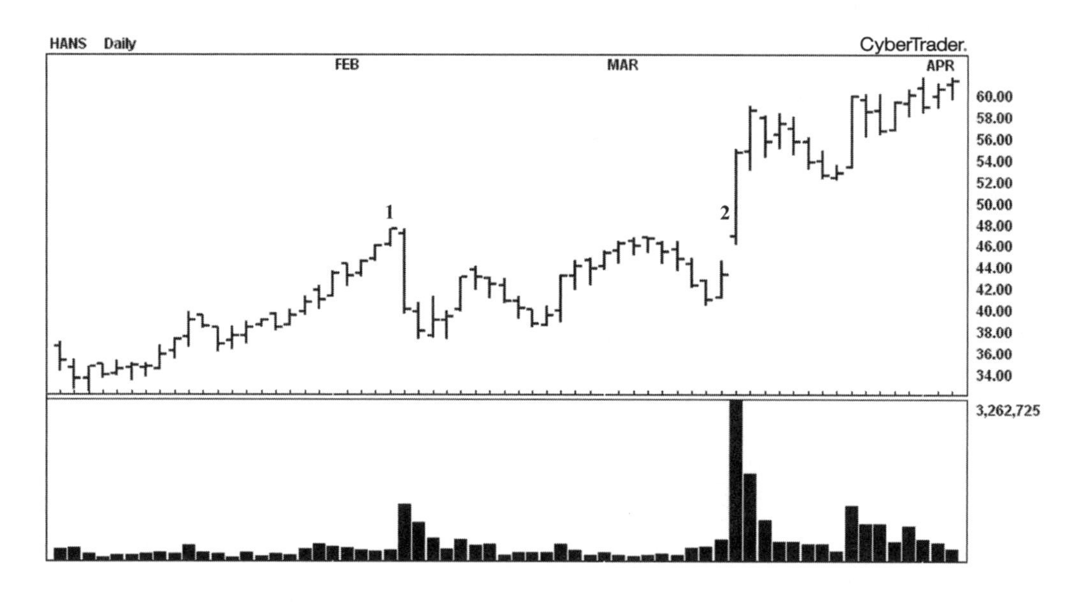

Figure 10-6: ***Swing High Taken Out*** **with** ***Volume - Hansen Natural Corp. (HANS)***

(1) *On February 7, 2005, HANS formed a swing high at $47.49 on 241 thousand shares.*

(2) *The February 7th swing high was taken out on March 14th on 3.3 million shares (monster volume!) with the equity closing at $54.57. Note the subsequent price ascension.*

Now what happens if a previous YES swing high is taken out on significantly lighter volume? Usually that is an indication that YES's price is being extended - a huge road sign telling you that its price cannot stay up forever; i.e., look for this equity to go south. Something to remember is that the longer the stock stays above the high on lighter volume, the deeper that it will pull back once it starts to drop.

Figure 10-7 illustrates our example where a swing high is taken out with lighter volume. Note the stock's price cannot be held up any longer and what follows is a subsequent decline.

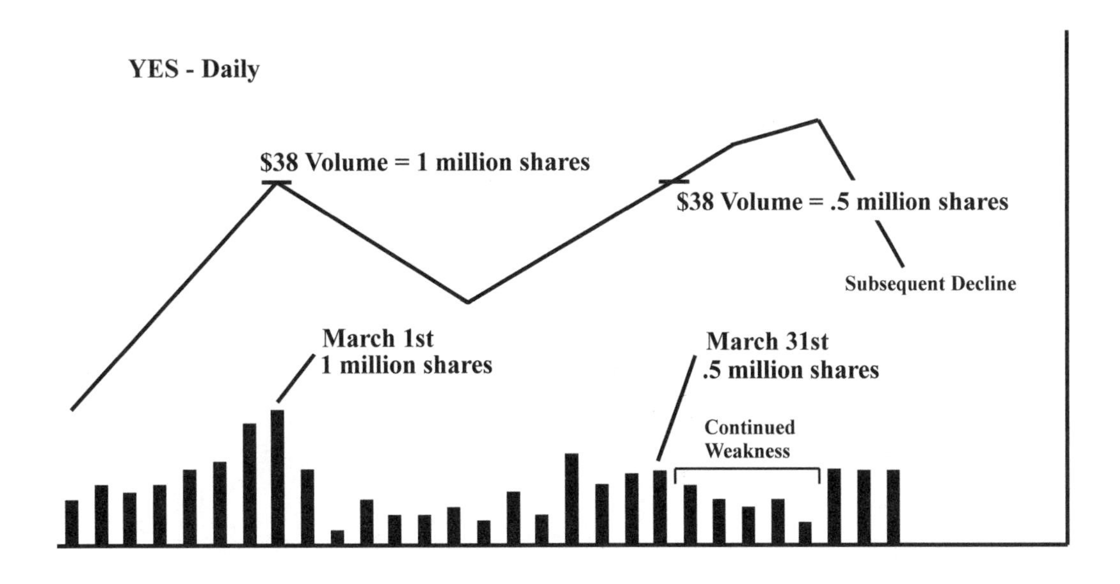

Figure 10-7: ***Swing High Taken Out Without Volume***

Throughout this section we have covered examples where there is a swing high that is taken out. Indeed, the same principles apply with swing lows, with volume being the key determinant of whether the stock will continue dropping or turn around. If a swing low is taken out on volume, the stock is very likely to continue in its downtrend. If a swing low is taken out on lighter volume, don't expect a continuation of the move for long.

Figure 10-8 includes a real example of a swing high being taken out without volume. Note the subsequent movement due to the lack of volume conviction.

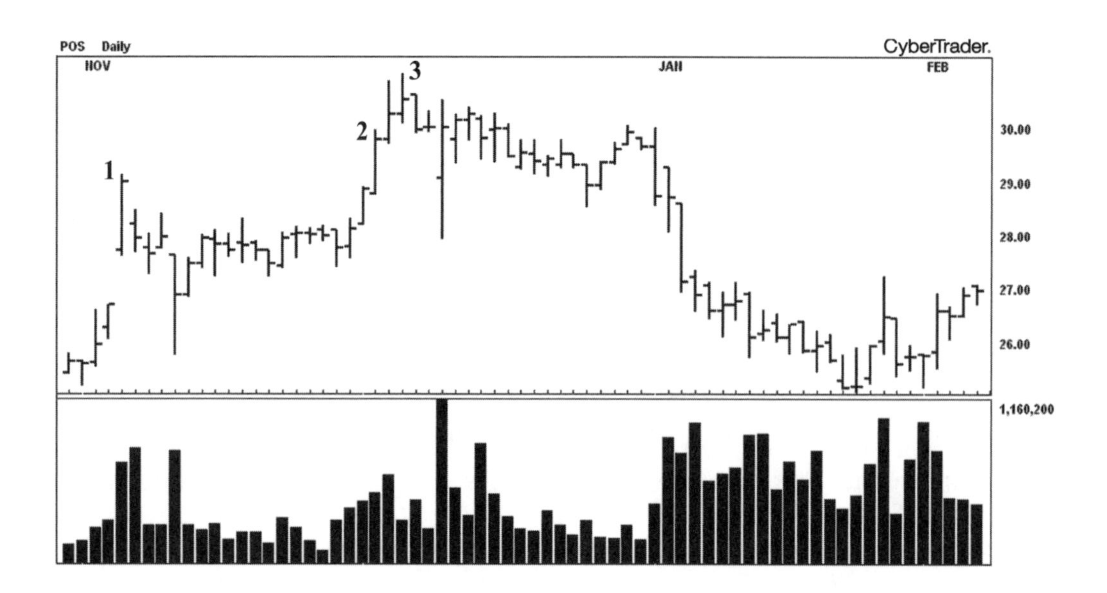

Figure 10-8: ***Swing Highs Taken Out Without Volume - Catalina Marketing Corp. (POS)***

(1) *POS forms a swing high on November 4, 2004 at $29.11 on 718 thousand shares.*

(2) *The November 4th swing high is taken out on December 2nd on 510 thousand shares (compared to 718 thousand shares of November 4, 2004).*

(3) *After a small phase of unnatural price extension, POS tops out on December 6, 2004 at $31.00 and begins a steady roll downhill.*

Movement on stronger volume implies that the movement will continue.

Movement on lighter volume implies that the movement will reverse.

Hitting Swing Points Head-on

So far, we've covered swing point dynamics (i.e. approaching swing points, taking out swing points with or without volume, etc.) from similar directional perspectives. That is to say that when a stock has approached a swing point, it has done so from the same direction or manner that the swing point developed. Example: our stock YES is at $27 and is approaching a $30 swing point (established as a swing high); the stock is *still* below the $30 benchmark and is approaching it the same way a climber approaches a mountain peak.

What if YES were at $33, moving downward and fast approaching the previously-set swing high of $30? In this case YES is challenging the swing high benchmark of $30, but from the other side or "head-on". Here too, volume is important. Figure 10-9 illustrates this example:

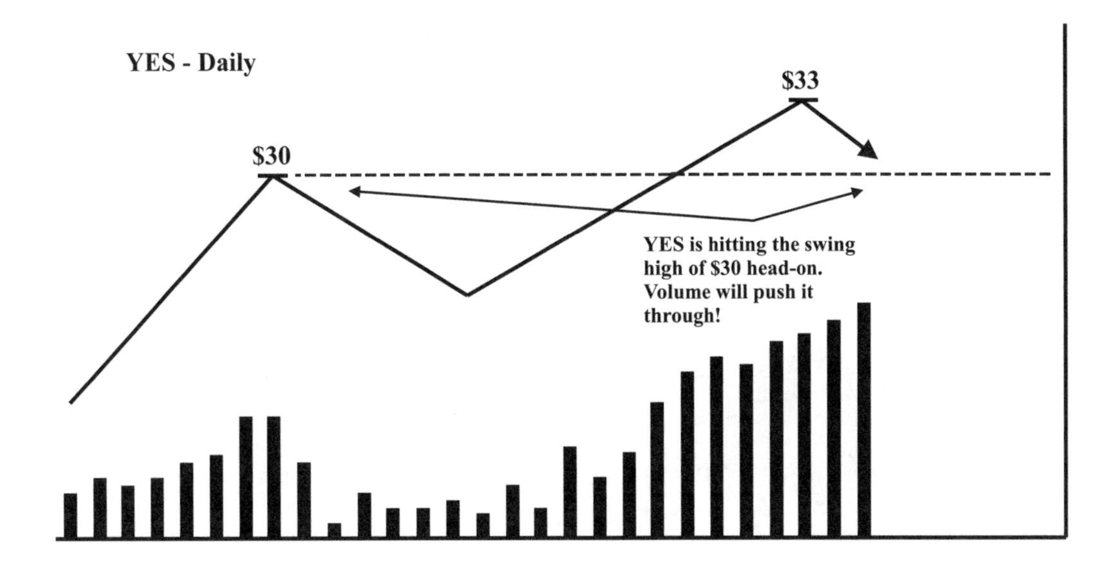

Figure 10-9: ***Hitting a Swing High Head-on***

Conversely, a stock can push a swing low head-on. Suppose YES were at $27 and approaching a previously-set swing low of $30 head-on. Here again, volume will determine whether or not the swing low will be taken out.

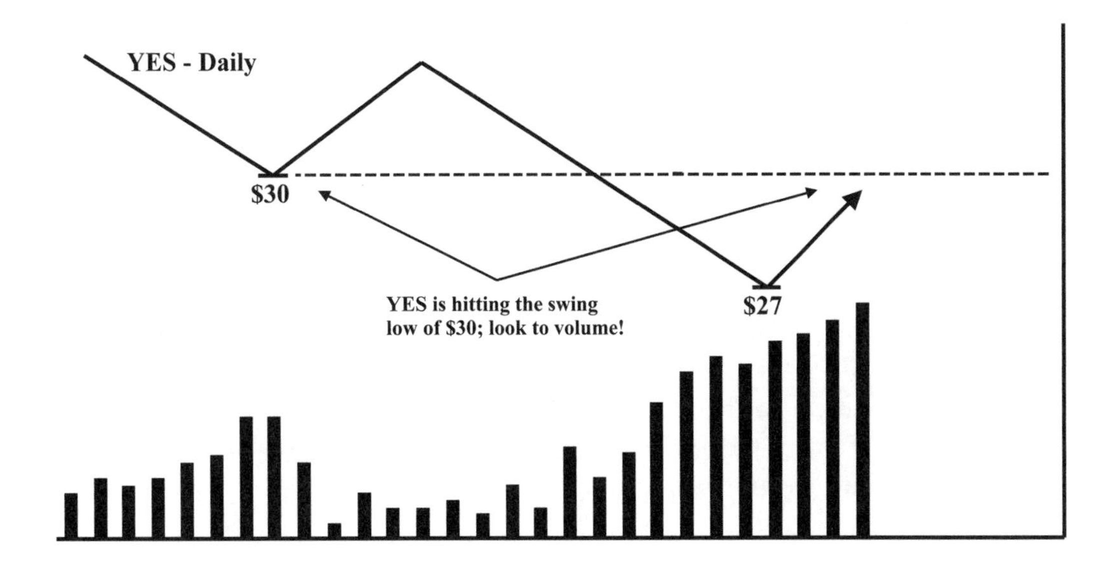

Figure 10-10: ***Hitting a Swing Low Head-on***

Figure 10-11 shows Patterson Energy hitting a swing high . . . head-on!

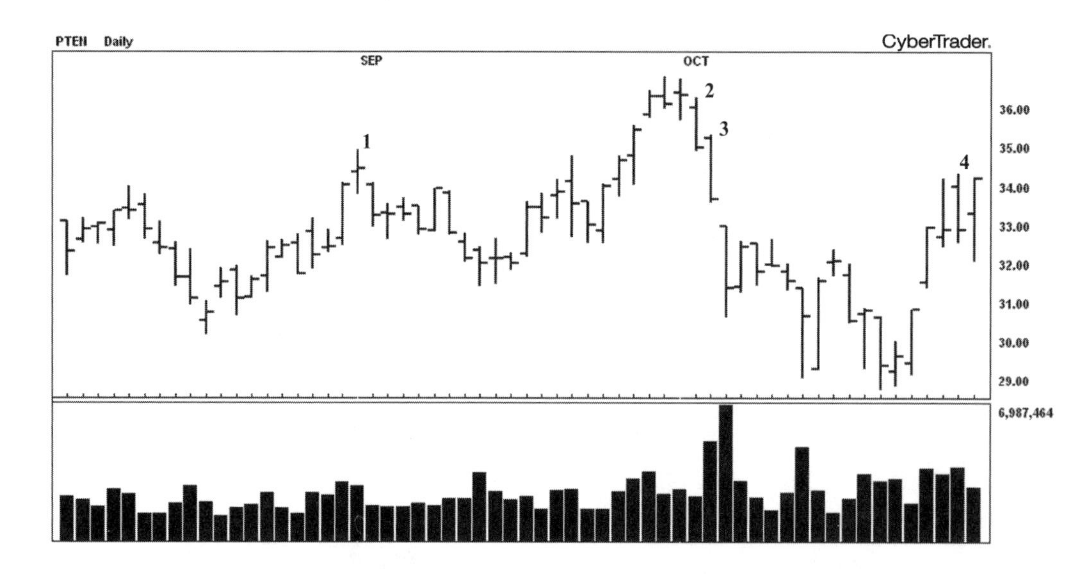

Figure 10-11: ***Challenging Swing Point from Opposite Direction - Patterson-UTI Energy, Inc. (PTEN)***

(1) *On September 1, 2005, PTEN forms a swing high of $34.91 on 2.9 million shares.*

(2) *The September 1st swing high of $34.91 is initially challenged "head-on" on October 4th with PTEN pushing down on the benchmark $34.91, hitting $34.92 on 2.3 million shares.*

(3) *The September 1st swing high benchmark gets blasted through with volume on October 5th with PTEN down-drafting on 5.1 million shares.*

(4) *PTEN struggles to overcome the October 5th downdraft price range "head-on" on October 27th. Volume this day totals 3.1 million shares – not quite the 5.1 million shares seen on October 5th.*

Swing Points with ABCs, Fibonacci and Confluence

In this book I have devoted entire chapters to ABC structures, Fibonacci expansion and contraction theory, and confluence. These concepts are greatly influenced by swing points and your ability to recognize them and nail their actual price points (in addition to determining their relative volume occurring on their particular trading day, week, month, year, etc.). It is these price points that create the "joints" of a stock's ABC structure. These points are also integral to the calculation of Fibonacci contraction and expansion projections, as well as to calculating a stock's area of confluence. It's at these very points where you'll be making your critical buy and sell decisions. Very, very important. Figure 10-12 identifies certain major swing points.

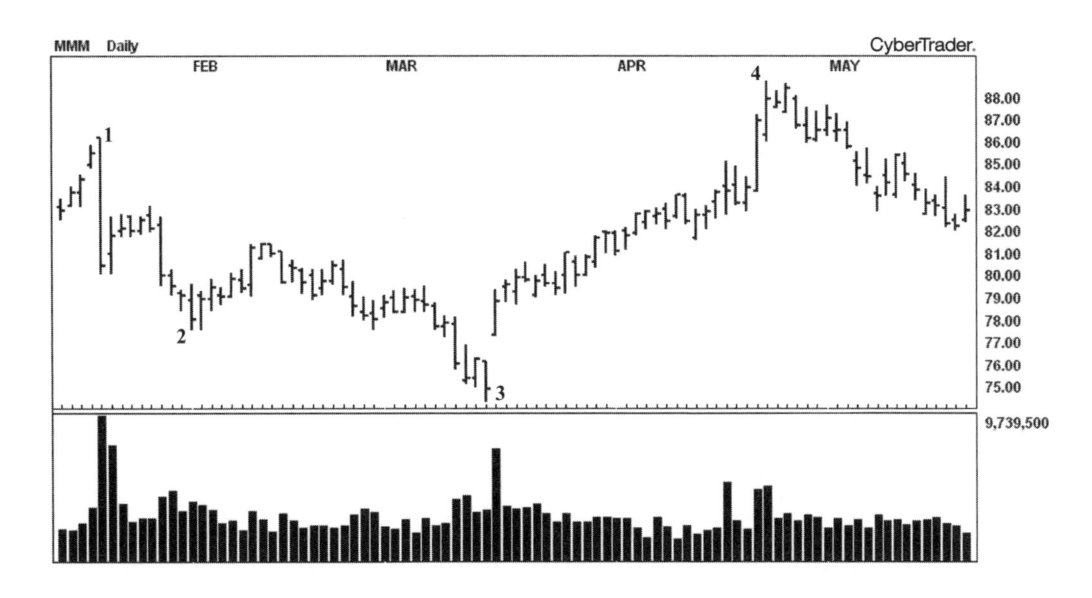

Figure 10-12: ***Major Swing Points – 3M Company (MMM)***

(1) *January 20, 2004 – 3M opens at its high of $86.20 before experiencing a monster downdraft hitting $80.10 the very same day on volume of 9.7 million shares.*

(2) *3M hits a short term bottom on February 2nd of $77.57.*

(3) *March 15th – 3M strikes $74.35 on volume of 3.4 million shares.*

(4) *April 23rd – 3M goes back to $88.70 with volume of 5 million shares, going against the swing point of January 20th on lighter volume (versus 9.7 million shares). Note the decline that follows.*

Swing points are turning points in the supply and demand equation. Major swing points, as opposed to minor swing points, provide greater meaning by revealing stronger levels of support and resistance.

Swing Point Key Points

What follows are some simple expectations for price behavior around swing point price levels (based on related volume of course) and how they can help your decision-making process.

Approaching a Swing Point:

- Higher volume - Expect the swing point to be surpassed.

- Lighter volume - Odds are the swing point will not be surpassed (at least not in the short term).

Surpassing a Swing Point:

- Higher volume - Expect a continuation of the price move.

- Lighter volume - The move will not hold.

Sitting at a Swing Point:

- Swing high - If a stock sits underneath a swing high for a few days without pulling back, the equity is building strength to take the swing high out (surpass it). Volume may not be very intense during this phase.

- Swing low - As with a swing high, if a stock sits over a swing low and continues in a sideways manner, the stock is building cause to break the low.

  - In either case volume is the determinant. Look to the stock's volume history as it previously approached the swing highs and lows.

Setting Up a Trade:

- Identifying a recent swing point can uncover a level of support or resistance.

- Determine your entry and stop price points accordingly using swing point price levels, all the while staying mindful of *volume*.

Important: Throughout the book, I use *higher, stronger, lighter, lower,* etc. to qualify volume when comparing amounts. My rule-of-thumb minimum (or benchmark) for considering these terms is 10%, i.e., the difference between two amounts must be at least 10%, otherwise the two are *relatively* the same.

11

Gaps

The suspense is horrible... I hope it'll last!
~ Willy Wonka

Another invaluable tool and characteristic of technical analysis that I find extremely useful in interpreting stock price behavior is that which is encompassed in the field of *gaps*. Surely you've seen the term gap used in many different contexts: such as the space between two objects, like my two front teeth, or how about all the gaps that you run across when traveling through the mountains or on the Blue Ridge Parkway – those of you with RV's know exactly what I'm talking about.

Here, we will look at gaps as they relate to the empty space between the price ranges of two trading days or periods. Their interpretation and application to trading is not an exact science; however, they can be appreciated and applied to *Timing the Trade* just as powerfully as swing points.

Gaps Defined

Now, as I mentioned above, a gap, as it relates to technical analysis, is basically the space between the price ranges of two trading days (or periods depending what time frame you're using, e.g., day, week, month, etc.). Let's take a look at a gap in Figure 11-1:

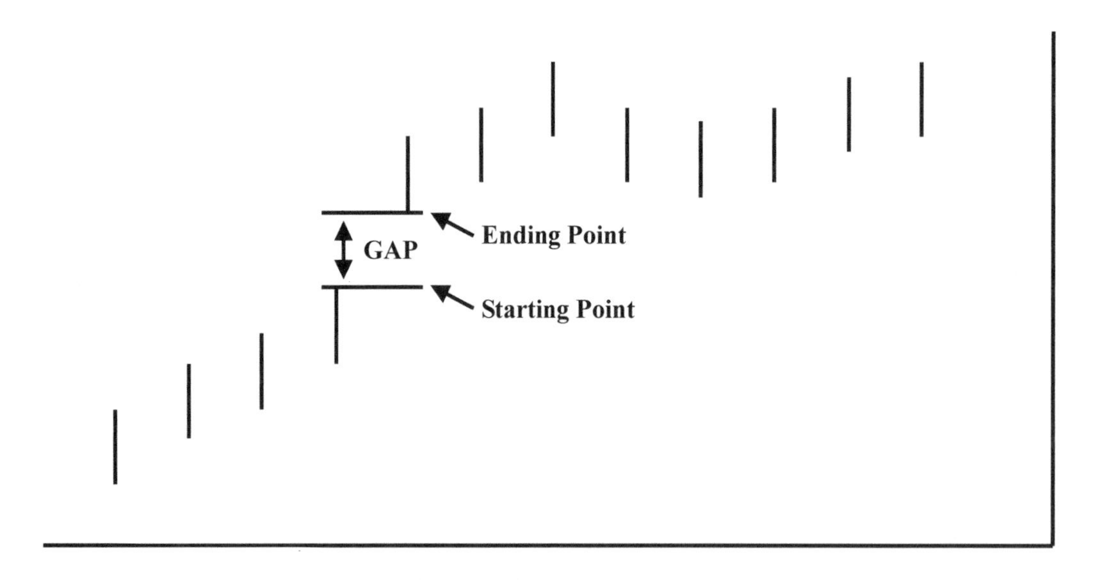

Figure 11-1: ***Simple Gap***

Do you see the price range between the two trading days where no trades were fired off? Well, this is a textbook example of a gap. It's basically something of an empty price area where there are no trades, and perhaps a void of ownership.

Question: How often do gaps occur?
Answer: Not very.

Q: What causes gaps?
A: Gaps are typically due to events that cause the supply and demand dynamics of a particular equity to change or shift immediately and dramatically. These events create a price spread between two trading periods (going forward, we will look at them as they occur on a daily time frame) where no transactions took place. Example: If a stock is moving upward in price and has a high of $10 on Day 1 and then on Day 2 has a low of $12, that stock has created a gap of $2, essentially a void of ownership in this $2 area.

Q: What is their significance?
A: In a sense, gaps will raise eyebrows and their significance can vary; as for exactly what meaning they hold, "time will tell" (i.e., you have to wait to see how the stock trades afterwards). I'll get into their possible influences and impacts in short order.

Q: What are the critical points of a gap?
A: The beginning and ending of a gap are the only points we should be concerned

with; they are the *starting point* (typically the high or low price of the previous trading day) and the *ending point* (again, typically the high or low price of the subsequent trading day; by "high or low price" I mean that which is closest to the gap itself). Figure 11-1 outlines the starting and ending points of a gap.

Q: What about 24 hour trading? Doesn't this impact gaps insofar as we're concerned?
A: No. With after-hours trading there is a noticeable decline of trading liquidity (i.e., volume) and stock charts that are expressed in daily terms will only include trading activity (price and volume) for trades that are executed during market hours.

A Perfect Gap Example

Let's say for example that there is a newsworthy event that will affect the trading price of Cancer Cure, Inc. (CCI). Suppose CCI is in the business of laboratory research and development and they are working on a complete cancer cure. Trading of CCI stock ceases at four o'clock on a particular Friday afternoon and over the weekend that follows, a press release hits the wires (Reuters, AP, etc.) that CCI has discovered a certain enzyme found in South American banana trees that can eradicate the spread of *all* types of cancers. CCI has filed the appropriate documents to patent the extraction process to harness the enzyme.

Well this would certainly be positive news. Not to mention all the lives that would be saved and the physical and emotional tolls that would be eliminated, CCI stands to make a considerable windfall if their discovery is fruitfully (no pun intended here) brought to market through an FDA-approved medicine that is globally accepted and distributed; and if CCI itself doesn't do this, it can certainly license the process to a multinational pharmaceutical outfit for a decent amount of money.

Q: As a result of the press release, what happens to the perceived value of CCI?
A: It goes up!

Q: How does this affect the trading price of CCI?
A: It too goes up!

Q: Will CCI's opening price on Monday or the following trading day be the same as the previous trading day's (Friday's) closing price?

A: No way! More than likely, the equity should open significantly higher than Friday's close.

Q: How will the opening price be established?

A: Market makers and specialists will mark up the price according to the perceived increase in demand for CCI; the greater the perceived demand, the higher price that CCI will command during the market's open.

Q: What does this higher opening price create in technical analysis terms?

A: A gap!

Q: Could this press release have an effect on other equities?

A: You bet! Sympathy plays exist when peers (similar companies in the same industry, business or "space") experience reactive trading pressures thanks to the initial news. Let's say that YES is also in research and development and YES is working on a cure for leukemia. The fact that CCI found a natural cure through South American banana trees may open the door for YES to look for other enzymes in similar trees for its potential leukemia cures. Let's also not forget about the multinational pharmaceutical companies that may have a competitive advantage insofar as acquiring the technology from CCI, not to mention their enhanced production economies, marketing potential and distribution might. Their stock's opening prices may gap up as well (the terms "gap up" and "gap down" are commonly used for disparities between opening and previous closing prices) because of an increased demand in their stock. And let's not forget the agricultural companies out there growing banana trees!! Their stocks may gap up as well!!

Q: Does it take a significant news item, such as CCI's discovery, to cause an equity to gap up or gap down?

A: Not always. Typically you'll see uncommon news events such as earnings releases or takeover announcements spur market makers or specialists to mark a stock up or down; the news events may also simply cause fundamental shifts in market dynamics, i.e., supply and demand, to move the opening price.

Q: Could an external news event, not directly related, create a gap in CCI's trading activity?

A: Absolutely. Consider what happens each time there is significant news item regarding world stability.

Q: Does it necessarily take a news item to create a gap?
A: No. Fear and greed during powerful bear and bull markets can create imbalances in the supply and demand equation and as a result, create gaps.

Meaningful Gaps

The creation of a gap is usually the result of a trigger (e.g., news item, euphoric fear, greed, etc.) that leads to a dynamic shift in the supply and demand fundamentals of an equity (or commodity for that matter). The development of a gap creates additional dynamics that can impact a stock's future trading behavior going forward; before we get into why a gap creates additional dynamics (basically their characteristics), let's look at a fundamental price behavioral tendency that is brought on by gaps.

Gaps get Filled

Gaps typically get filled (there are a few exceptions that I will cover later).

Q: Tom, what do you mean when you say that gaps get filled.
A: Well, as I mentioned before, a gap is an *empty* price range. This price range is typically filled during future trading activity. It is *filled* by trades that go off inside of the gap's range up or down to the starting point of the gap (also known as the "fill point"). See Figure 11-2 for an example of a gap getting filled.

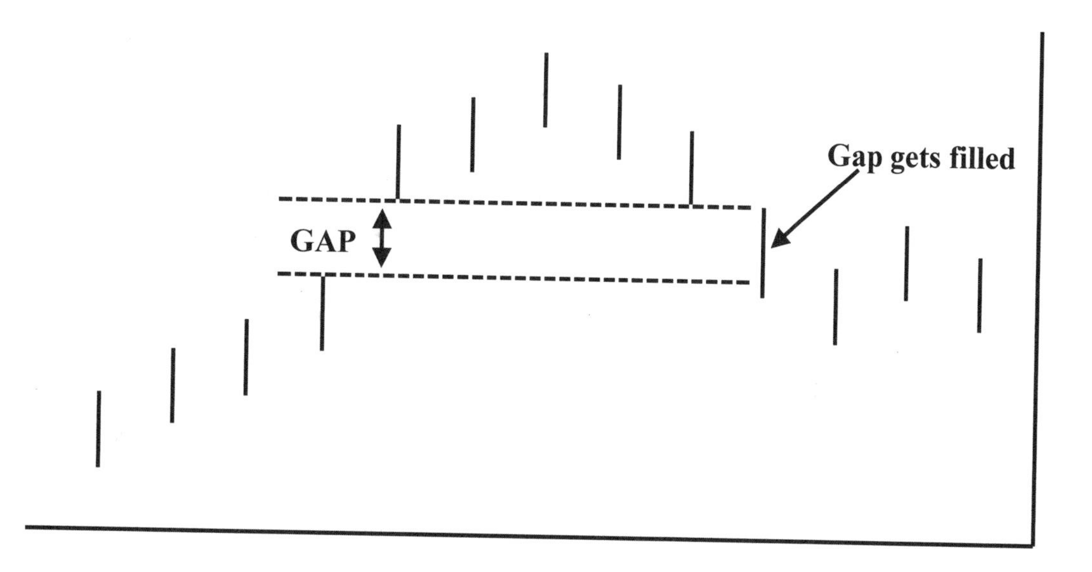

Figure 11-2: ***Gap Getting Filled***

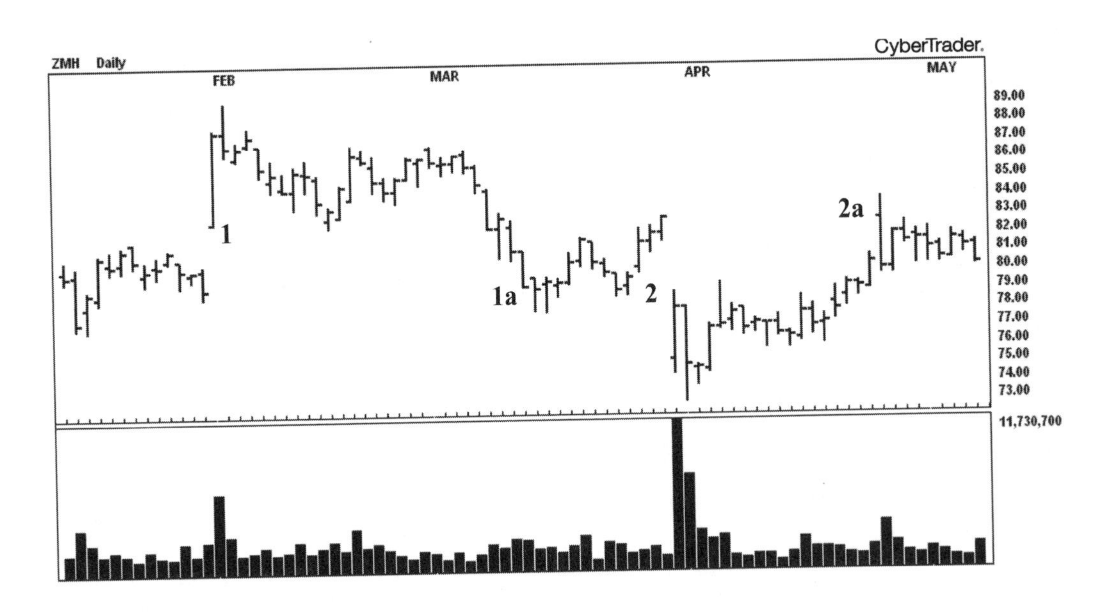

Figure 11-3: ***Filling Gaps - Zimmer Holdings, Inc. (ZMH)***
ZMH creates a gap up on February 1, 2005 (1) *that is subsequently filled on March 11th* (1a). *ZMH then forms a gap down on March 31st* (2)*; this gap appears to be filled on April 26th* (2a)*; unlike most market technicians, I don't regard a gap as being filled until the equity closes beyond the fill point – in this case it did not.*

It is important to note that a gap formed as a stock is moving up will get filled as the stock comes back or down to that level. Conversely, if a gap is formed while the stock is moving down, the gap will not be filled until the equity has gone back up to meet the gap (this is very similar to the concepts we will cover in Chapter 13 - *Jumping the Creek, Coming Back to Ice*)

Q: Is a gap completely filled if it surpasses the fill point intraday yet does not *close* beyond the fill point?
A: I differ with most market technicians in this aspect, not to mention others. I do not regard a gap as being filled until the equity or commodity has *closed* at a price that is beyond or at the fill point.

Q: Tom, why would a stock's gap *not* get filled?
A: More often than not, a gap will not get filled when there is a paradigm shift in the perception or outlook for the company whose stock is being traded. An example would be the announcement of a bankruptcy or takeover.

Some important notes on the filling of gaps:

- Gaps have a tendency to get filled.

    - The likely exception is a dramatic gap down caused by a significant fundamental reason(s), paradigm shift, etc. It would take a seriously greater dynamic force to take the stock back to its original pre-gap levels.

    - The further away your equity is from a previous gap, in a *price* sense, the less likely that the gap will be filled.

    - The further away your equity is from a previous gap, in a *time* sense, the more likely it will take a market turn to fill the gap.

Some important things to note about the last two items above concern the time and distance since previous gaps:

- As for *time*, if your equity experienced a gap 12 months ago that has yet to be filled, it becomes increasingly likely that it will take a turn in the market for the gap to be filled.

- In a *distance* sense (as it regards price), if your equity experienced a gap last month between $10 and $12 and is currently at $30, it is very unlikely that the gap at $10 will be filled any time soon but it may happen at some point in the future.

Incidently, gaps in candlestick terminology are referred to as "windows" and the filling of a gap is regarded as the "window" being "closed".

Characteristics

<u>*Support and Resistance*</u>

Gaps usually act as price magnets and more surprising than not, as price points of support and resistance. Does this sound familiar? Well it should because the same principles apply to the characteristics of swing points. Again, a likely exception to this is when there is a dynamic *paradigm* shift that obviously keeps a stock from heading back to the gap.

Let's take a look at gaps and the levels of support and resistance that are subsequently born.

Support Created from Gaps

Gaps to the upward side will create levels of support, namely two. The first level is created at the *ending* point of the gap, where trading picks up after leapfrogging a price span. In a logistical sense, there is a void of ownership in the price span that is gapped. What creates the level of support at the other side is the rush of volume that meets the stock once trading commences; this rush creates a price point with significant ownership thus forming a significant level of support. What will crack this support with conviction? Volume. What happens if the level of support is broken? There is another support level (second) occurring at the *starting* point of the gap. Figure 11-4 gives us a great illustration of this concept.

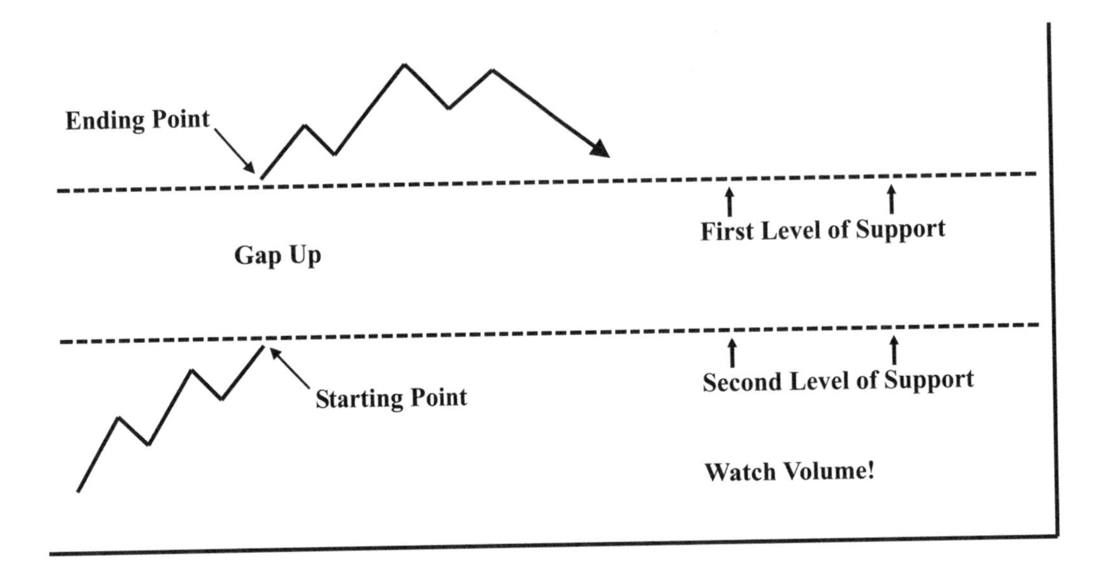

Figure 11-4: ***Gap Up Creating Support***

Figure 11-5 gives us a real example of gap-up support levels in action.

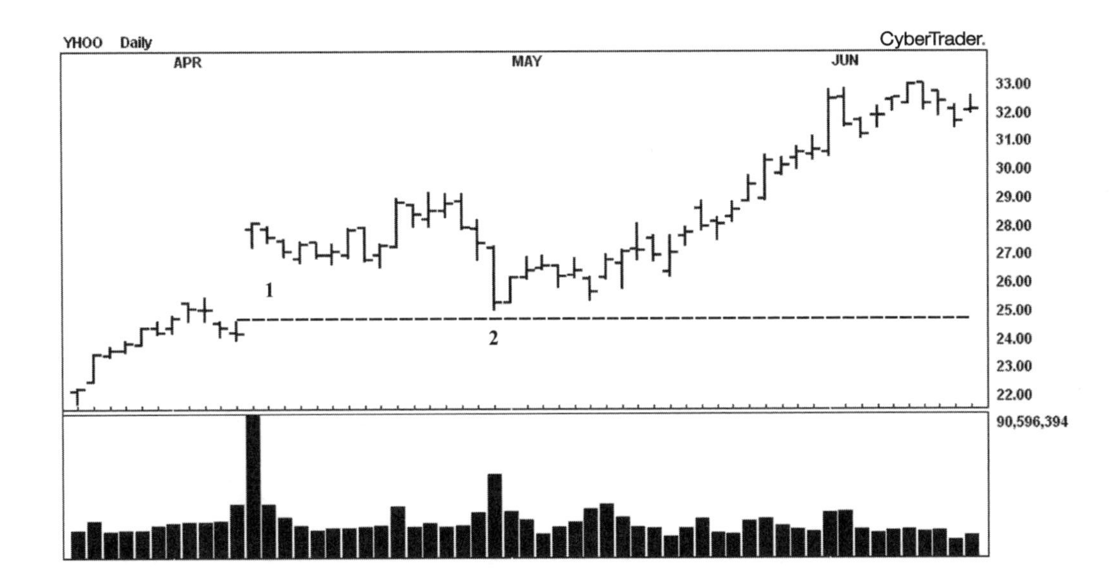

Figure 11-5: ***Gap-up Support – Yahoo! Inc. (YHOO)***
On April 8, 2004 (1), *YHOO gaps up to the tune of $27.89 and finishes above the open at $28.10, all the while having a monster volume day of 90.6 million shares. The first level of support comes in at the lower end of the day, $27.25 (gap's ending point) and is somewhat "violated" in the days that follow but on much lighter volume. The second level of support was established the day previous to the gap (starting point) at $24.62. YHOO makes a run for this level on April 30th* (2), *but comes up short by thirty-nine cents, on volume of 53 million shares – far short of the 90.6 million shares on YHOO's April 8th gap-up day. The second level of support held and YHOO turned around to head back north.*

<u>*Resistance Created from Gaps*</u>

Gap-down situations typically create two levels of resistance with the first one occurring at the ending point of the gap and the second at the beginning (this is similar to a gap-up scenario). Figure 11-6 gives us an example.

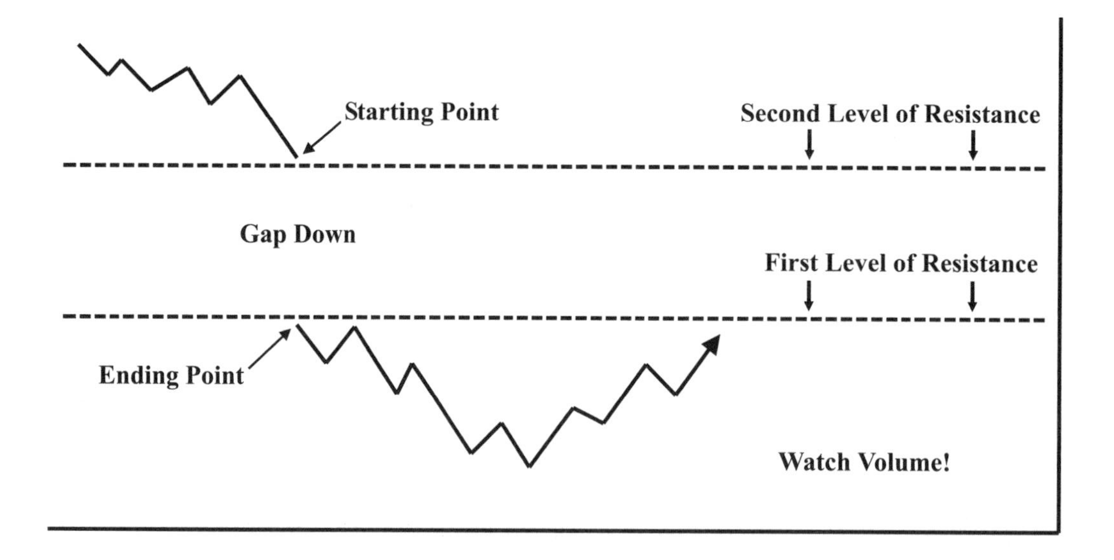

Figure 11-6: ***Gap Down Creating Resistance***

Figure 11-7 gives us an excellent example of the resistance from a gap-down situation coming into play.

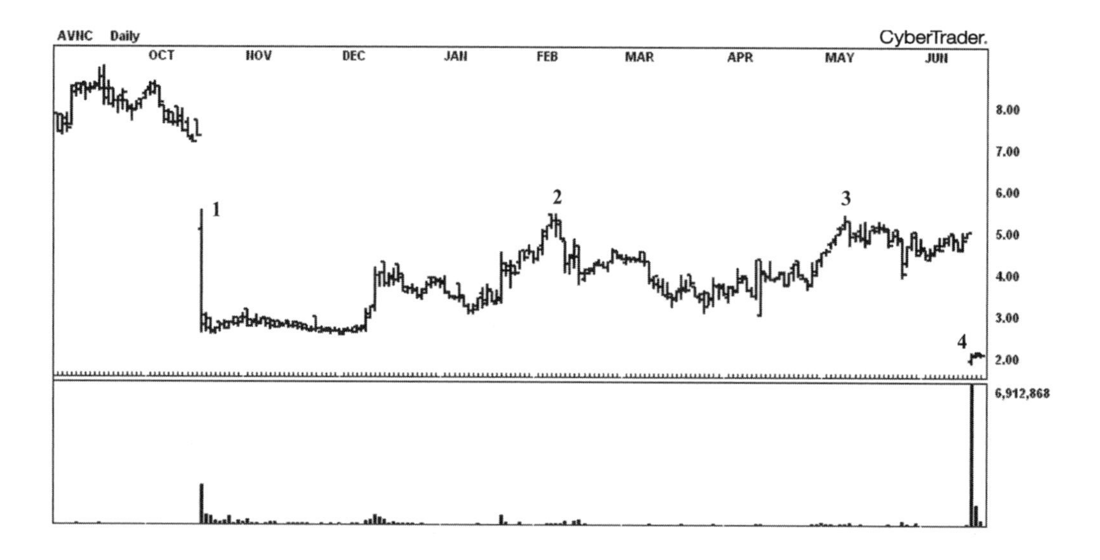

Figure 11-7: ***Gap-down Resistance – Advancis Pharmaceutical Corp. (AVNC)***

(1) *On October 19, 2004, AVNC has a monster down day with the stock gapping down substantially. Volume totaled 1.9 million shares; compare this to the previous day's volume of only 14 thousand shares. The high for this particular day was $5.50 and it's at this price point that a significant level of resistance is born.*

(2) *On February 7, 2005, AVNC strives to test resistance of $5.50 and reaches $5.41 on just 83 thousand shares. It fails the test, does a "one-eighty" and heads lower.*
(3) *On May 9th, AVNC tries yet again to test resistance and makes it to $5.40 on 91 thousand shares.*
(4) *On June 16th, AVNC creates another gap down to $1.92 on 6.9 million shares.*

You can see how powerful AVNC's $5.50 resistance level became.

The Psychology of Gaps

Psychologically, gaps represents areas and instances where there may be new holders of a particular stock. Say for example we have a sudden demand in a stock, such as CCI in the earlier example. Obviously, you will have new holders in the stock as your Aunt Mary and Uncle Joe scramble to pick up some shares. So a gap definitely can define a period of new ownership. Another way to look at gaps is that they can represent instances where there are voids of ownership with holders on either side deciding when to recover losses, take their losses or fulfill their greed. Think about it.

The Size of Gaps

As it regards the size of gaps, the rules here are pretty simple. A large gap up is more likely to be filled than a large gap down. However, you should definitely consider the size of the gap in relative terms to the overall price of the equity. An example would be a gap measuring $5; this is a significant gap for an equity trading in the $20-$50 range, but to a stock that is trading at $25,000 a share (think Berkshire Hathaway, as an example), this gap is fairly, not to mention *relatively*, insignificant.

Volume!

As with everything else in the trading world, volume is fiercely important when combined with gaps.

Remember, volume provides conviction:

- If a gap is filled with light volume, look for the stock to go the other way. Also, look to the fill point to act as support or resistance.

- If a gap is filled with strong volume, look for the fill point to be blown through!

Similar to the effect of volume on swing points and levels of support and resistance, volume will tell you whether the price action will blow through the price point or simply do a "touch & go" (and go the other way, of course!)

12

Channels

We love to overlook the boundaries
which we do not wish to pass.

~ Samuel Johnson

Throughout the countless stock and commodity trading charts there exist countless trading patterns. Most of these patterns can be identified as occurring within one or more trading channels which are basically walls that more or less "house" the recorded trading activity of a particular stock, commodity or index. These trading channels also act as outstanding road signs in identifying additional trading opportunities for tremendous profits.

Channels, What are They?

O.K., what are channels? As I mentioned, channels are essentially walls that surround and border trading activity. Let's look at examples of channels in Figure 12-1:

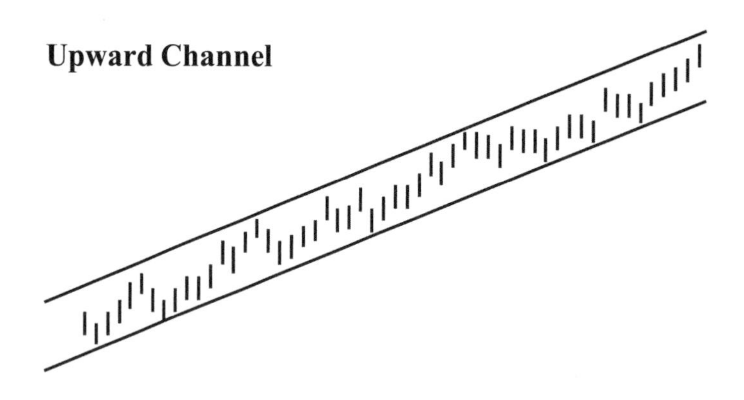

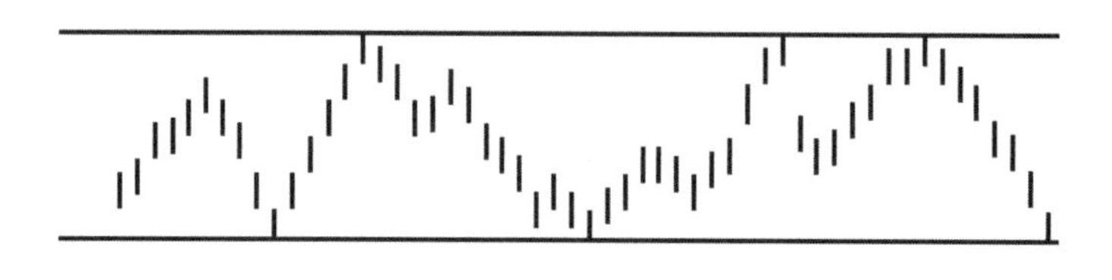

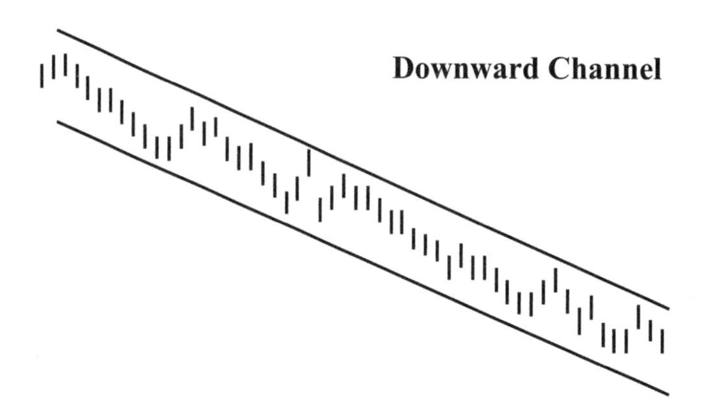

Figure 12-1: ***Basic Trading Channels***
Notice how you can have channels that define upward trends, downward trends or consolidations that build steam for the next move up or down.

Plotting Channels

The first step in plotting a channel is to spot or identify an overall trend. Let's say that you are looking at a stock in an upward trend. To plot the channel corresponding to this trend, simply use three or more highs and three or more lows to draw two trend lines that should be roughly parallel to each other. Typically the channels will not be consistent with the high and/or low points simply because these levels may represent instances where the price jumped out of the true channel but only for a short while.

Check out Figure 12-2. The channels here are pretty clean.

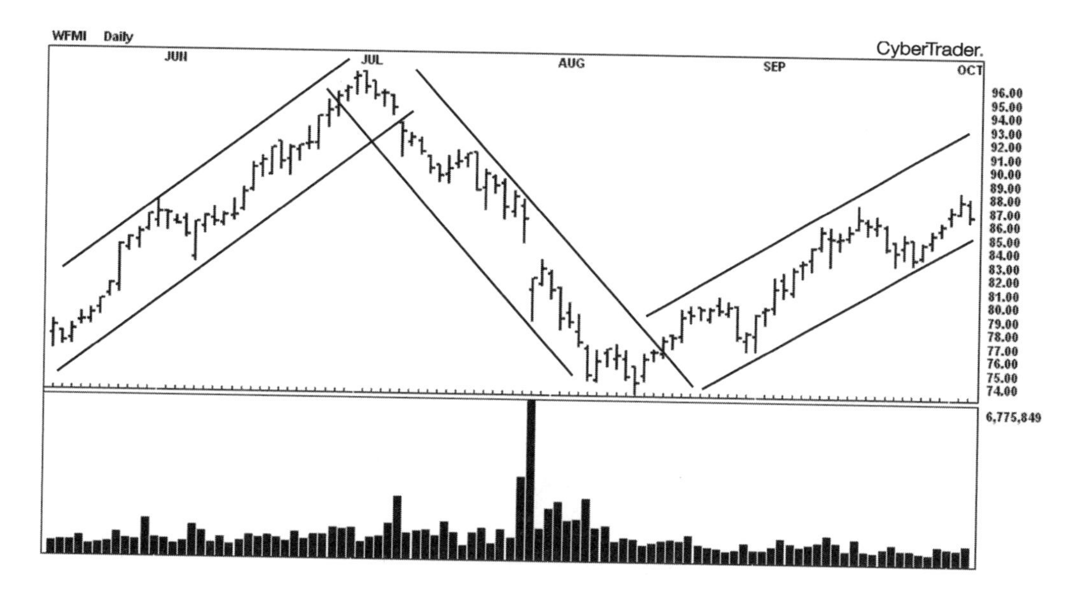

Figure 12-2: ***Channels - Whole Foods Market, Inc. (WFMI)***

One thing to note is that true channels have parallel lines. Not always will you find true bona fide channels, but when you do, they become powerful trading allies.

Breaking the Channel

All right, let's take a look at the significance of a stock breaking a channel wall and typically what happens during this process.

Given the fact that channels act as corridors or boundaries for an overall trend, and the notion that these trends themselves contain significant gravitational energy (i.e., prices tend to stay within or close to these trends), a break outside of a channel can create a certain cataclysmic event. What do I mean? Well, if there is a break beyond a channel and the break comes with conviction (i.e., volume) the break can signal a change in the overall trend of the stock, be it for the short or long term. And when you have a change in direction, you have a simply fabulous point in which to enter a trade!

Now let's suppose that YES is beginning to show signs that it wants to break its lower channel and subsequently it does (anytime you have a break in a channel, that's an indication that there may be a change in the overall trend just around the corner). Typically what you'll see are small breaks in the channel wall with the stock immediately returning back to the trend or channel. The break of the channel and the subsequent return can be very meaningful when stacked against the volume of the corresponding moves. Take a look at Figure 12-3 below:

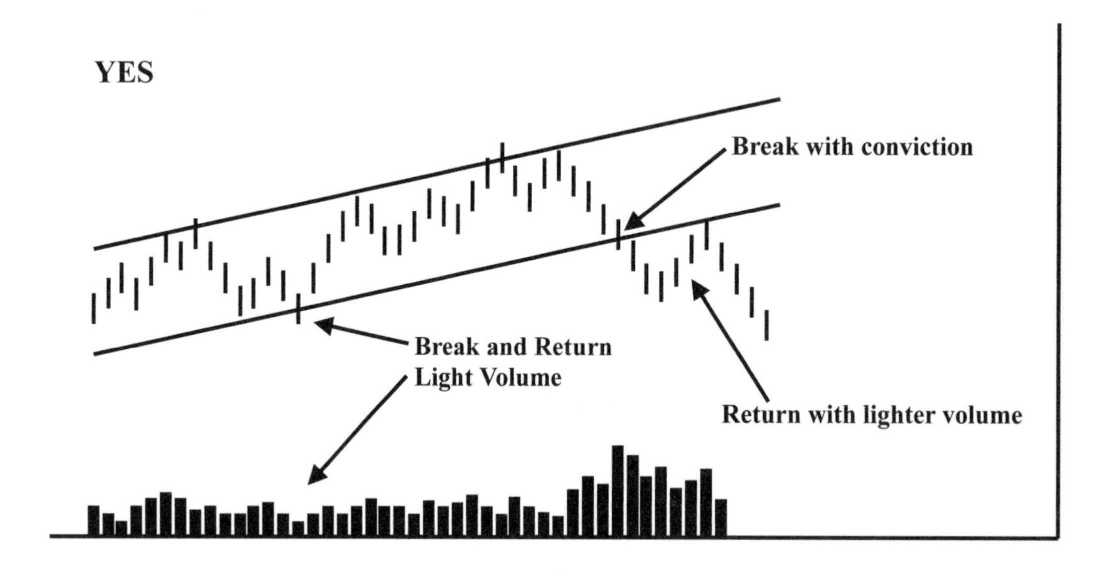

Figure 12-3: ***Breaking a Channel – (YES)***
This diagram illustrates two different price moves within a channel with volume being the key determinant of their subsequent behavior. The first move involves a break of the lower channel wall and it occurs on fairly light volume – the result is a return to the trading channel (the move had no real power or conviction). The second involves another break of the lower channel wall but this time on heavy volume. What we see is a return to the channel occurring on lighter volume. Just as a previous level of support becoming resistance, the equity hits its head on the channel wall, turns around and continues to the downside. The common denominator in both of these moves is volume; the uncommon denominator is volume strength. Remember, strong volume (yielding price moves with strength and conviction) will break a channel wall, level of support or resistance. Your confirma-

tion of the break (at least for the short term) is shown via light volume on the retracement back to the channel wall, without a definite or prolonged re-entry into the channel. This behavior is similar to the "jumping the creek, coming back to ice" dynamic discussed in the next chapter.

Remember, conviction on a channel break is the key and conviction comes in the form of volume. A couple points to remember:

(1) Look for strong volume on the way out of the channel; this is the first sign that there may be conviction and that the move may be real,

(2) On the return to the channel, look to volume for conviction:

  (a) If volume is light, then there is little conviction as to the stock's return to the channel; look for the stock to subsequently change its overall direction. This is similar to a quality volume move where volume is strong on the A to B leg and light on the retracement (B to C) with a powerful move coming after the C point.

  (b) If volume is strong on the way back into the channel, then there is conviction for the return; look for the stock to stay and continue its current trend for the time being or until there is a subsequent break in the channel wall.

The channel break rules that I've outlined above, apply to all channels regardless if they house uptrends, downtrends or consolidations.

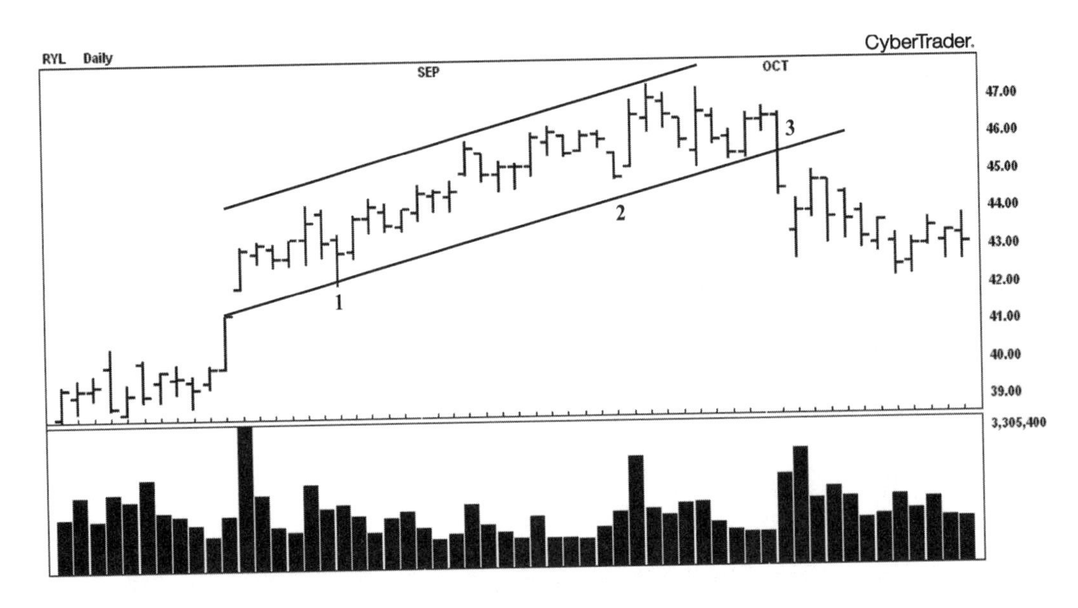

Figure 12-4: ***Break of Channel – The Ryland Group, Inc. (RYL)***
Ryland Homes gives us an example of a stock breaking a channel. On August 25, 2004 (1), RYL makes a drive down to $42.03 on 1.5 million shares but is rejected and returns to its trend; its downward move and retracement reinforces a lower channel wall. The wall is revisited on September 20th (2) but this time on 1.3 million shares – the result is the same with RYL staying within the channel and continuing further in its trend. On October 4th (3), the equity makes a determined drive downward and breaks the channel wall with conviction, blasting through on 2.6 million shares. RYL makes a brief attempt to return to the wall, but on lighter volume. Light volume, in this case, equals lack of conviction and the return to the channel is rejected.

Consolidations

Typically, a stock will either trend up, trend down or stand still, in a relative sense. The process of standing still or trading in a sideways pattern represents a consolidation phase that the stock is undergoing.

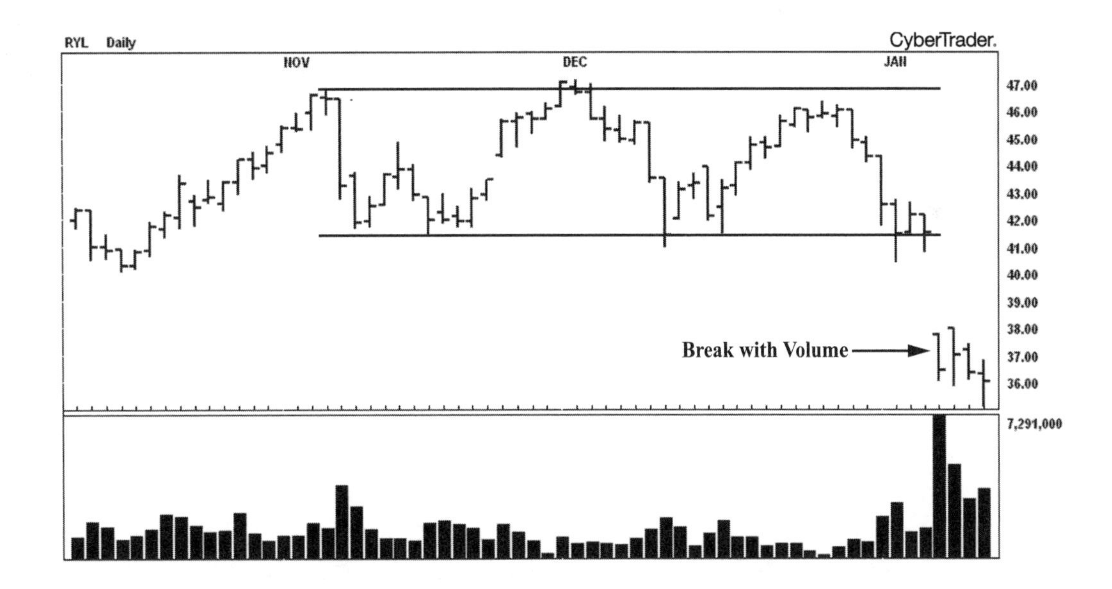

Figure 12-5: ***Sideways Channel – The Ryland Group, Inc. (RYL)***
You can see the channel that formed from the trading activity in Ryland Homes (RYL) during November and December 2003. RYL made attempts to convincingly break through both sides during this time frame but failed each time with the stock returning to the channel. The real break with real conviction came on January 8, 2004 when RYL dropped $5.05 with volume ballooning to 7.3 million shares, up 460% from the previous day's volume of 1.6 million shares. A simple phrase to remember: "If they can't bust it up, they'll try to bust it down".

A consolidation phase can occur at the bottom of a trend, the top or anywhere in the middle of an uptrend or downtrend. This consolidation period generally allows a stock to build up steam for its next move.

Do you remember my discussion on cause & effect? Indeed, the more time that a stock spends in a consolidation phase, the more cause is built and thus the more effect there should be once there is convincing movement beyond the consolidation phase. While in the consolidation phase, the presence of a channel becomes more and more obvious as time goes on without a significant move beyond the trend.

Think of what could be happening during this phase. You basically have a stock that is going back and forth between buyers and sellers with no real imbalance in a supply & demand sense; that is, there is no preponderance of sellers or buyers; there is no real "rush to buy" or "rush to sell". There is literally a changing of hands marked by a gradual increase in quiet accumulation or distribution; it is quiet because it typically occurs somewhat inconspicuously, or at least the general public isn't in on it.

It is also during this phase that you'll see a shifting of ownership from weak to stronger hands (or vice versa). Once the shifting ceases and the accumulation (or distribution) has run most of its course, the stock should begin to experience certain shifts in the supply and demand balance thus giving it direction. Couple this shift with surges in volume and you have a recipe for a potential breakout from the consolidation phase. Refer back to my discussion on accumulation and distribution in Chapter 2 - *Quality Volume* if you need to.

Volume on a Consolidation Breakout

While a stock is in a consolidation phase it pays to note the importance of volume. Once again, volume!

As a stock is making headway to the outer limits of one of its channel walls defining its consolidation phase, you should pay close attention to its volume. If volume is strong on upward surges towards the upper wall and light on no moves or downward moves, clearly the stock is building steam for an upward move. This should be the first "heads-up" for you that the stock is wanting to bust out of where it's been for while (ever get that feeling?).

Now here's an important matter to remember on consolidation channel breakouts. *If there is no volume conviction on upward or downward moves within the consolidation's channel, then there is little, if any, clarity in regards to where the equity will move; therefore as a trader you should postpone trading the stock.* Remember, conviction (which is essentially strong volume) is the name of the game.

Figure 12-6 includes an example of a stock with little conviction during its "wanting to break out" phase. Notice how volume remains relatively steady during its consolidation phase.

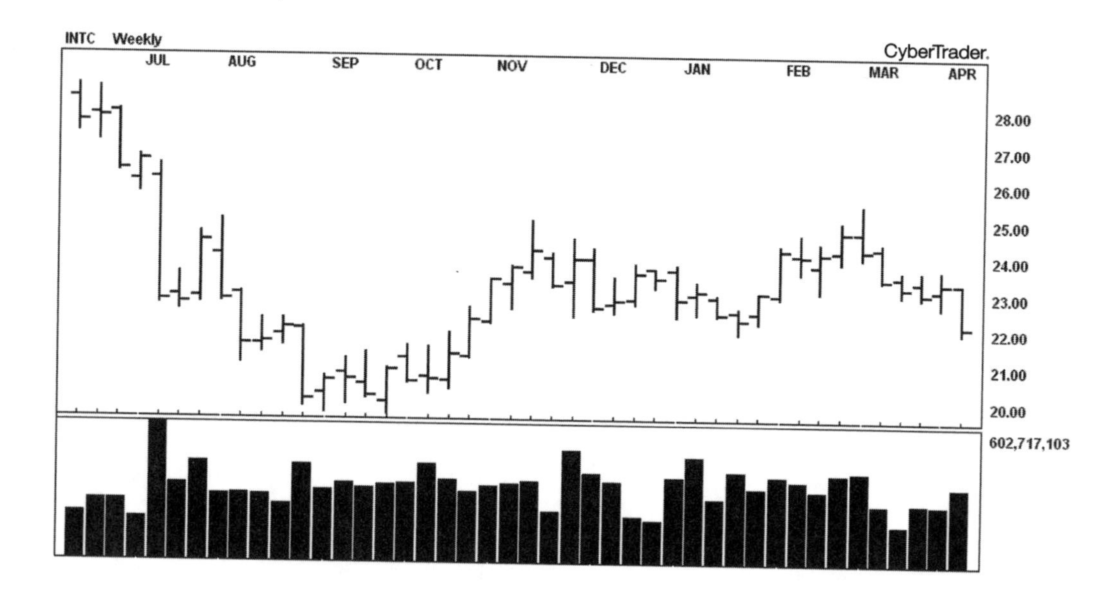

Figure 12-6: ***Consolidation with Steady Volume - Intel Corp. (INTC)***

Trends

In addition to "housing" consolidation phases, channels also mark the outer boundaries of trends. Trends are essentially made up of trading energy or momentum that propels a stock either up or down.

What happens in a trend? As a stock is firing off buys and sells, there is clear direction of the movement in its price with the stock basically following a path of least resistance which is where energy tends to direct itself. Again the path may have an upward, downward or sideways direction. You can always judge the integrity of a trend based on how it moves through levels of support or resistance. These levels can be based on previous ownership levels (e.g., overhead supply) or swing points, which are basically the same thing. If powerful volume is maintained during a move through one of these levels, you can count on the fact that the trend, not to mention the price move, is real.

13

Jumping the Creek, Coming Back to Ice

Never try to leap from a standstill.
~ Mason Cooley

With one look at this chapter's title, you're probably thinking that I'm off my rocker. Well, I hear that everyday and who knows? Maybe I am!! "Jumping the creek" and "coming back to ice" are actually two terms used by perhaps the greatest (and possibly the least known) technical analyst of all time, Richard Wyckoff.

First of all, Richard Wyckoff made his (silent) mark in the world of stock and commodity trading by identifying and articulating the meaning and clarity behind the science of analyzing price movements and their corresponding volume relationships. Does this sound familiar? Well it should. Mastering the science of price and volume movements should be your ultimate objective.

Wyckoff, in an uncanny manner, was able to dissect and draw meaning from volume strengths and weaknesses and how they affected price. He also focused on the meaning of price retracements and the ensuing price power that a subsequent surge in volume would precipitate. Unfortunately, his knowledge and teachings were never made widely available.

I'll get into the terms "jumping the creek" and "coming back to ice" in more detail, but I first want to give a general explanation as to how these terms apply to my approach to trading stocks.

First of all, "jumping the creek," as Wyckoff defined it, merely refers to a particular price pattern that has maintained or hugged a steady line (also a line of support or resistance and in this context, the "creek") for quite some time and then suddenly exploded beyond it – similar to a "breakout".

Ideally, a breakout should be followed by a retracement occurring on lighter volume, taking the stock back to the support or resistance line that it hugged. Usually on the way back to the "creek" the stock's price will *not* break through the "creek" and should turn around and head up. Wyckoff referred to this retracing movement as "coming back to ice". Why "ice"? It could be that the line which was originally the "creek" has become impermeable so that a subsequent piercing of this price level will not occur, much like jumping over the creek in the summer and coming back in the winter to find it frozen.

If I haven't mentioned this before, Wyckoff's teachings essentially form the backdrop to which I base most, if not all, of my trading decisions, essentially the related price moves and the volume tendencies that accompany them. Wildly enough, the concepts covered in this chapter pretty much underlie most of what's covered in this book. So while this chapter may seem a little short on pages, it's definitely not short on substance!

"Jumping the Creek"

Why don't we look at an example of a stock formation that resembles a "Wyckoff creek". Take a look at Figure 13-1. Notice the trend line (also a resistance line) that has formed. This line represents the "creek" in Wyckoff's "jumping the creek" analogy.

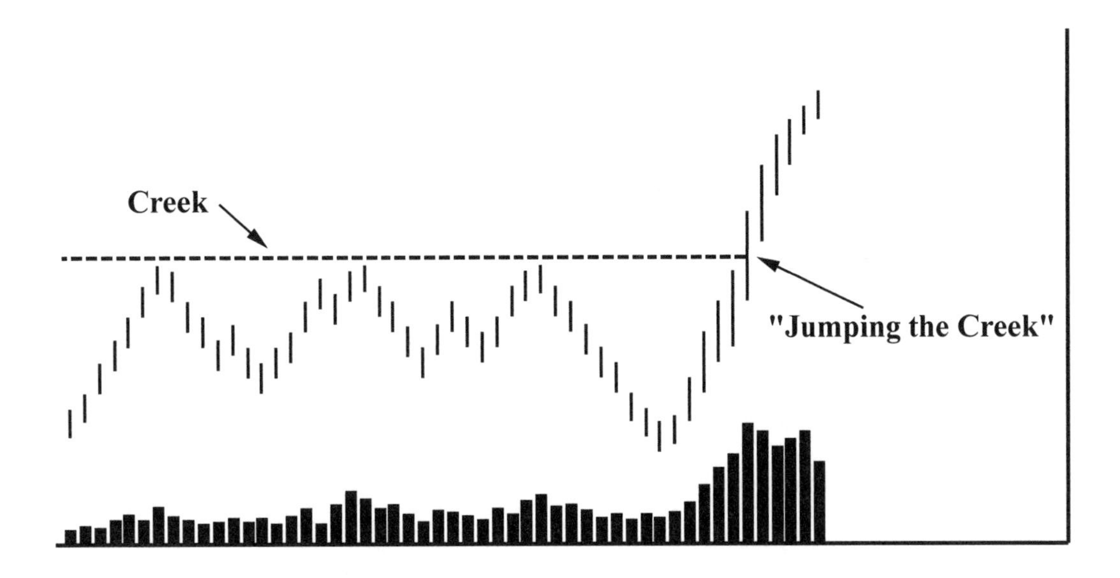

Figure 13-1: *"Jumping the Creek"*
Notice how in this case, the "creek" is identified through a line of resistance which is formed by the peaks of previous swing points. In this early phase, volume stays relatively quiet then quickly accelarates to a feverish pitch with the stock's price spreads getting wider as well. Utilizing a "cause and effect" way of thinking, volume moves price which ultimately propels the stock to "jump the creek".

Take particular note as to how the "creek" or trendline is formed. Do you see how a resistance line was formed by several attempts to break a certain price level. The line may not be clearly defined but in a general sense it's there.

Now take a look at the breakout or "jump". See how volume is fairly consistent while this stock spends time at the creek and then a sudden rush propels it beyond the creek much like a springboard would launch a diver into the air. It is during this breakout that the stock may experience a buying or selling frenzy (depending on the direction of the breakout). Also, notice the larger price spreads (i.e., the difference between the highs and lows of each trading session or price bar) showing the strength of the move. Larger price spreads are also an essential component of the "jumping" aspect of "jumping the creek".

Let's say for example that we've run into a situation where a stock has hugged a resistance line or "creek" (in essence, also building cause) and suddenly has exploded on price and volume (effect), what do we do now? Do we hop into the buying frenzy? No. Do we watch the stock explode, let anxiety build up, then finally reach a point where we should throw caution into the wind and buy the stock (i.e., chase it)? No way. Should we exercise patience and wait for the stock to retrace? Yes!

There is a Zen philosophy that states that "we always chase that which retreats". Well in our context we should do our best not to chase a stock that explodes and gets out of hand but rather follow the belief that "patience is the virtue of all virtues" and wait for our stock to retrace to a better price level. At the very least, we should wait for the buying frenzy and chaos to cease. Here at least, you can act rationally and make clearer and better formed and informed decisions. Remember, don't chase a wild stock!

> *It never was my thinking that made the big money for me. It always was sitting. Got that? My sitting tight! Men who can both be right and sit tight are uncommon. I found it one of the hardest things to learn.*
>
> "Reminiscences of a Stock Operator"
> Jesse Livermore

Back to our example. Once the buying frenzy eases, natural forces may cause the stock to slip in price. As I mentioned in a previous chapter, people who bought into the stock may decide to hold on; many previous holders may decide to take money off the table. Whatever the case may be, if there is a retracement, it should be accompanied by lighter volume. Such a retracement begins the "coming back to ice" phase.

"Coming Back to Ice"

The "coming back to ice" term is used to describe the retracement behavior of a stock that has recently broken out of a resistance level. Check out Figure 13-2 and note how the stock's price movement retraces its steps back to the "creek" line which has now become "ice".

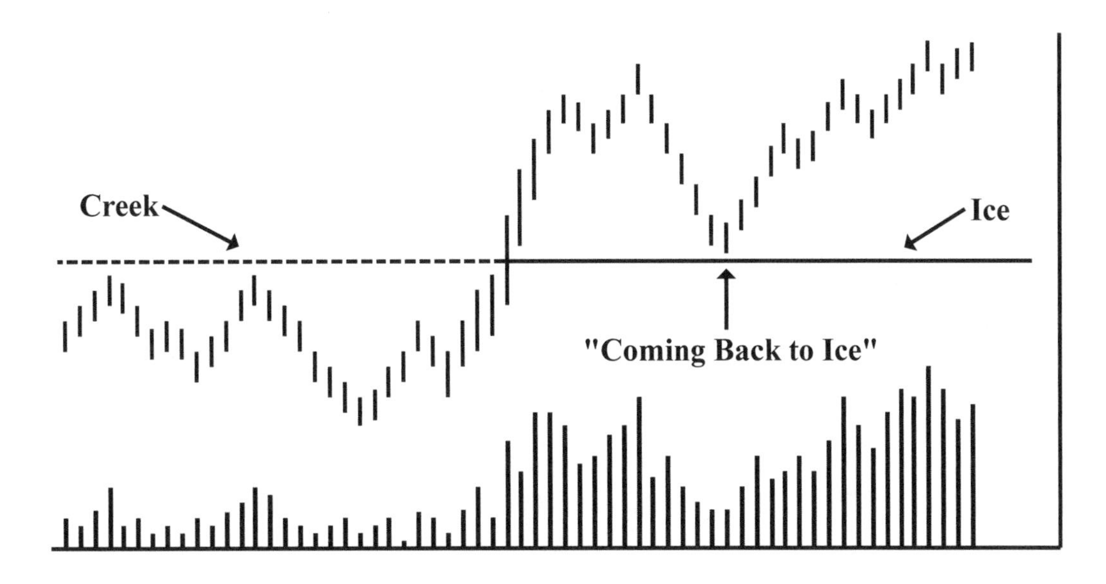

Figure 13-2: *"Coming Back to Ice"*
Here our stock comes back to the previously surpassed line of resistance (the "creek") which now has become a level of support (now "ice"). Volume is fairly critical throughout this phase. On "jumping the creek", volume should be heavy. On the "coming back to ice" phase volume should be light - if not, the stock may crash through ice.

Notice how during this retracement phase, there is definitely lighter volume than as there was during the breakout. This light volume behavior is key, because it demonstrates quality volume as well as the good possibility that there are no major sellers (at least not presently) in the stock. With no major sellers, the trip back to ice should be short-lived.

Now, it's at this particular point that things can get interesting. With a stock that has experienced a breakout and is currently retracing its way back to ice, history has shown that *most* stocks will reach a point near or at "ice" and then turn around for a much more protracted price move, accompanied by strong volume (don't forget also that lines of resistance that are surpassed with volume become lines of *support*!). This may sound very similar to my preachings in an earlier chapter, but I've already warned you that this chapter virtually incorporates much of what is written in this book.

Also, the closer a stock gets to "ice" before turning around or, better yet the closer to "ice" that you are able to get off a trade with this stock, the better your risk/reward ratio. Why? Because your stop will be at a point just on the other side of "ice" (just as with confluence).

So what now? While staying mindful of where "ice" is, it's good to go ahead and calculate confluence (just in case, go back to the confluence chapter for a refresher). If you run this exercise on several "creek" examples, you'll notice that "ice" more or less falls at or just below confluence! Amazing, isn't it? Knowledge is power!

Figure 13-3 below includes a real example of a stock "jumping the creek" and "coming back to ice":

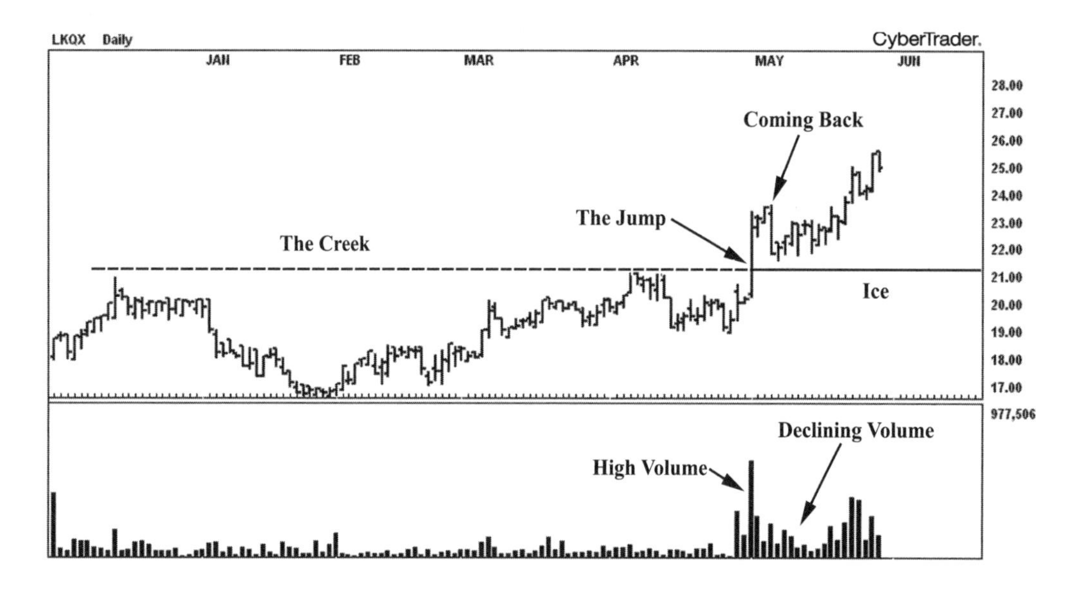

Figure 13-3: *"Jumping the Creek" - LKQ Corp. (LKQX)*
LKQX gives us a textbook example of "jumping the creek" and "coming back to ice". Notice how the presence of two swing highs close to the same price point create a level of resistance (the "creek") and how volume is fairly steady from January through mid-April. Suddenly volume begins to pick up steam and LKQX's price starts to move creating wide price spreads in the process. Strong volume propels LKQX through the "creek" and then tapers off once price reaches a peak and starts to retrace or "come back to ice". The equity seemingly bounces off "ice" and demonstrates a great example where previous resistance has now become support. Volume once again powers up and the stock continues north.

Applying the "Creek" and "Ice" to your Trading

Learning to recognize instances and situations that lead to "jumping the creek" and "coming back to ice" might take some time but once you get the process down pat, these Wyckoffisms become extremely powerful trading tools. History has demonstrated that stocks that break out from a line of resistance and retrace back to the previous line of resistance *on lighter volume* do have a tendency to change directions near or at "ice" and head further *away* from the line of resistance; remember again that lines of resistance that have been surpassed with volume become lines of *support*!

How do we benefit from "jumping the creek' and "coming back to ice"?

Assuming that we will trade a stock after it has "jumped the creek":

(1) The first challenge is to recognize a "creek" set-up:

> (a) The "creek" is a line of resistance that has been established through several attempts by a stock to break through a general price area.
>
> (b) The line will be generally flat (horizontal) but may slant up or down, but not substantially.

(2) The next step is to watch volume:

> (a) Volume is typically consistent with slight surges on approaches on attempts to "jump the creek".
>
> (b) When volume spikes dramatically on the way up, expect the stock to "jump" and blow right through resistance.

(3) When it jumps, you should notice stronger volume and wider price spreads (buying frenzy).

(4) Do not chase the stock (i.e., don't buy while the stock is going through its own price explosions) and

(5) Again, keep an eye on volume; if it starts to lighten, expect it to begin its "coming back to ice" phase.

Once a stock is in its "coming back to ice" phase:

(1) Keep a vigilant eye on volume; it should be lighter than when it "jumped the creek",

(2) Calculate a confluence area; "ice" should be close to or at confluence,

(3) Place a buy order just above the higher of "ice" or confluence; naturally, the closer you can pull off the trade to "ice" the better your risk/reward parameter,

(4) Place your stop just below the lower of "ice" or confluence – here too, the closer you place your stop to "ice", the better your risk/reward.

This process will be covered in detail in Appendix I – *Case Study*.

Facing the Other Direction

Throughout this chapter, we've seen how Wyckoff's "jumping the creek" and "coming back to ice" apply to long scenarios, that is, buying low then selling high. These concepts however also apply to the short view, or selling high *then* buying low. Just as we covered in the chapter addressing confluence, the short view simply involves a reversal of the application of the entry and stop points.

When looking at a downward stock that has "jumped the creek" (here you merely think of it in an upside down manner), simply place the sell short order below "ice". Your stop should fall just at or above "ice". Very simple. But remember, as I've hopefully impressed upon you throughout this book, keep a watchful eye on volume! If your stock is in the neutral zone (between entry and stop) and volume all of a sudden surges with price moving to the upward side, get out!

Figure 13-4 includes an example of a downward "jumping the creek" and "coming back to ice".

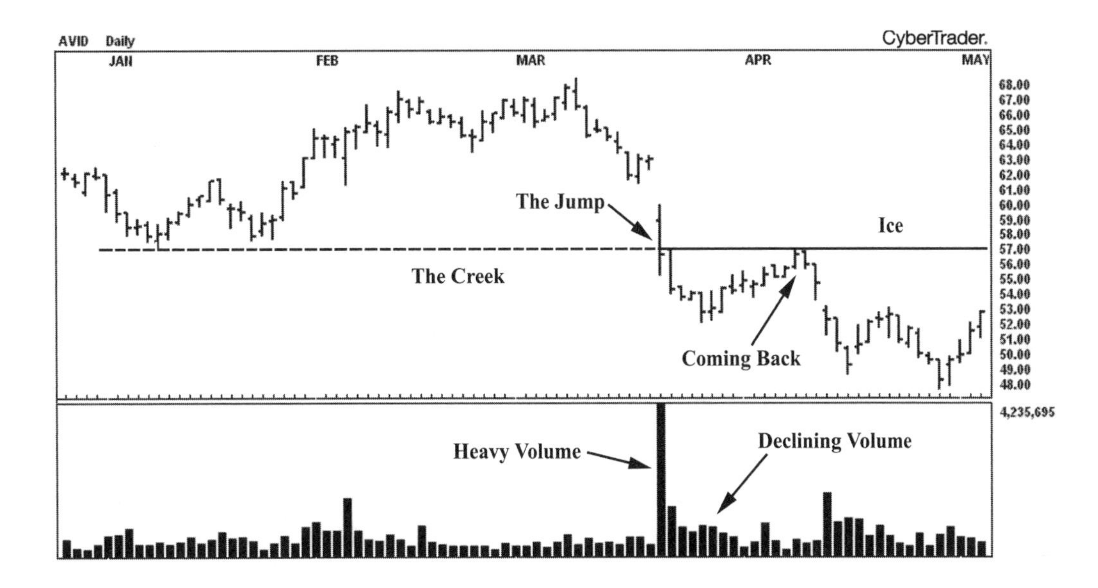

Figure 13-4: *"Jumping the Creek" (down) - Avid Technology, Inc. (AVID)*
In this example, AVID slams through a level of support ("creek") on heavy volume and then retraces a portion of its downward move (the "coming back to ice" phase) on lighter volume. Its price barely kisses "ice", turns around and continues in a southerly direction.

14

3x3 DMA & MACD

If you come to a fork in the road, take it.
~ Yogi Berra

So far, we've covered several important concepts with each one in its own right being full of enough detail to fill entire books; for our purposes, I have presented enough information on each which I believe is crucial to *Timing the Trade*. The sequencing of the presentation of these concepts (i.e., chapter order) was predicated on their complexity and more or less the order to which I use them to pull off successful trades (in Chapter 16 – *Setting up the Trade*, we will go through a step-by-step implementation of the concepts using a real example).

Useful Indicators

There are two technical indicators that I use as part of my *Timing the Trade* process. They are fairly known in the technical analysis and trading communities; they are the three-by-three displaced moving average (3x3 DMA) and the moving average convergence-divergence indicator (MACD).

I use the 3x3 DMA and MACD right before I pull the trigger on a trade. Up to the point of actually entering a trade, I've done *all* of my homework, calculated the Fibonacci retracements and confluence (the whole routine will be covered in Chapter 16 – *Setting up the Trade* and later in Appendix I – *Case Study*) and I'm ready to enter the trade; here is where I look for an "all systems go" signal, almost like looking out the window to make sure the weather's clear before heading out for a picnic. The 3x3 DMA and MACD indicators help me confirm my assumption on the direction my stock is trending and also whether my stock has truly bounced off "ice" (telling me that its retracement on lighter volume is over and the stock is turning around to head in my direction!).

This chapter is devoted to the 3x3 DMA and MACD, how they are calculated and their relevance to *Timing the Trade*. I won't be getting in terribly deep insofar as how they are calculated since they can be accessed through most internet charting sites and services.

3x3 DMA

Before getting into the intricacies of the 3x3 DMA, it's important to understand what a moving average is.

We should all know that a simple average is merely the summation of a number series (components) divided by the amount of numbers making up that series.

Let's say you took the average of the last three days of a stock's closing price and computed the amount to be $48.50. Suppose then we perform the same computation tomorrow. The difference would be that the 1st day of the first computation (the oldest day) would fall off and tomorrow's price (the new day) would be included. This is the basis for the moving average. Moving averages are typically plotted on a stock chart as a line or curve.

	Closing Price	3-Day Moving Average
Day 1 (Today)	$ 49.00	$ 48.50
Day 2 (Yesterday)	48.50	
Day 3 (Day Before Yesterday)	48.00	

Figure 14-1: ***Computation of 3-day Moving Average***

As I mentioned before, you can easily find moving averages offered as a technical study on most internet charting sites and services. Some will prompt you to enter a time frame; in our example we used three days. Some more common moving average time frames include the 200-day and the 50-day.

Displaced moving averages are moving average curves that are *moved* either forward or backward. The effect of doing so gives greater meaning to a particular trading day. In my case, I rely on the 3x3 displaced moving average. The first "3" represents the time frame (three days) and the second "3" denotes the number of days I'm displacing the moving average curve in a forward direction.

By moving the curve forward three days, I am able to make sure that the current trading price is on the right side of the trend I'm after. Figure 14-2 provides an example of its computation.

Google, Inc (GOOG)	Closing Price	Computed 3X3 DMA
April 20, 2005	$ 198.10	$ 189.79
April 19	191.40	192.77
April 18	186.97	193.37
April 15	185.00	
April 14	191.45	
April 13	192.93	
April 12	193.95	
April 11	193.23	

Figure 14-2: ***Computation of 3x3 Displaced Moving Average***

The 3x3 DMA in the above diagram is computed as $189.79. If I choose to enter a trade and go long, I want to make sure that the trading price for my stock is above $189.79. What this will say is that the current trend is still in place.

Visually, the 3x3 DMA looks like the curve in Figure 14-3; note how the curve looks like it's pushed forward.

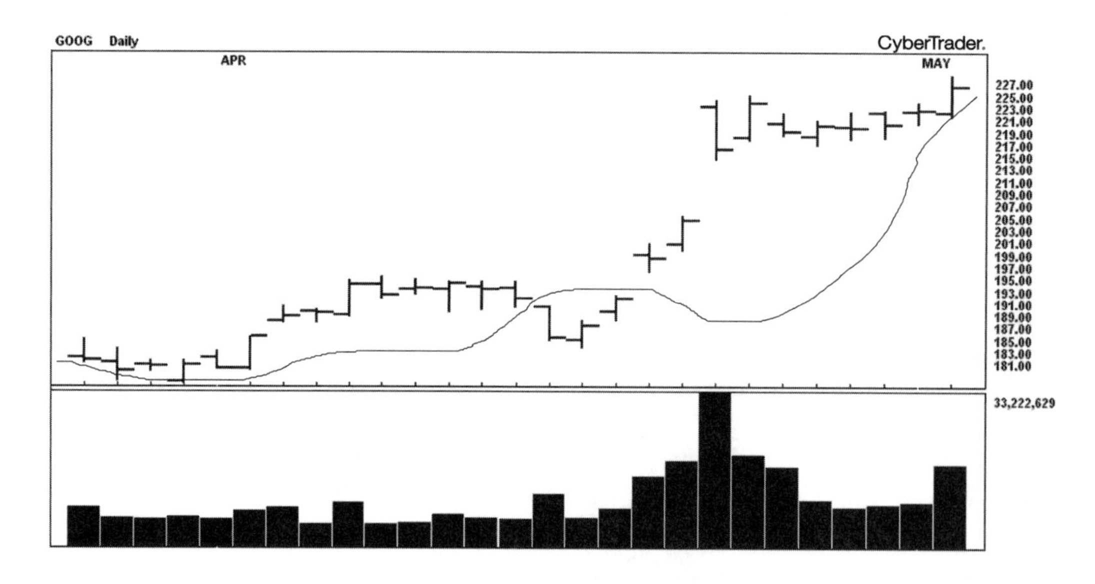

Figure 14-3: ***3x3 DMA Curve - Google Inc. (GOOG)***

The 3x3 DMA can also be used for selling short. Current price merely needs to be on the "south" side (below) the moving average curve.

Let's take a look at RDC; Figure 14-4 below includes its 3x3 DMA computation. Notice how its closing price falls below the computed DMA on September 22, 2005 (does its crossover).

Rowan Cos, Inc (RDC)	Closing Price	Computed 3X3 DMA
Sept 22 (price enters "bearish side")	$ 36.55	$ 36.82
Sept 21	37.41	36.42
Sept 20	37.28	36.04
Sept 19	37.49	
Sept 16	36.53	
Sept 15	36.43	
Sept 14	36.31	
Sept 13	35.39	

Figure 14-4: ***Computation of 3x3 DMA - Rowan Companies, Inc. (RDC)***

From a visual perspective, Figure 14-5 demonstrates RDC's crossover. Notice how RDC's price crosses over the DMA curve on September 22nd (as computed in Figure 14-4's table).

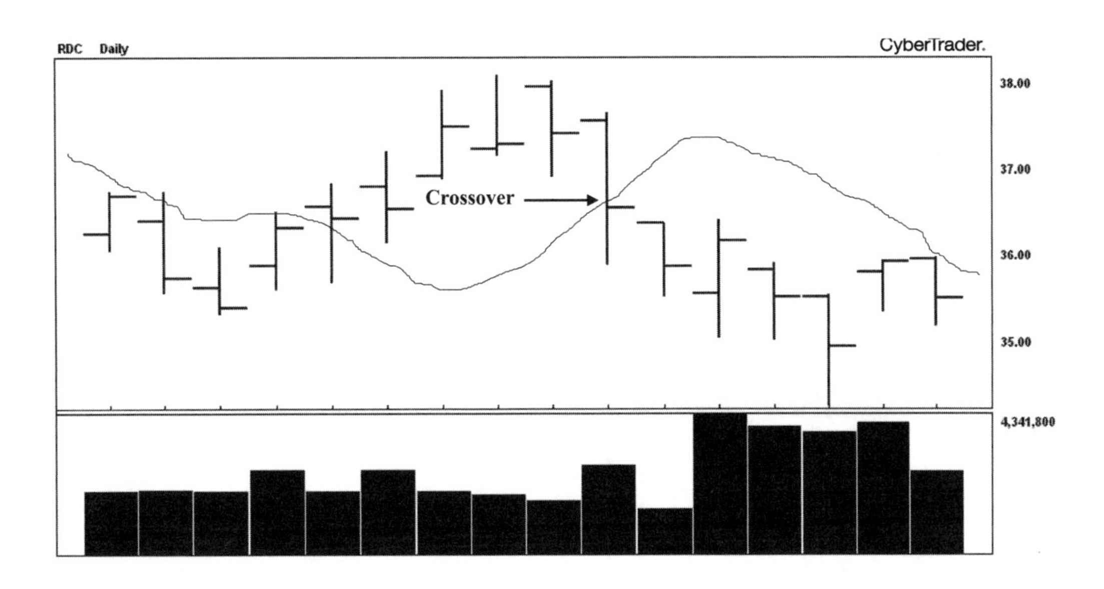

Figure 14-5: ***3x3 Displaced Moving Average Curve - Rowan Companies, Inc. (RDC)***

The 3x3 DMA is an effective tool for entering trades, both long and short, ... particularly when combined with the MACD!

MACD

The MACD was developed by Gerald Appel and is one of the most reliable indicators available in the market. It basically combines two moving averages to create a momentum oscillator. The faster average will oscillate above and below the slower average and each crossover creates a buy or sell signal.

The standard formula for the MACD (using the more popular parameters) is the difference between the 26-day and the 12-day exponential moving averages. I utilize the two-line MACD which has a 9-day exponential moving average included in the calculation. We could go through the motions of computing an actual two-line MACD (it is possible) but it's much easier to come up with it using a free charting service on the computer.

Figure 14-6 includes an example of the MACD:

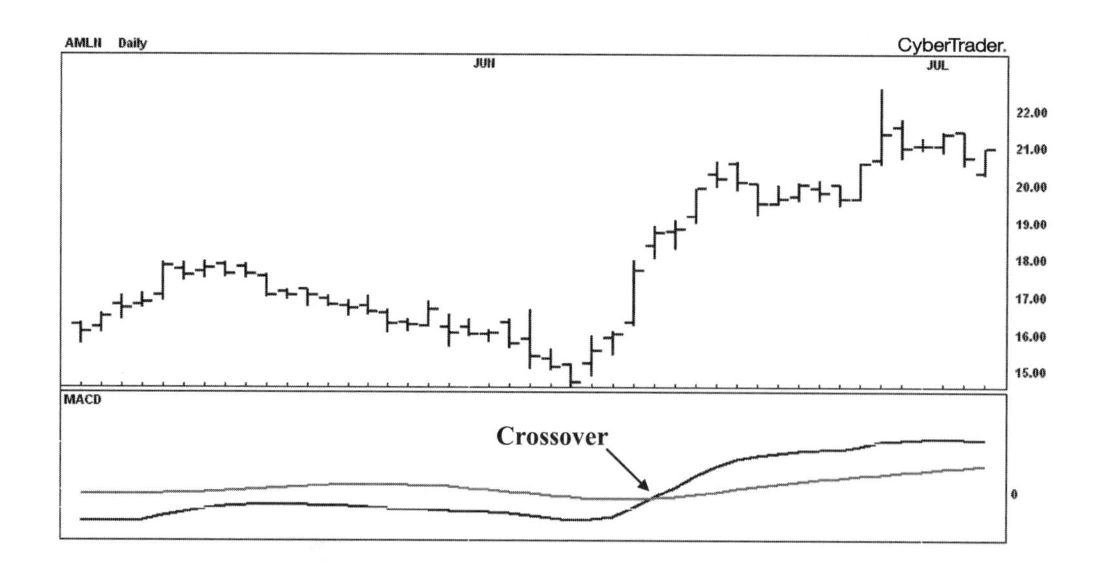

Figure 14-6: ***MACD Curve - Amylin Pharmaceuticals, Inc. (AMLN)***

Note how there are two curves, one oscillating faster than the other. When the fast curve crosses the slower curve, this occurrence is referred to as a "crossover". Crossovers are interpreted as signals for buying or selling. When there is a crossover with the fast curve moving north of the slower curve, this creates a buy signal. A sell signal is created when the fast curve crosses the slower curve in a southerly direction.

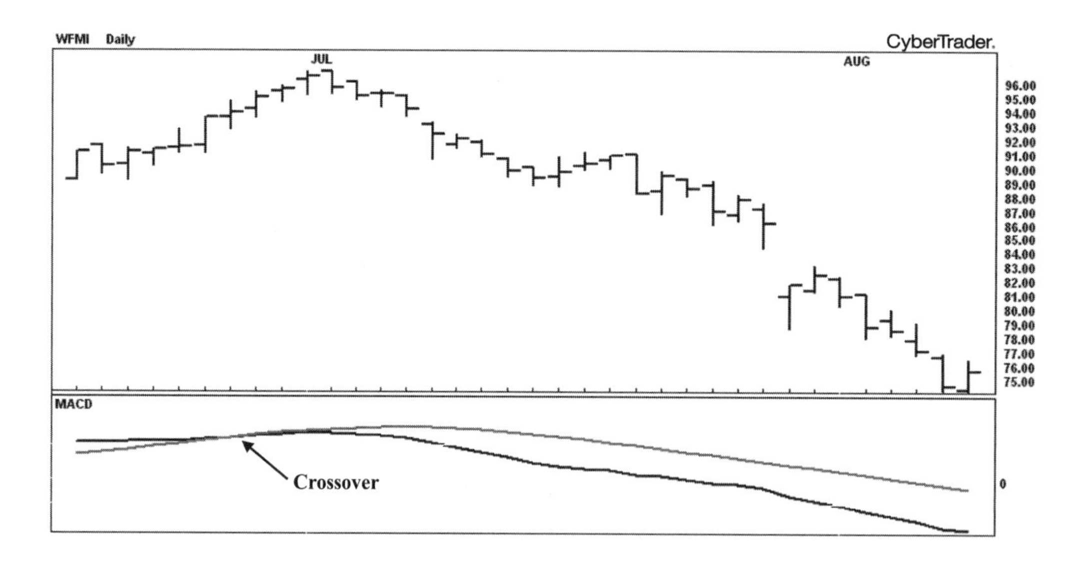

Figure 14-7: ***MACD Curve - Whole Foods Market, Inc. (WFMI)***

Relevance to Timing the Trade

As it regards my own trading and *Timing the Trade*, the 3x3 DMA and MACD give me the "all systems go" indication before firing off a trade. The 3x3 tells me that I'm on the right side of the trend and the MACD confirms the stock has turned around (also bounced off of "ice").

With the 3x3 DMA and MACD it is possible to predict buy and sell signals in advance of their occurence.

Together, these two indicators provide the final go-ahead and are wonderfully integral to the *Timing the Trade* approach!

15

Identifying the Trade

The real voyage of discovery consists not in seeking new landscapes, but in having new eyes.

~ Marcel Proust

I'm often flooded with questions concerning the stocks I pick for trades. If you're a subscriber of my daily newsletter, you'll see that I am, more times than not, in several trades. Many of the questions are of the same nature, "Tom, how do you pick stocks to trade?" Well, my selection process is very basic and simple. I merely look for stocks that are poised to move!

How do I spot them? Easy. I look for relationships between movements in the market versus movement in individual stocks. To get to this point, I first look for strength or weakness in the market and then in particular sectors. Why do I do this? I look for stocks that simply are going to move! Movement is the name of the game! Remember:

> *You'll want to trade the stocks that you believe are going to move, the soonest, the furthest and the fastest!*

Market Analysis

To spot strength or weakness in the market I ask myself, "What is my time frame for this trade? Am I looking at a daily, weekly, monthly or yearly view of the market? Do we have a bull or bear market? Do the yearly and monthly charts look bearish despite the weekly and daily charts showing bullish activity? Are the daily, weekly, monthly, and yearly charts showing prices going in the same direction?" Needless to say, when you have congruence in charts of all possible time frames, that is, prices and volumes acting in concert, you have the makes for an optimal atmosphere to be timing your trade!

The approach to understand where a market is going, either up, down or sideways (consolidating) is to first take note of the amount of volume on each leg or trend, then compare the amount of volume as the highs and lows (swing points) are crossed. This isn't terribly different from what we do at swing points to gauge where an individual equity is going.

Keep in mind that in the United States there are three major markets for equities: the New York Stock Exchange (NYSE), the NASDAQ and the American Stock Exchange (AMEX). Now as for the markets I focus on, the NYSE and NASDAQ are definitely critical; I also gauge U.S. market strength using the SPX, an index used to represent the Standard & Poor's 500 (S&P 500), a composite of 500 equities from the NYSE, NASDAQ and AMEX. Given its composition (the fact that its components come from the three major U.S. markets), the SPX gives a genuine indication of what the U.S. markets are doing, as a whole. Also, the SPX is the hardest to manipulate because the NASDAQ, Dow and AMEX must be open to calibrate the SPX number (this might seem silly until you consider the impact that a bunch of operators can have on an individual equity or market). The SPX does not trade as the SPX futures do at the Chicago Mercantile Exchange. (Also, the SPX futures market can be moved very quickly any time during the day by an operator buying or selling one to two hundred contracts to either push the market higher or lower hitting stops, breaking support or resistance levels in the short run.)

My favorite approach to gauging the strength of the market combines metrics from the SPX and the NYSE – I take the price from the SPX price index and combine it with volume from the NYSE. The SPX can only moved when all of its 500 stocks are bought and sold. By combining it with volume from the NYSE, you get a good broad market view of the largest companies in the world to arrive at a solid overall trend. I use it and it works.

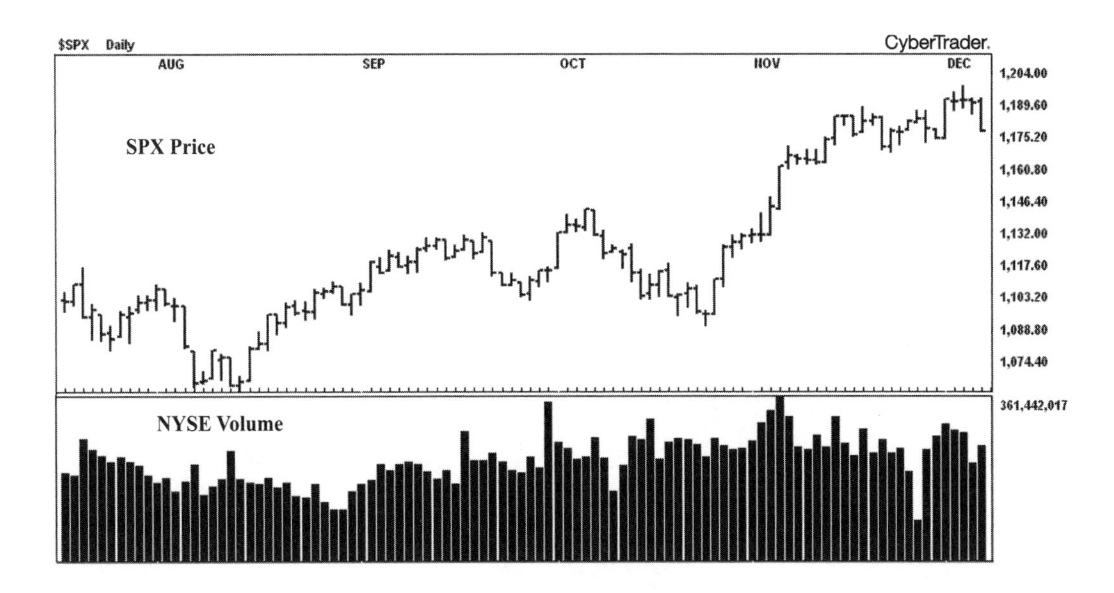

Figure 15-1: ***S&P 500 Index (SPX) Combined with NYSE Volume***

Sector Analysis

Sector analysis involves both fundamental and technical analysis. As for fundamental analysis, I look for sectors that are poised to make strong moves either to the upside or downside based on one or more fundamental reasons. An example of a fundamental reason would be a promising future for a particular company or sector. Without a doubt, this is an important place to start. But more important than adopting a fundamental perspective, it is critical to look at how sectors move in a technical relationship to the market as a whole. One example is the S&P 500. If it has a very strong move, I look to sectors that have even stronger moves. If the S&P goes up 5%, it would be wise to look at sectors that move more than 5%.

Conversely, if there is weakness in the S&P, for example if it goes down 5%, I look for sectors that drop more than 5%.

In either case, I look for sectors that have greater moves than the S&P.

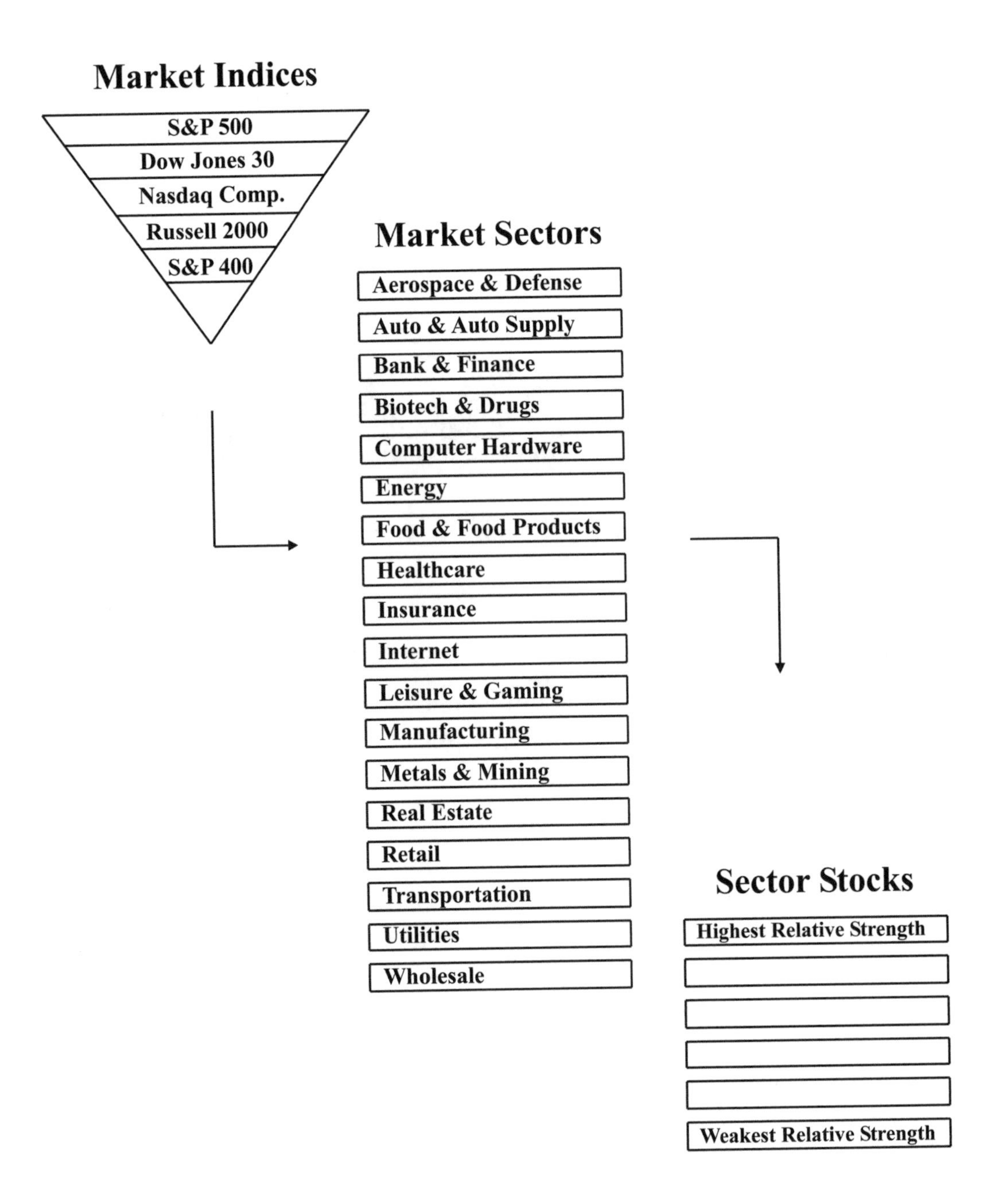

Figure 15-2: ***Identifying the Trade - Market, Sector and Stock Analysis***
This diagram provides a visual interpretation of the process I use for identifying a trade. I first look to the market indices to determine an overall trend. I then look to market sectors and then to individual stocks within favorable sectors, all the while using relative strength as a screening tool.

Intrasector Analysis

Once I have identified the sectors that merit attention, I look to those sectors for stocks that have moves greater than movement in the sector overall. Another way of saying this is that I look for stocks with greater or weaker relative strength. An easy and surefire way of obtaining this information is by looking up a stock's related relative strength via a publication entitled *Investor's Business Daily*. A strong relative strength for a stock in a strong sector is a good sign – so is a weak relative strength for a weak sector (for going short).

Another way to look for greater or weaker relative strength in regards to a particular sector is to superimpose a stock's chart on to its related sector's chart. You can get a sector's chart through any charting service available on the internet.

This approach will ensure identifying stocks that will not get dragged down as much as the market (in the case of strong stocks) and those that will not rise as much when the market shows strength in a long or upward sense.

Looking at Individual Stocks

After I've identified candidates for potential trading, I look to each of their price and volume movements. Particularly, I look for them to break swings on volume (refer back to the chapter on swing points for additional clarification of "breaks of swing points with volume"). If there does not appear to be a break of a swing point with volume, I place the stock on a backburner for future analysis (or until that stock demonstrates a "break of a swing point with volume").

When a stock is pushing against swing highs or swing lows, volume will give you an indication whether it will break through those levels. If a swing point had volume of 2.5 million shares and the stock is pushing to the upside with 2.3 to 2.6 or 2.7 million shares right below the break point, you can expect the swing point to be taken out with volume. If a swing low had volume of 3.2 million shares and the stock is pushing down on that with volume of 2.8 to 3.5 million shares, you can expect that low will be taken out. It is important to understand in both cases that the market is building strength in these cases to take that price point out. This technique works not only with individual equities but with the broad market as well.

When looking for either an entry or exit point, start with a monthly, then a weekly, and then a daily chart to get a clear understanding as to where your equity is heading. A monthly chart will provide a longer term picture of the market while the weekly and daily charts will give you a more immediate perspective.

Figure 15-3 gives us a daily, six-month view of Caterpillar Inc. (CAT). Notice how in Figure 15-4 and Figure 15-5 (a weekly, two-year view and a monthly, six-year view, respectively), wider perspectives convey a clearer, more pronounced and concise message as to where the stock has been and where it is going.

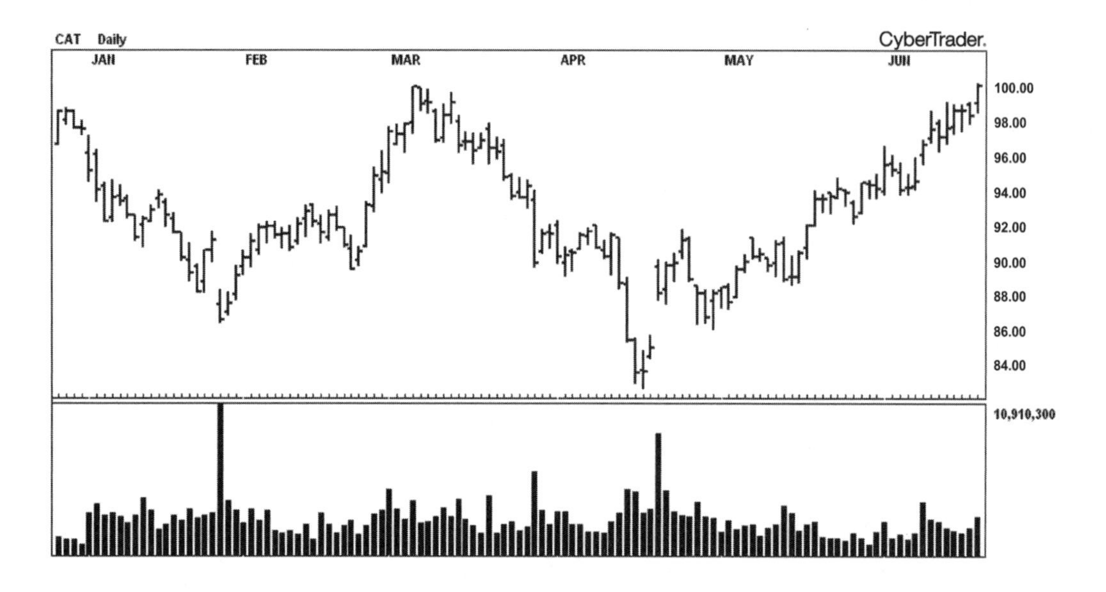

Figure 15-3: ***Six-month Daily View - Caterpillar Inc. (CAT)***

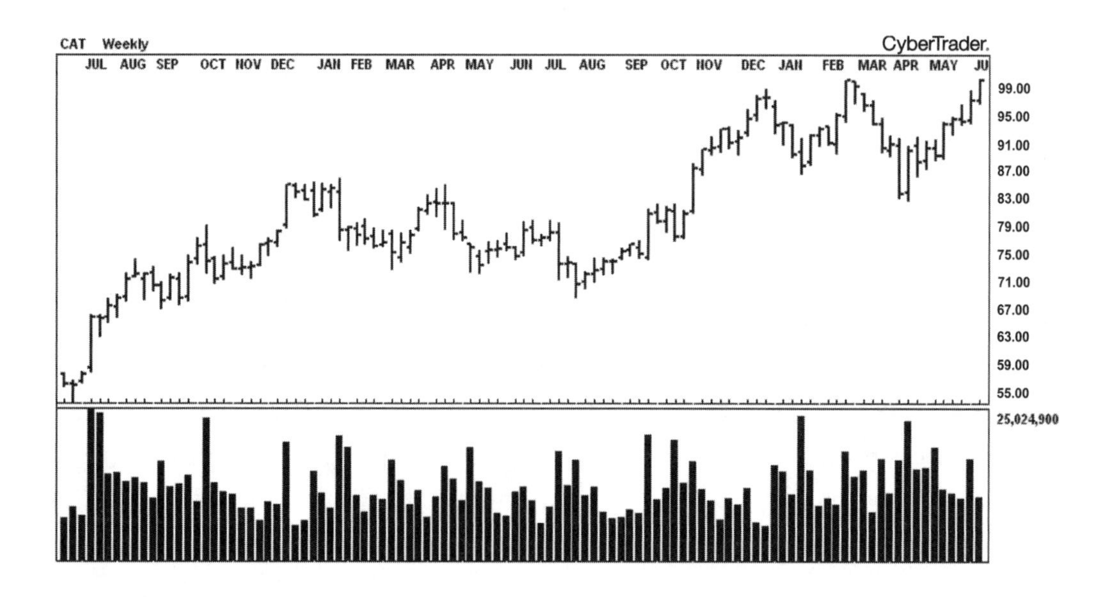

Figure 15-4: ***Two-year Weekly View - Caterpillar Inc. (CAT)***

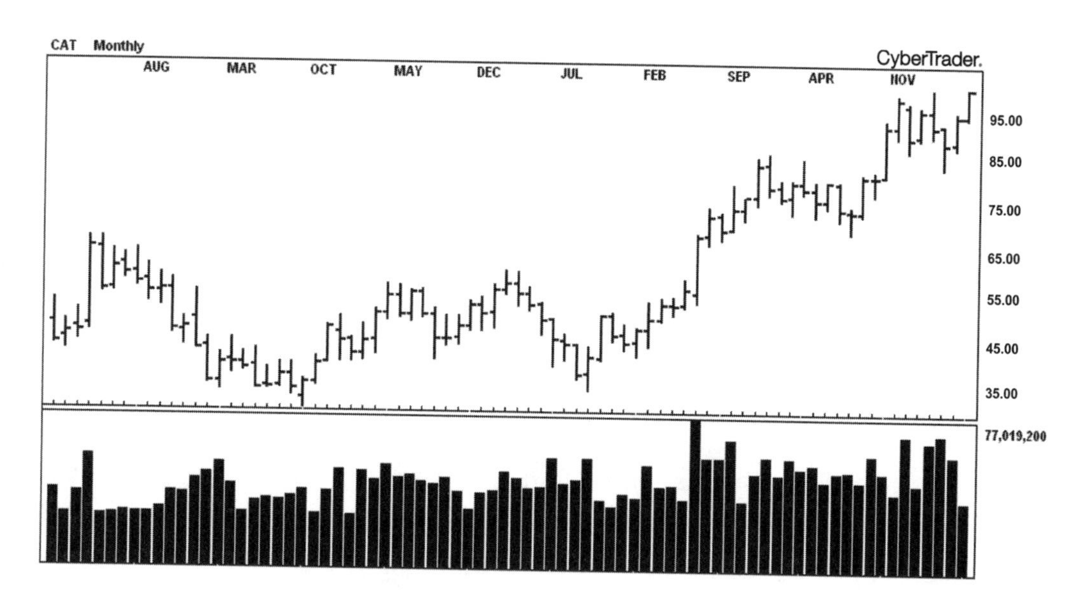

Figure 15-5: ***Six-year Monthly View - Caterpillar Inc. (CAT)***

Notice how Figure 15-3 (daily view) conveys a choppy, volatile picture of CAT's price direction whereas the movement in Figure 15-5 (monthly view) is more clear and direct.

> *Swing points are where decisions are being made. Am I buying or selling? Patience is the key; wait for the trade. Be the market.*

Other Aspects of Identifying the Trade

As I mentioned before, it is a good idea to hone in on about twenty stocks in your selection process. If all stocks break swing points with volume, you certainly do not want to trade all twenty stocks! Despite your candidates having strong relative strengths, a down day in the market could spell disaster with so many positions on the table. Also, don't forget that having many open trades at one time may hamper your decision-making process. Will you have the mental fortitude to check the volumes, prices and swing points before you start unloading positions in a panic sale? It's a good idea to have your trades in different sectors; this will help when you encounter rotation in the market. Many times you'll see different sectors correcting at different times. If you have too many positions going at any given time, you probably will burn your mind out trying to track them all mentally. Say you notice volume behaving contrary to your expectations on some of your positions. Are you going to be able to keep making the right decisions regarding staying in those trades?

Conversely, you will not want to trade just one stock. It is very possible that your one stock will not move in up or down days in the market despite having a very strong or weak relative strength.

It's a good idea to keep it simple and down to a reasonable amount of trades (say four to eight stocks), particularly those which you feel are the best candidates. As I mentioned before, too many trades will keep you from maintaining mental clarity and could spell disaster on a down day.

Spikes in Your Back

Have you ever heard the phrase, "spikes in your back"? Well, I use it to speak of the distractions that impair our sense of clarity as well as the amount of awareness that we exercise at any given time.

Throughout your selection process in identifying a trade, you should pay very close attention to any amount of uncertainty that you encounter. You should strive to maintain a minimal amount of uncertainty at all times; if you encounter more uncertainty than you're accustomed to, then by all means, halt your selection process, regroup, and determine the cause for the added uncertainty. If you can't do this, then you should not trade at this point, but rather, wait for a better day.

Remember: always manage your distractions, expectations and most importantly, your money!

16

Setting up the Trade

The two most powerful warriors are patience and time.
~ Leo Tolstoy

O.K. You identified twenty or so stocks based on relative strength and now you are sifting through their charts looking at their price and volume movements. Let's say you've selected two stocks that have recently surged (in this case let's consider them as being "long" candidates) and have broken a previous swing high on volume. What are you going to do next?

Retracements

Do not chase stocks! In other words, don't be tempted to get into rising stocks while they keep surging higher and higher. Patience here is the name of the game!! While they are surging, keep an eye on them, particularly on their volume. Does volume continue to be strong as your candidates are surging ever higher? If so, good. Don't do anything yet, though; just keep watching. Remember, a rising stock cannot keep rising and rising. Make a list of the equities that have broken swings on volume and set your alarms on your trading platform (a trading alarm can be a useful tool providing you alerts based on predetermined triggers such as trading price or volume).

Let's say your stocks are rising and one in particular, YES, is surging on strong volume. It moves from $10 to $15. Remember, this is only an example (it would be very nice to find stocks that make 50% moves like YES). Upon reaching $15, volume strength begins to drop and the stock starts to move down, slowly. This is the "retracement" move of our stock's recent price move.

Retracements can be analyzed in different manners, but my favorite is to look at the related volume and focus on the "integrity of the retracement". Remember, when stocks make substantial price moves, they do not always move in a straight line. Their movements and trading rhythms are comprised of a "surge, retrace, surge, retrace" pattern before resting or consolidating on a price level before their next substantial move, be it up or down.

It is during the retracement phase that we look to our stock's volume strength. As long as volume is noticeably lighter during its retracement, as opposed to volume during its surge, quality volume is being demonstrated and accordingly the overall price moves are real (remember quality volume?).

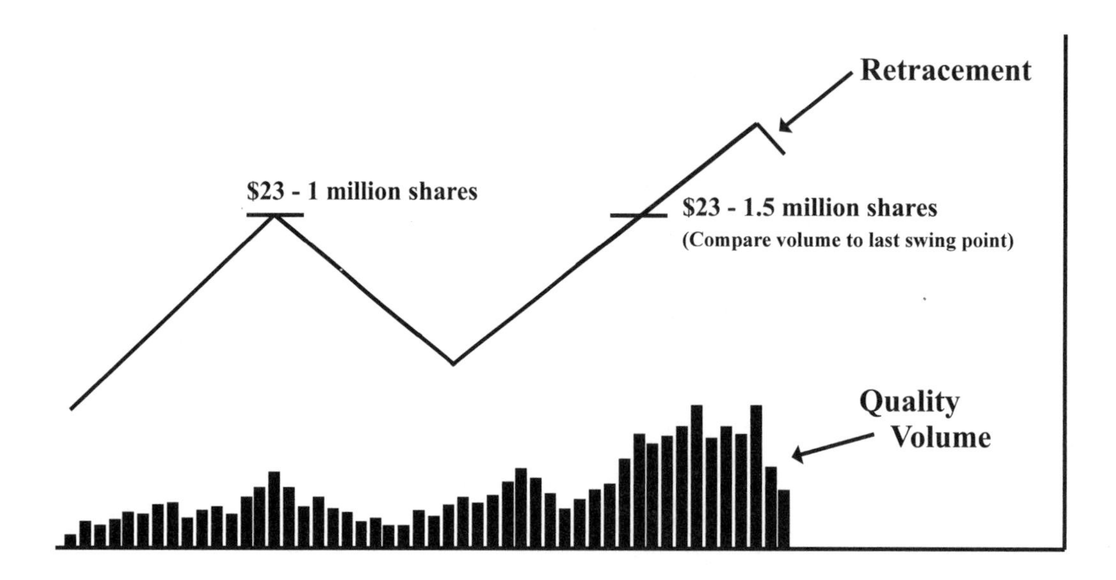

Figure 16-1: *Retracement on Lighter Volume*
This figure includes an example of a stock taking out a swing point with stronger volume followed by a retracement accompanied by lighter volume.

What happens during a retracment in real, everyday terms? Well, the surge of buying energy doesn't come in one continuous flow, just as water gushes out of your faucet. Rather, it comes in waves, just like the waves that crash onto the shore. After a wave, which in essence is the beginning of a retracement, the buying energy that caused the surge in the first place begins to wane or slow down. Additionally, people who got in early (before or during the early phase of the price surge or mark-up) are tempted to "take money off the table", i.e., sell their shares to make a quick profit. The shares sold into the market without a compensating buying interest create a temporary imbalance in the supply and demand equilibrium. What is the result? A drop in price! Will prices continue to drop? Answer: Keep an eye on volume!

I can't stress enough how important it is to keep an eye on volume during the retracement. If it is light, then you can safely bet that the stock is merely taking a breather. If volume is strong during this move down, all bets are off! The stock may have already turned a corner and is heading downward mostly because of heavy selling pressure.

Remember, look for the retracement on a stock that has made a considerable price move and pay close attention to its volume! With volume being light during the retracement, what happens next? Well, those traders/investors/operators that took money off the table are tempted to get back in.

How Far Will it Retrace? Fibonacci!

Your stock has completed a surge and is now in a retracement phase. Question is: how far will it retrace? Well, it depends. Assuming that the stock is indeed retracing in preparation for its next move up and is not heading lower on strong volume, the stock can retrace a little or a lot. One thing to keep in mind here is that the smaller or tighter the retracement, the stronger the stock is in its current trend.

Using what we learned in the chapter covering Fibonnaci ratios, it would be helpful to calculate the Fibonacci retracement levels using your stock's recent price expansion (in the case of our YES stock, $10 to $15). The retracement levels are calculated using the price points associated with the ABC designations. Remember how we calculate Fibonacci retracements? If not, refer back to Chapter 6 – *Fibonacci* for a refresher.

Let's say that at this point you have calculated the .382, .50 and .618 retracement levels for your stock. Will your stock retrace necessarily to these levels? Not necessarily. These levels merely represent targets residing in price *areas* where stocks typically retrace to. Again, you should refer back to the Chapter 6 – *Fibonacci* for discussion on the relevance of each of these levels to the subsequent price expansion and their relationships to one another.

In the following example (and also in the case study included in Appendix I – *Case Study*), we will assume that we have calculated the Fibonacci retracement levels prior to calculating confluence.

Setting up the Trade

Alright, we have an equity that has taken off to the upside or downside (possible short trade). What's next?

As the equity begins its retracement phase:

(1) **Market Trend** - We check the SPX, Dow and NASDAQ markets (their recent point moves and volume strengths) and make sure our stock is moving with the broad market trend.

(2) **Volume** – We open our eyes to volume keeping mindful of quality volume!

(3) **Last Swing Point or Support/Resistance Level** - We take the equity's last major swing point or breakout level (basically using this to build our "staging area") and make note of its price point and trading volume for that day (assuming we are looking at a daily chart); on a going-forward basis, all observations of our equity's price and volume behavior will be compared to the last swing point. Also, we use this level to target our entry point.

(4) **Strong Price Move** - We look for our equity to make a strong price move through a major swing point or support/resistance level ("jumping the creek").

(5) **Retracement on Lighter Volume** - We look for the commencement of a retracement that occurs on lighter volume ("coming back to ice").

(6) **Confluence** - We identify the A1 and A2 points as well as the Focus point (the end of the recent price move) and calculate confluence taking particular note of its closeness to the last swing point; this can be pretty key because if confluence is close to or sits right on the last swing's price point, you have the making of a strong resistance level where the likelihood of your stop being hit decreases substantially. At this point we also calculate our projected expansion point and identify our stop (being on the other side of confluence).

(7) **Risk/Reward** - Using our stop and expansion points, we calculate our risk/reward ratio and make sure we have at least a 3-to-1 ratio (I'll elaborate on this in short order).

As the equity gets close to confluence we continue to keep an eye on its volume making sure it continues to be light. We also look for a reversal candle formation – this isn't crucial to entering the trade but it definitely stacks the probability in our favor. With our current risk/reward ratio being at least 3-to-1 and volume on the equity still being light, we look to the 3x3 DMA and MACD for the final go-ahead. We note that we're still on the right side of the trend (3x3 DMA) and that the stock has begun to turn around to head where we want it to go (MACD). Time to enter the trade.

You're in it. You've done your homework, you've picked out a great candidate, more than likely you've entered your stock at a very fortuitous price point and now you've logged onto your online broker and your order for your equity has been executed. Now you're ready to see how your equity trades!! Are you done? No way!! Did you forget your stop? Have you entered or given your stop loss amount to your broker? Forgetting to perform this step is like forgetting to wear clothes to church! Don't forget your stops!!

Risk vs. Reward

As part of setting up the trade, it's important to calculate and stay aware of your possible risk/reward scenarios while aiming for a minimum ratio. The concept of risk vs. reward is extremely important and accordingly I've devoted an entire chapter to the topic as well as share sizing and money management (Chapter 18 - *Risk & Money Management*). I do however want to further discuss the benchmark risk/reward ratios I use in my trading.

I want to quickly point out that I present these parameters as reward to risk or reward/risk which will structurally seem different from the way the concept is typically expressed: risk/reward. Throughout the book I'll be using the more common "risk/reward" terminology even though the reward will be numerically expressed before risk.

I personally like to achieve a minimum 3-to-1 risk/reward parameter for trades (that means that I should stand to either make $3 or lose $1).

Sometimes, you'll identify a potential entry point only to discover that it may be too late!! Well, if your equity has established its C point (or the end of its retracement) and has inched away, don't give up on it right away. Look at where its price is and recalculate the risk/reward ratio as if you were getting into it at its current price point. If the risk/reward ratio is still better than our benchmark 3-to-1, then by all means, it's not too late!

Typically what I do is calculate risk vs. reward *early* in the process so that I'll identify appropriate entry points.

A Real Example of Setting up the Trade

Figure 16-2 gives us a four-year chart showing recent trading history for E.I. du Pont de Nemours and Co. ("Dupont") which has built substantial cause over a substantial amount of time.

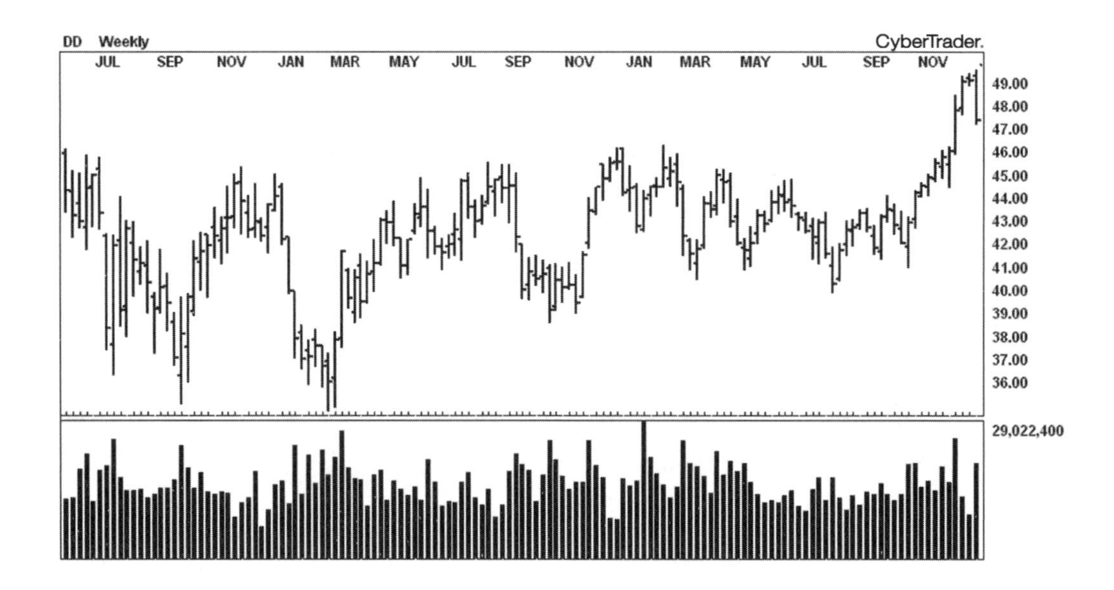

Figure 16-2: ***Recent Dupont Trading History - Dupont (DD)***

Let's take a look at how we could have effectively set up a trade following our guidelines and using Dupont as our stock.

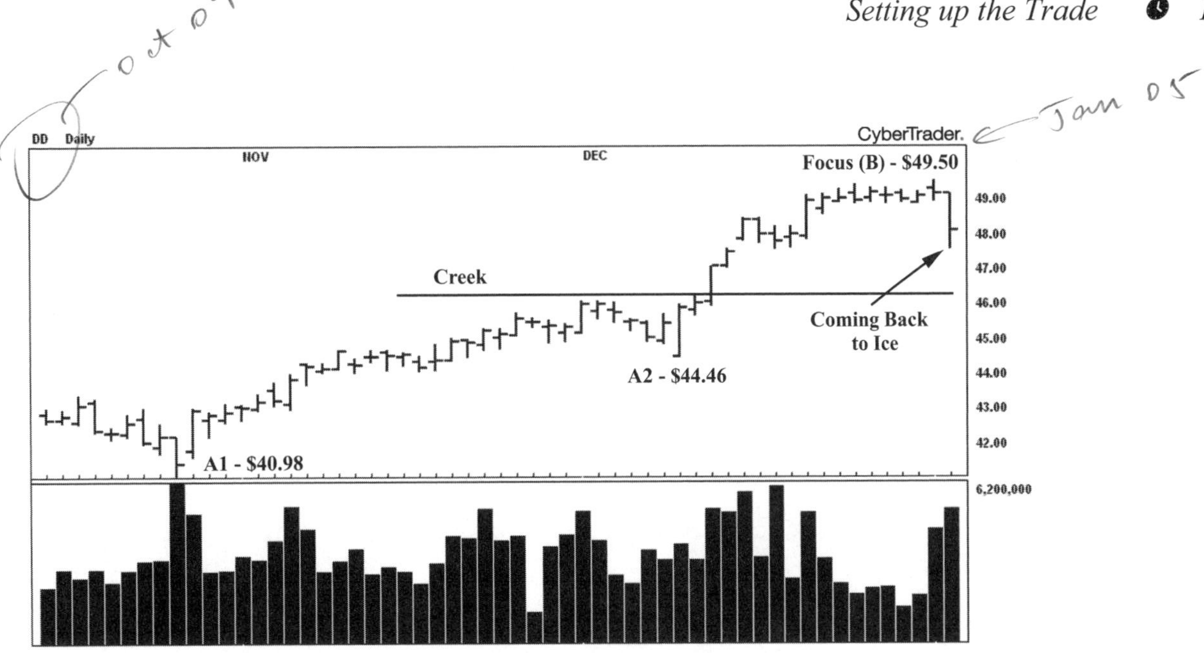

Figure 16-3: ***Setting up the Trade - Dupont (DD)***

(1) **Market Trend, Volume -** The first thing we note is Dupont breaking out of a long consolidation with volume in early December, taking out old swing points in the process. The price movement continues onward and reaches it focus point and begins to retrace on lighter volume.

(2) **Last Swing Point, Strong Price Move** – Here we note that our staging area is built using information from the swing point level which happened to take place at the December 1st swing point of $46.05 (volume was 4.0 million shares). DD breaks through this level on December 13th on volume of 5.2 million shares.

(4) **Retracement** - We allow DD to complete its run and await a retracement on lighter volume.

(4) **Confluence** - Given the price movement and simple identification of an A1 ($40.98 on Oct 26, 2004), A2 ($44.46 on Dec 9th) and Focus point ($49.50 on January 5, 2005), confluence is calculated as $46.25 to $46.39. Notice how A1 in this case is clearly defined and how confluence happens to occur at the breakout price level.

(5) **Risk/reward** – Our entry price would be above confluence and at the breakout level, possibly $46.40 or thereabouts. Theoretically we'd place our stop on the other side of confluence. Optimally however, we want to place it at a

previous support level (still beneath confluence) such as a previous swing point or breakout level. A good spot in this case would be $44.76 which happens to be at strong support and just on the other side of an early 2004 swing high. With these entry and stop amounts, our potential risk is $1.64 ($46.40 - $44.76). Our potential reward is arrived at by taking A1 ($40.98) to B ($49.50), yielding $8.52. Our risk/reward ratio comes up as 5.2-to-1, which is greater than our desired ratio of 3-to-1.

Risk / Reward Calculation

Reward	**Risk**	
A1 = $40.98	**Target Entry**	**$46.40**
B = $49.50	**Stop**	**- 44.76**
A1 to B = $8.52 (Projected Expansion - Reward)	**Potential Loss =** (Risk)	**$ 1.64**
"Risk/Reward Ratio" equals Reward divided by Risk		
$8.52 (Reward) / $1.64 (Risk) = 5.2 [Greater than 3 to 1]		

Figure 16-4: ***Risk/Reward Calculation - Dupont (DD)***

(6) **3x3 DMA & MACD** – We turn to the 3x3 DMA and MACD for the final go-ahead. Looking at the 3x3 DMA we note that we are not quite on the right side of the trend; we wait. DD finally enters into the "bullish" side of the 3x3 DMA on January 27, 2005; we notice this as DD closes *above* the 3x3 DMA.

Dupont (DD)	**Closing Price**	**Computed 3X3 DMA**
January 27 (Price crosses into DMA "bullish side")	**$ 46.97**	**$ 46.65**
January 26	**46.48**	**47.10**
January 25 (Originally planned entry date)	**46.58**	**47.36**
January 24	**46.01**	
January 21	**46.71**	
January 20	**47.23**	
January 19	**47.38**	
January 18	**47.49**	

We take a look at the MACD and notice that the fast curve is fast approaching the slower curve and is about to make its crossover (it's O.K. to speculate that the crossover will occur, if it doesn't later on, you definitely want to get out of your trade). We aim for a good entry price and arrive at $47.00 which is 60 cents greater than our previously planned entry. From a risk/reward perspective we have given up 60 cents of reward (now $7.92) and added 60 cents to our risk, taking it from $1.64 to $2.24. Upon recalculation, our risk/reward ratio has moved from 5.2-to-1 down to 3.5-to-1, still above our 3-to-1 benchmark. We now have an "all systems go" and we fire off the trade.

What was the broad market doing at this time? The SPX and Dow were both going through retracements, incidentally on lighter volume.

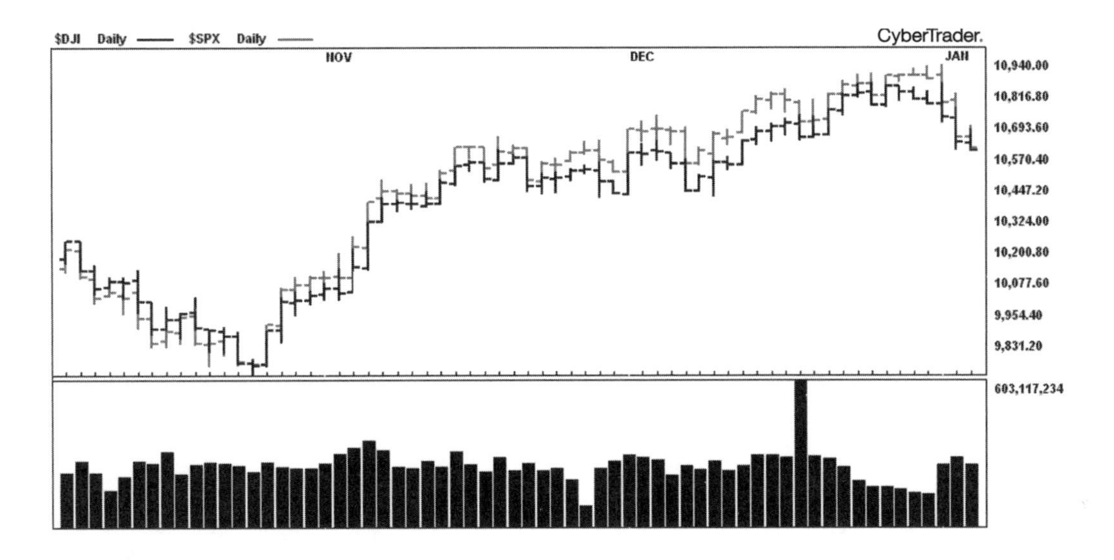

Figure 16-5: ***SPX and Dow***

What did Dupont end up doing? It hit confluence on extremely light volume and then took off. Take a look at Figure 16-6.

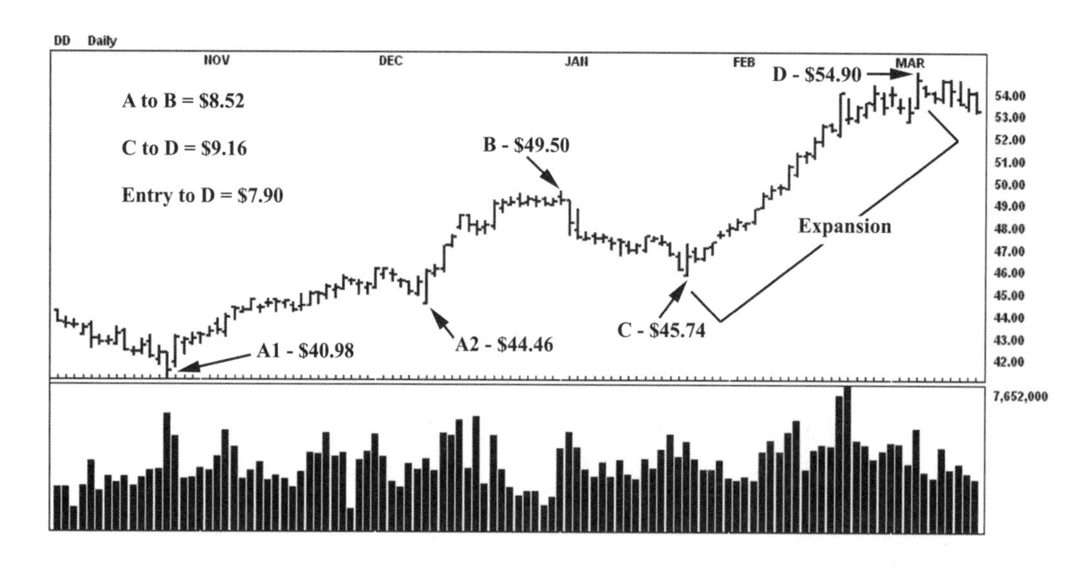

Figure 16-6: ***The Whole Picture - Dupont (DD)***

With our entry point equaling $47.00 and our projection point equaling $54.90, our actual expansion totaled $7.90, lower than the planned $8.52 (A to B) due to the simple reason that we waited for the appropriate entry signal from the 3x3 DMA & MACD and got in at a higher price. A good trade nonetheless!

Confidence is preparation. Everything else is beyond your control.

~ Richard Kline

17

In the Trade

What lies behind us and what lies before us
are tiny matters compared to what lies within us.
~ Ralph Waldo Emerson

You've done all your homework, read *Timing the Trade* upside down, waited for a breakout followed by a pullback on lighter volume, planned your trade and pulled off your entry; now finally, you're in the trade.

This is where the head game comes on with all cylinders firing. Are you going to be able to live with your trading decisions? Your stomach starts to rumble, your head starts thinking about the money you're going to make, but then, "what if I lose money?" You have this uncomfortable feeling running through your body. This is where you'll find out that the real battle is not in the market but perhaps within yourself.

What type of person are you? What sort of discipline do you possess? How are you going to respond to the motions of a deviant market that, on a drop of a dime, can move mercilessly against you? How about your emotions and doubts as you face these uncertainties? Are you going to take losses personally? Are you going to maintain your discipline and honor your trading plan, or will you start hoping and praying soon after you decide a stop isn't really necessary?

What about passion and perseverance over the long haul? What are you going to do when the market comes knocking on your door taking a substantial amount of your trading capital in short order. Are you going to pack it in and ask why you did this in the first place, or are you going to get up off the ground, collect yourself, and analyze your errors, not to mention yourself?

Welcome to the world of trading.

Being in a trade is a great opportunity for serious reflection; you'll have the opportunity to take a deep look into your makeup, maybe have some conversations with yourself and find out just what makes you tick. At a minimum, you should take note of your emotions as you're in a trade. If you feel cool, calm and collected, chances are that you've done your homework and that you're exercising discipline by sticking to your trading plan – actually an excellent place to be.

Realize that losses happen. Even the best traders in the world can end up having more losing trades than winners in a given year. What makes them profitable as well as great traders (not to mention what saves their sanity) is sound planning and discipline. By analyzing mistakes, honoring stops and letting winners ride, the best traders in the world are just that, the best.

Back to being in the trade.

Making Money

This is the sweet spot in the business. Your screen is green; you've been hunting for the right trade and it's paying off as you watch it head for your projected price point. You're holding fast to your expansion target and it seems that your trade may just in fact reach it. You've studied this book inside and out and you've paid close attention to the critical importance of *volume*. You're paying close attention to trading volume and you notice it beginning to dry up. Your trade is oh-so-close, yet volume doesn't give you conviction that the price movement or momentum will continue. What now?

You either stay in or get out. Staying in the trade is probably the lesser desirable of the two options simply because you're betting that an unnatural force, certainly not strong volume, will continue to push your stock up to its target; that's right, an unnatural extension of price, lack of quality volume… remember? If you are a true disciple of volume, you'll exit your trade. Yes, just simply get out. So far, you potentially stand to make a nice gain thanks to certain important variables that got you in the trade in the first place. Why then would you stay in this trade when the most critical variable that got you in is no longer there? If quality volume got you in, lack of quality volume should tell you to get out!

In sum, making money or at least being in a winning position is a good thing. If there are forces that should compel you to get out such as lack of volume or a change in market condition, then by all means get out, take your money, and take your family out for a nice dinner or vacation weekend.

Losing Money

When you pause and think of the odds of succeeding in a simple trade, wouldn't it make sense that your odds are fifty-fifty? You get in a trade and the trade should go either up or down, right? Fifty-fifty. Well, without employing sound trading principles and tactics, the odds of losing a great deal of money can definitely stack up against you. With such probabilities it makes sense always to employ fixed and sound stop-loss strategies. I've already covered the importance of these, but if you've forgotten, go back and review the chapter on stops.

At any rate, a stop will keep you from losing a significant amount of capital on a single trade, essentially giving you a chance to fight another day. Regardless, hitting a stop still involves the loss of some amount of money. Not a terribly rosy experience, would you say? Well, in Spanish there is a phrase that speaks directly to what you may experience when encountering a trading loss: *No hay mal que por bien no venga.* Roughly translated the saying is: "there is no bad from which there can't be good" (very similar to the "look for the silver lining" expression we use in English). In our context, there is still a positive element to experiencing a loss. The most obvious is that we can all learn from our mistakes, that is, of course, if the mistakes are readily there to take note of.

Traders, however, will many times incur losses, period. These types of losses do not necessarily come about because of trading mistakes but, still, it makes sense to analyze all your trades and try to uncover any isolated mistakes and/or common patterns. Are you jumping the gun and getting in too early? Are you paying attention to those important candlestick formations or 3x3 DMA & MACD? Have you an itchy trigger finger that keeps you from allowing a stock to prove itself? Keeping tabs on trades gone wrong helps you in the long run, and the returns you stand to make based on your growing trading experience will come back to you in spades.

This is a good place to stress the importance of maintaining a log to track your trades. Your log or diary should include each trade, the day you entered, execution price, designated stop and your final exit price. You should also include some qualitative information such as reason(s) for entering and exiting trade. Such a log will not only help uncover shortcomings to your trading decisions, it will also tell you what's working for you!

What about ending a losing trade prematurely? Definitely this is not a bad practice particularly if the road signs are there signaling you to get out. Again, the road signs I'm talking about here involve volume and price movement. If you notice volume behaving in a manner that will spell a greater loss, then without hesitation, get out. Psychologically this is a tough decision to make, but being able to systematically get out of losing trades (i.e., not pondering the decision) when signals are more than obvious will help you become a master trader!

I learned much from my teachers, more from my books,
and most from my mistakes.

~ Anonymous

Breaking Even

Getting out "flat" is not a bad thing.

If your stock is not reacting the way it should, then get out. Again, getting out is the thing to do simply because your expectation of the stock's movement was originally formulated into your decision-making process. If it's not behaving as you had predicted or as it had previously, take your money and run. It doesn't matter how good the stock looked yesterday; what matters is what the stock is telling you *now*.

Remember, pay close attention to price and volume movements and particularly to what your mind is telling you insofar as the money you have invested is concerned.

Although breaking even also gives you a chance to fight another day, stop and analyze your trading behavior if you find that you are getting out too often just to break even. This may point either to a lack of patience or a need for money, or simply to some emotional or psychological force saying you shouldn't be trading at the present time.

Mental Dynamics

This is a good time to talk about what goes on in your head while you have a trade in place, or better put, what are the mental dynamics involved in your trade?

Being in It

You've executed your trade, you've set your stop and now you feel a sense of euphoria and excitement. You've basically placed a bet and you're wondering how your horse will do. Well, it's not that crude but still you have money at risk, and this can create quite a stir of emotions, particularly if you're new to trading. It's important to realize that you've done plenty of homework. You've identified a stock worthy of trading based on its price and volume movements, calculated your stock's risk and reward parameters, and have created a sense of conviction that was sufficient to make you decide to pull off the trade. You've followed through on placing a stop order in the event that your planning was flawed or that unforeseen forces, such as operators, will move your stock in an unanticipated direction. With the stop in place, you have already planned the amount of money that you stand to lose. You've perfected your decision making process so that entering and exiting a trade is practically mechanical.

With all this analysis, preparation and risk management you may ask, "Hey, what's the worry"? It really doesn't make sense to lose sleep at night over your trade, but that doesn't mean that you can pack your bags and head to the French Riviera either. What may serve you well is to monitor your trade but make sure that you do not become obsessed. You'll be faced with many factors that may hamper your trading plan once you're in a trade, internal as well as external – the key is to stay focused.

The internal factors I'm talking about mostly comprise fear and greed. These factors are motivated through many other variables which are driven primarily by external stimuli, so many that it would be impossible to list them all in this book. A good example would be a related news event. Suppose you're trading YES and you hear over the wire that their employees are considering a strike in order to get better pay. This news may affect the trading price of the stock. On the other hand, it's very possible that this news event has already been factored into the price of the stock (i.e., people already knew ahead of time about the strike and traded the stock accordingly.) That being said, it pays not to worry about news or any other form of external noise. Do your best to ignore message boards, news flashes, etc.

An important thing is to make sure that trading does not control your life, but rather enriches it. Trading can be quite a passion, but it can also become an obsession. Remember, there is a difference between passion and obsession. Passion leads to a desire to learn more. We are never done learning. Our entire lives are spent learning lessons. These lessons make us better, more whole. Obsession is the result of the agony of not knowing what comes next. By making calculated decisions and consciously ignoring "what if" and "what could be" you'll be more systematic in your decisions and make more concrete moves.

If there is some level of obsession that you must have or maintain regarding your trade, then let it fall or rest on monitoring your stock's volume and corresponding price move, nothing else. If you focus accordingly, you'll be able to notice the right road signs that will tell you whether your trade is on the right track or if you should be taking the next exit and get off the highway!

Keep in mind that it pays to stay conscious of your own state of mind, and trade accordingly.

Clarity

Being in a trade can be a tough place to find yourself, and while you're in it you get a real chance to really *find yourself.* Take this chapter to heart. Make sure that you take trading as a serious pursuit requiring dedication. Exercise discipline (plan your trade and trade your plan) and patience (wait for your trade). Not only will you be well on your way to becoming a successful trader but an individual controlling his or her own destiny.

18

Risk & Money Management

Risk is always present whereas reward is possible but not guaranteed.
~ Robert Rotella

John from Denver liked to consider himself as being a savvy investor. He was up to speed on mostly all facets of investing including the due diligence aspect of it (i.e., researching potential stock purchases); he was up to date on all the terms and metrics used to analyze stocks and their companies' financial positions, earning histories and capabilities. John even knew something about reading charts, understanding moving averages, and calculating Fibonacci retracement levels, etc.

The Plunge

With about $20,000 of his hard-earned cash to invest, John was looking to purchase 1,000 shares of DTI stock at $20 per share. DTI (Down the Tubes, Inc.) was a long-standing plumbing supply manufacturer and looked good by all accounts. Nonetheless, John had performed boatloads of due diligence and research on DTI and analyzed DTI's daily, monthly and yearly charts. The company had a stable earnings history, new and exciting products in the pipeline, not to mention patented technologies and a solid management team to boot. In technical terms, DTI stock had just risen above its 200-day moving average and was poised to go much higher. By golly (and certainly by John's efforts and convictions), DTI was the stock to buy . . . and John bought it.

John was proud of his purchase. Just days after buying it at $20, John's DTI stock was up 10% or $2 at $22, not bad. As a reward for picking such a winner, John treated himself to a last minute, super-saver weekend trip to Costa Rica which he found on the internet. With his bags packed, sunscreen in tow and his DTI stock up a handsome 10%, John made for the white sandy beaches of the Pacific on an early Friday morning. ¡Pura Vida!

The Disaster

"Margaritas are absolutely wonderful!" A joyous thought danced in John's mind that Saturday afternoon as he soaked in the sun, the breeze and the seductive sounds of the playful waves breaking off the edges of the vast blue Pacific. Life was great and John knew it as he relished the sweet oblivion of being away from all the cares of the world. Why, at this point, John's greatest concern was what to have for dinner: lobster or stone crab? Hmm, very tough. Why not both?

John grabbed his towel and sunscreen, and in a slow, lazy cadence made his way back to his room for a shower and then . . . dinner! He briefly flipped on the television, turned to CNN (the only English speaking channel other than MTV) and . . . and . . . "what the...?!"

To his total and utter amazement, Wolf Blitzer (typically a political correspondent) is reporting live from the smoldering explosion site of Down the Tubes, Inc.'s primary manufacturing facility. "Explosion site?!"

Fortunately no one was hurt during the Friday lunch-time explosion, but the flaming truth was that millions of dollars in PVC pipes and high-tech, robotic manufacturing equipment had gone up in smoke.

John could not pinch himself out of this bad dream. What will happen to the company? What about its new products? What will happen to DTI stock? Or better yet, what *happened* to DTI's price on Friday afternoon?

His fears were realized when he learned through a very expensive operator-assisted, international call that DTI hit $18 at Friday's close, down $4. John froze. You can imagine how the rest of his trip was. He returned Monday afternoon and saw that DTI had gapped down to $15 and continued its slide closing at $10.

John's investment was now down 50%. He was also down 50% on his total capital base. In other words, his entire base of $20,000 was now at $10,000. After fearing further losses, John pulled the plug on his investment and got out.

The Lessons

Money Management

You've heard the metaphor, "don't put all your eggs into one basket". Indeed, this is precisely what John did. His entire $20,000 was sunk into one stock. The malaise of this approach is that when your one stock goes down substantially, so does your entire capital base.

In John's case, his investment went down 50%. Can you figure what sort of increase DTI stock would have had to experience in order for John to recover his potential loss had he stayed in the stock? Answer: 100%. Yep 100%. $10,000 grown 100% equals $20,000. Figure 18-1 includes a loss recovery chart:

Loss %	Recovery %
10%	11%
20%	25%
30%	43%
40%	67%
50%	100%
60%	150%
70%	233%
80%	400%
90%	900%

Figure 18-1: *Loss Recovery Chart*
This chart conveys the gain percentage required to make up for a particular loss. The column on the left lists various loss percentages and the column on the right includes the gain percentages required to recoup the corresponding loss. Example: if your capital base goes down 40%, it would take a gain of 67% to get back to even.

John should have divided his $20,000 into several amounts and invested those amounts (not necessarily all) into different stocks. We'll dive further into money management, but for now let's take note that John invested his entire bankroll into one stock, the stock did a nosedive and so did John's bankroll. And let's also not forget about what John (and many other people in a similar situation) may have gone through both emotionally and psychologically.

Risk Management

Another cardinal sin committed by John was that he did not employ risk management by executing a stop with his trade. With a stop-loss, John would have been out before his stock slid considerably and he would have lost a small, manageable amount rather than 50% of his trade (not to mention 50% of his portfolio by not employing sound money management).

With a stop loss you are basically quantifying your exposure to risk and giving yourself peace of mind in the process. If your trade begins to go against you, the stop-loss mechanism will ensure a small loss rather than one of gigantic proportions. And what's unique about a stop-loss is that you know *ahead* of time how much you will stand to lose. With this dynamic, you'll even be able to size your trades (number of shares) given the amount you're willing to risk along with the size of your stop spread (difference between entry and exit). We'll get into sizing trades in short order.

One thing to note: even if John had set a stop at $17 (which would not have been hit on Friday unless a trade fired off at the amount or lower), on the following trading day (Monday), John still would have gotten out around $15 and would have saved himself the agony of selling at $10. The reason he would not have gotten out at $17 is because DTI *gapped* down on Monday (close on Friday was $18, DTI opened at $15 on Monday). A basic market stop would have sold his stock at market once DTI hit $17 or any lesser dollar amount. Sure the difference between what could have been a stop at $17 and Monday's opening amounts to a two dollar difference. . . it's still better to have a total $5 loss than a $10 loss! (Getting caught in a gap - down situation is an example of *uncontrollable risk,* which I discuss later in this chapter.)

Money Management

Slicing the Pie

Dividing the amount of your capital base for trades is much like slicing a pie. It is fundamentally sound to divide up your capital base to a certain amount of trades for profit. Unfortunately for John, he used up his entire "pie" for his one trade and suffered as a result.

Your "pie" is basically your at-risk capital. How much of your "pie" are you going to devote to how many stocks? The determination is systematic but mostly judgmental; that is, there may be a formula, but even coming up with a formula can be subjective.

I like to utilize 10 to 15% of my capital base for single trades – that's a maximum of roughly 6 to 10 different trades. I typically do not employ the entire pie because I like to maintain a reserve in the event that I run into a trade where I feel absolutely compelled to enter into. This practice ensures that I always have money in my back pocket for times I need it.

The important thing to remember with this approach is that it is strictly for trading purposes. With investing, you would be wise to have many more slices, as you would want your portfolio to be well-diversified. Remember, slice up your portfolio into manageable amounts for trades and keep money in reserve for ideal trading opportunities.

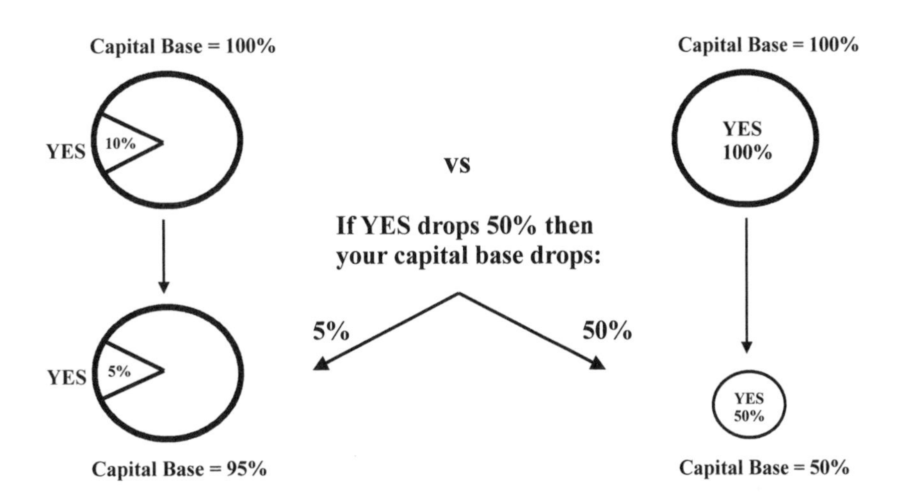

Figure 18-2: ***Slicing the Pie - (YES)***
This diagram basically demonstrates what happens when you "put all your eggs in one basket" with one stock and the catastrophe that results on the occasion the stock tanks. On the left, 10% of a given capital base is utilized to purchase shares in YES. On the right, the entire capital base is used. If YES drops 50%, the capital base on the left incurs a 5% drop or contraction with 95% of the starting capital

base still intact. The capital base on the right drops the entire amount of YES's collapse, 50%. The important lesson here is to diversify your trading allocations and utilize portions of your capital base, i.e., break up the pie and utilize different slices for your trades.

Risk Management

I am going to keep this section relatively simple, straight and forward. Employing stops allows you to size your trades while quantifying risk. Let's look at an example:

Sizing Your Trade

> Suppose you have $100,000 in total capital to put at risk and you decide to use 10% or $10,000 to trade a particular stock. You have identified a potential stock to trade and you have pinpointed the ideal entry spot, given and using the principles of *Timing the Trade* outlined in this book.
>
> Fieldco, Inc. (FCO) is the stock and you look to get in at $20. You have identified a stop point just on the other side of confluence and it's at $18. You roughly have a stop spread of $2 which means that you will stand to lose $2 on each share FCO that you purchase in the event your trade goes against you.
>
> With the $10,000 you have earmarked for the trade, you decide that the most you are willing to lose is $600 or 6%. Now, you have sufficient information to size your trade. The key variables to arrive at *how many* shares you should buy are the $600 you are willing to lose and the $2 stop spread.
>
> It should make perfect sense to us that if you stand to lose $2 per share and you only want to lose $600, the amount of shares you should buy are 300, basically $600 divided by $2 (this of course ignores the impact of trading commissions which in the present-day world of online trading, should be minimal).

<u>Another Example</u>

> You have $10,000 to trade in YES and figure a stop spread of $1 (the distance between your entry and your stop point, just on the other side of confluence) and you wish to potentially lose only $600.
>
> With these figures, the amount of shares you should purchase is 600 which is arrived upon by taking $600 and dividing it by $1.

I repeated the loss amount of $600 and reduced the stop spread to prove a point: *the tighter your stop spread, the more shares you'll be able to purchase and thus the more you stand to make as your trade moves in your direction.* Did you get that? If your stop spread is $1 rather than $2, you'll be able to purchase *twice* the amount of shares. If your stop spread is $1 instead of $3, you'll be able to purchase *three* times the amount of shares as opposed to maintaining the $3 stop spread. This is a very powerful concept that will make you further evaluate your entry and exit points.

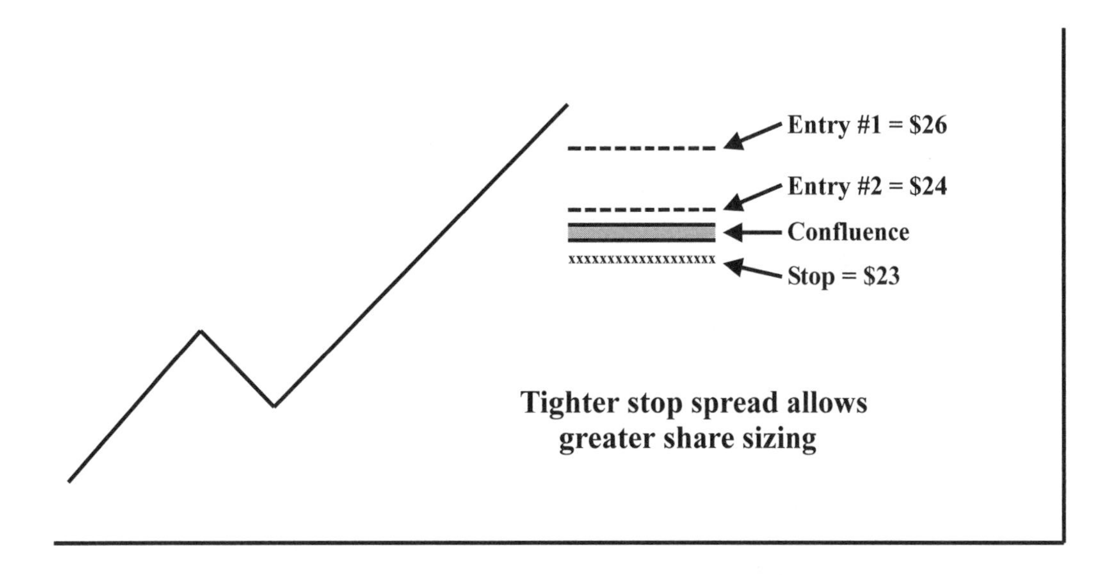

Figure 18-3: *Share Sizing*
With the stop being fixed at $23 (remeber that share sizing should not influence the postioning of your stop), the difference between the stop and entry #1 amounts to $3 of risk ($26-$23) and the difference between the stop and entry #2 amounts to $1 of risk. These differences in risk ($3 vs. $1) translate into different amounts of shares that you can purchase when your stop point is already defined. This highlights the importance of exercising patience and getting into your stock at a

price that is not only closer to confluence, but yields a tighter stop spread, thereby allowing you to purchase more shares.

Risk vs. Reward

Risk vs. reward is a very important concept with many books being devoted to the topic. Here, in *Timing the Trade*, I want to point out a few things related to it and keep everything short and simple.

Risk/Reward on Projections

In the chapter covering ABCs we learned how to project prices, given the thrusting movement of a stock. Without rehashing the chapter, remember that the A to B segment usually equals the C to D phase and that the C to D phase, in terms of planning your trade, is essentially your price projection.

When you know your price projection (or reward), be it $3 or $5 per share, you have one-half the equation related to the risk/reward parameter for your trade. Can you guess what the other half is? Well, it's basically the amount you set as your stop loss or your stop spread. Your stop spread is your risk. Here's an example:

> You've determined that the price projection on YES is $6 and your stop spread is $2. Your risk/reward parameter is 3-to-1; essentially $6 (reward) divided by $2 (risk) which is 3. ("Risk/reward" might seem like a misnomer since the parameter is numerically expressed as *reward to risk.*)
>
> If your projection on YES is $8 and your stop spread is $1, your risk/reward parameter is 8-to-1.

Desired Risk/Reward Parameters

A desired risk/reward parameter or DRRP will act as a filter for deciding on whether or not to enter a trade.

Let's say that you believe you've run through all the exercises to enter a *Timing the Trade* candidate. Have you considered the desired risk/reward parameter? If not, you're not quite ready to trade.

I personally use a 3-to-1 risk/reward parameter. A 3-to-1 parameter means that I have planned my trade to yield a reward of $3 for every $1 that I risk.

The reward is equal to the calculated expansion (remember A to B = C to D? Turn back to Chapter 6 - *Fibonacci* if necessary) and risk is the difference between your entry and stop price points. If A to B equals $3, then C to D will also equal $3; this is our targeted expansion and our planned "reward"; refer back to Chapter 6 - *Fibonacci* if necessary.

Controllable and Uncontrollable Risk

There are essentially two types of risk in trading and they are *controllable* and *uncontrollable* risk. The study and employment of stops addresses controllable risk. As the term implies, controllable risk involves the management of risk that can be entirely managed. In a perfect trading world, if you buy a stock at $20 and set a stop at $17, the most you stand to lose, in an absolute sense, is $3.

There are many elements however that keep our trading world from being perfect. One is slippage: it's what happens when your $17 stop is triggered and instead of being sold at $17, your stock is sold at the bid which is lower, say $16.90. Another element is a *gap* situation where a stock's opening price has "leapfrogged" your stop – if your stock closed at $18 on Friday and opened at $16 Monday morning, your $17 stop would get triggered and your stock would sell in the neighborhood of $16.

The difference between your entry price and designated stop makes up the portion of risk that is *controllable*; the difference between your designated stop and the actual stop execution price makes up that portion of your risk that is *uncontrollable*. Figure 18-3 provides a simple illustration of our example.

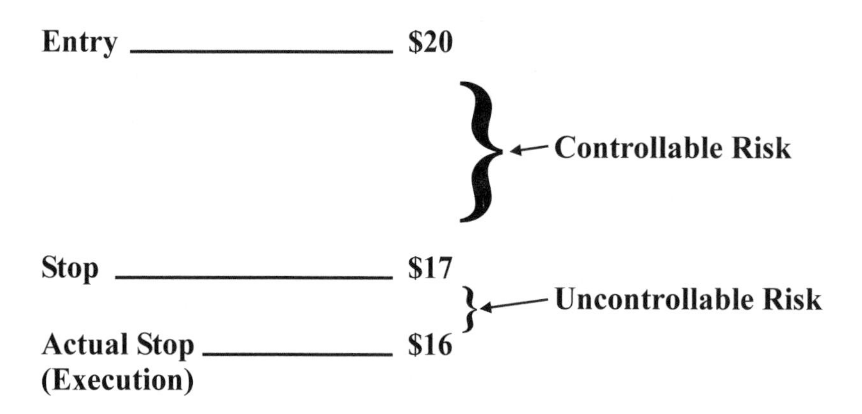

Figure 18-4: ***Controllable and Uncontrollable Risk***

Proper money and risk management techniques are critical to long term survival in the world of trading. Hopefully you will gain a mastery of these techniques and one day you (and hopefully John from Denver) will be able to enjoy the careless joys of a tropical vacation that will be *truly* stress and worry-free!

Appendix I

Case Study

Introduction

What would a dynamic book on stock trading be without a comprehensive case study? Well, here's one to help you cement the concepts I've introduced in this text and give you a model for implementing *Timing the Trade* tools.

We'll expand on our earlier Dupont (DD) example, see how it behaved during last quarter of 2004 and showcase the dynamics that made it an incredibly worthwhile stock to trade. We'll analyze its price behavior, essentially "paper trade" it and see how it performs, all the while utilizing certain concepts outlined in this text:

Identifying the Trade
- **Market Climate**
- **Cause & Effect**
- **Volume**
- **"Jumping the Creek"**

Setting up the Trade
- **"Coming Back to Ice"/Confluence**
- **Risk/Reward**
- **3x3 DMA & MACD**

In the Trade
- **Price Projection**
- **Mental Dynamics**
- **Success**

Throughout this case study, you'll be able to gauge your understanding of the *Timing the Trade* concepts. If you find yourself having any trouble, don't hesitate to go back to the pertinent chapter(s) to refresh your memory.

Identifying the Trade

How do I spot trades? Easy. I look for relationships between movements in the market versus movement in individual stocks.

For the sake of our case study, let's assume that Dupont has caught our attention.

Market Climate

The first thing we do when we first consider trading a stock is check out the climate of the market. What is the market telling us? Are we in a bull or bear market? This is very important since an overall market trend can have a direct impact on your stock. You've heard the phrase "the trend is your friend"; well, if you've ever been long in a bear market, you probably noticed that making money was much like swimming against a strong current. Ideally, you'll want to travel in the direction of the current.

Determining the trend can be fairly easy. Simply look to the last swing points. What has volume been doing since then? Is volume pushing price up or down?

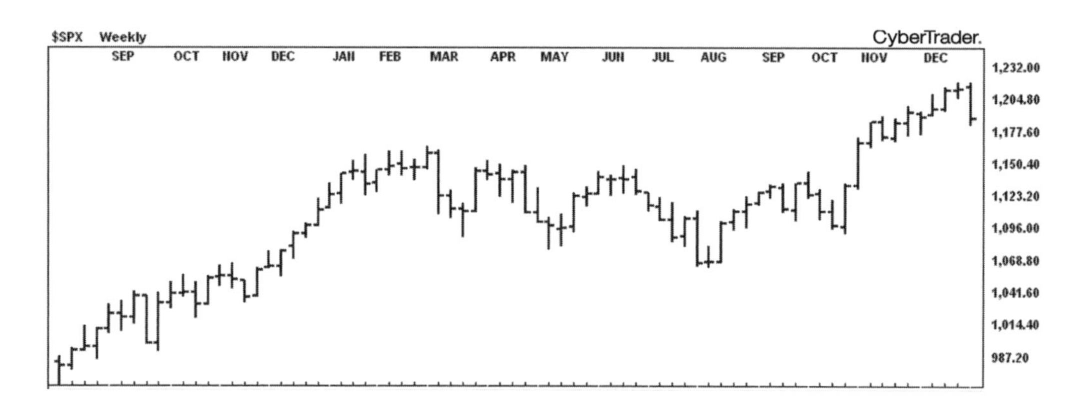

Figure AI-1

We're not done quite yet with analyzing the trading climate. Not only do we check out the major market to gauge the general climate, but we also look at our stock's more immediate climate and that is its own sector. What is the sector doing at the time? What is the stock (Dupont) doing vis-à-vis its sector?

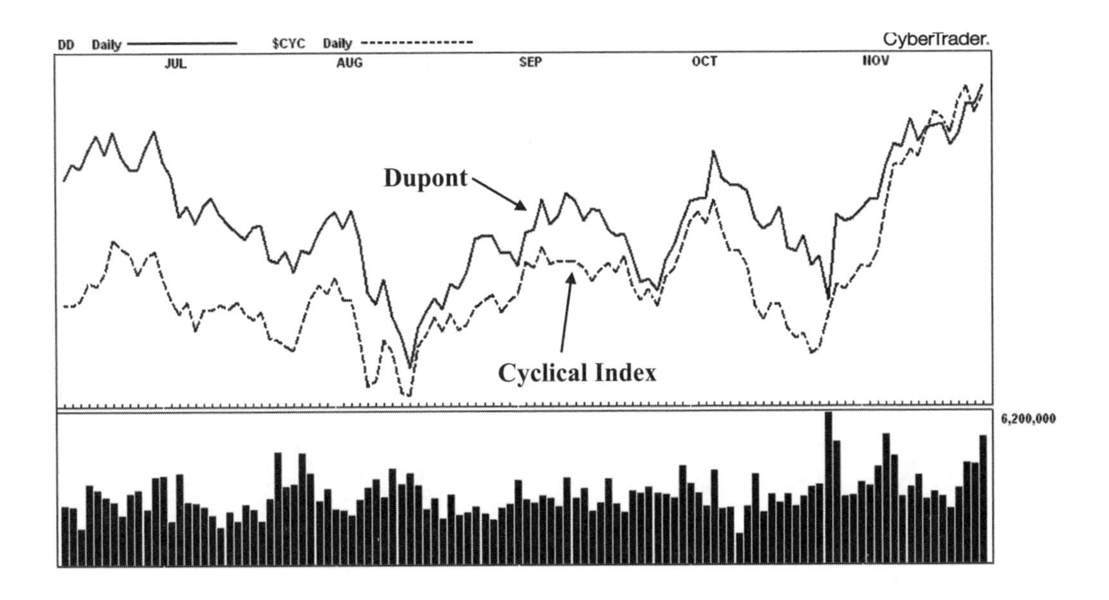

Figure AI-2

So at this point, we can see that the overall market climate is bullish as well as Dupont's sector, tracked by the Morgan Stanley Cyclical Index ($CYC). The overall and immediate climates appear conducive to going long.

Cause & Effect

If we look at Dupont on a standalone basis, we can see the amount of cause that has been building up through Dupont's trading pattern. It has basically traded sideways within a range for the last few months. Also, a level of resistance has developed with Dupont. Check out the cause (sideways movement) and resistance in the Figure AI-3:

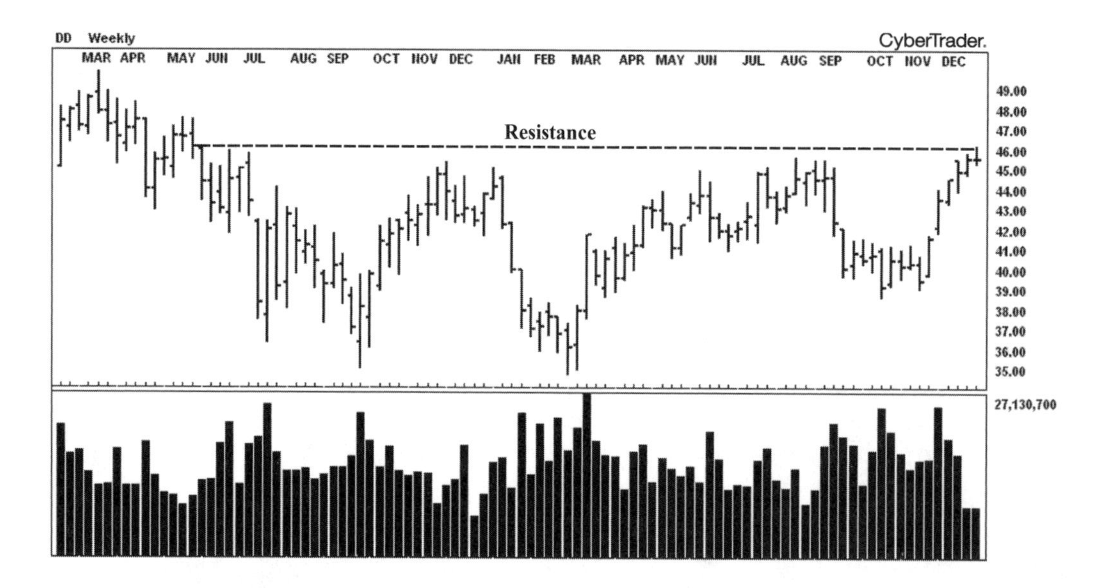

Figure AI-3

Volume

We get our first trading cue with Dupont when its volume begins to get strong and *stays* strong. If you check out Figure AI-4, you'll note around November 1st, volume begins to pick up after a long phase of building cause on relatively steady volume.

The equity begins to approach the line of resistance that previously developed and volume appears to ramp up, building steam to propel it right through. During this phase, the stock's price spreads get wider and wider. Dupont picks up steam and thrusts its way through resistance (the "creek").

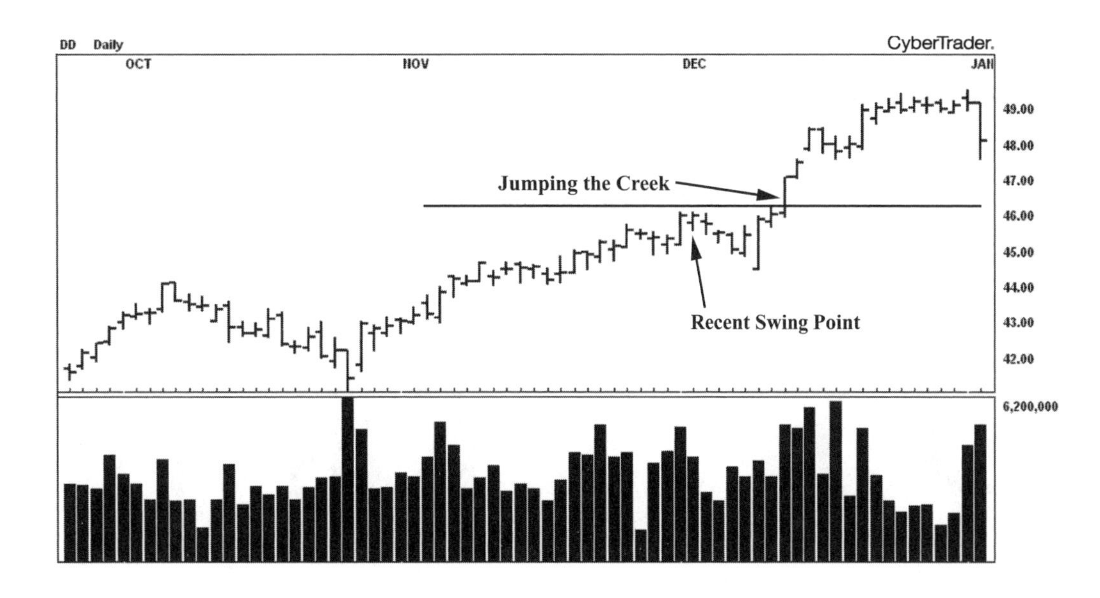

Figure AI-4

"Jumping the Creek"

Well, Dupont has proven to be a worthy stock and now its volume is giving indication that it wants to move! Dupont has broken through resistance or "jumped the creek". Again, let me point out that as it "jumps the creek", its price spreads are wider as compared with those in the "building cause" phase. Also, if you take a closer look, you'll see that it also passed a recent swing point with volume.

After crossing the line or jumping, the stock's price movement doesn't just stop right away. The energy from the momentum of the jump will keep the stock going, much like tossing a ball into the air – the ball doesn't immediately stop but keeps going until gravity slows it down and overtakes it.

As the stock slows down and turns around to come back, volume gets lighter; this starts the "coming back to ice phase". This turnaround also marks our potential B or Focus point. The distance from B back to the lowest low, A1 gives us a distance of $8.52. Assuming that A to B equals C to D, our potential reward if we enter this trade amounts to $8.52.

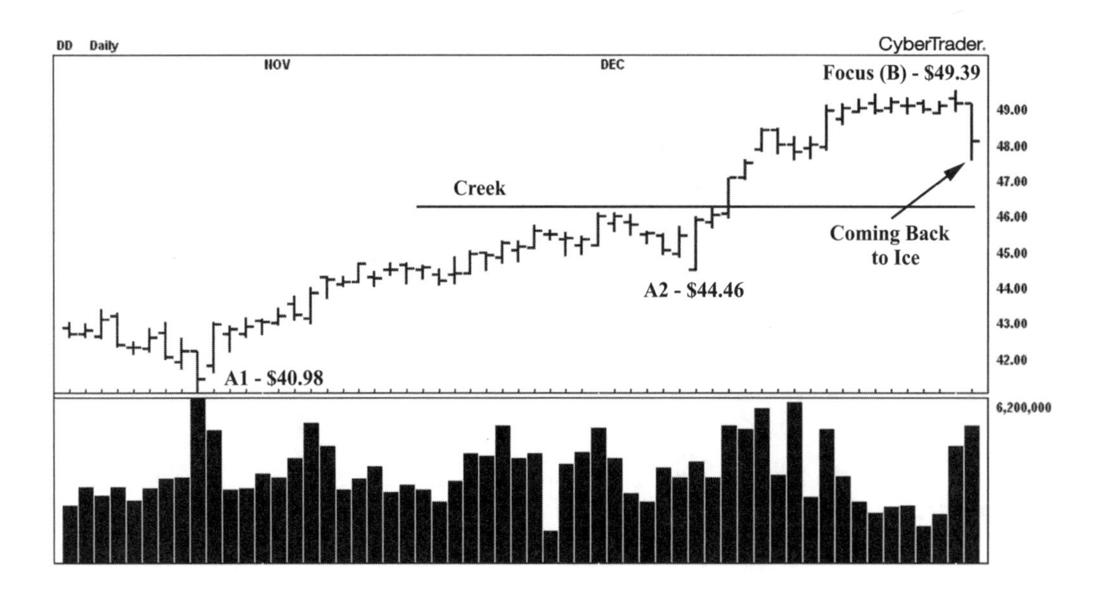

Figure AI-5

Setting up the Trade

Up to this point, we've spotted Dupont, checked out the general market climate and Dupont's trading behavior against its sector climate. The stock's volume has accelerated and it has broken through a line of resistance ("jumped the creek"). We've basically identified our trade. Next we want to set it up.

"Coming Back to Ice"/Confluence

As a stock is in its "coming back to ice" phase, its movement should be accentuated with lighter volume (a significant component of quality volume). This return movement is essentially the stock's retracement phase; at this point we calculate the Fibonacci retracement levels. We identify the stock's A1, A2 and B (Focus) points and (referring to Figure AI-5) come up with $40.98 as A1, $44.46 as A2 and $49.50 as the Focus point (B).

With our A1, A2 and Focus (B) numbers intact, we calculate confluence.

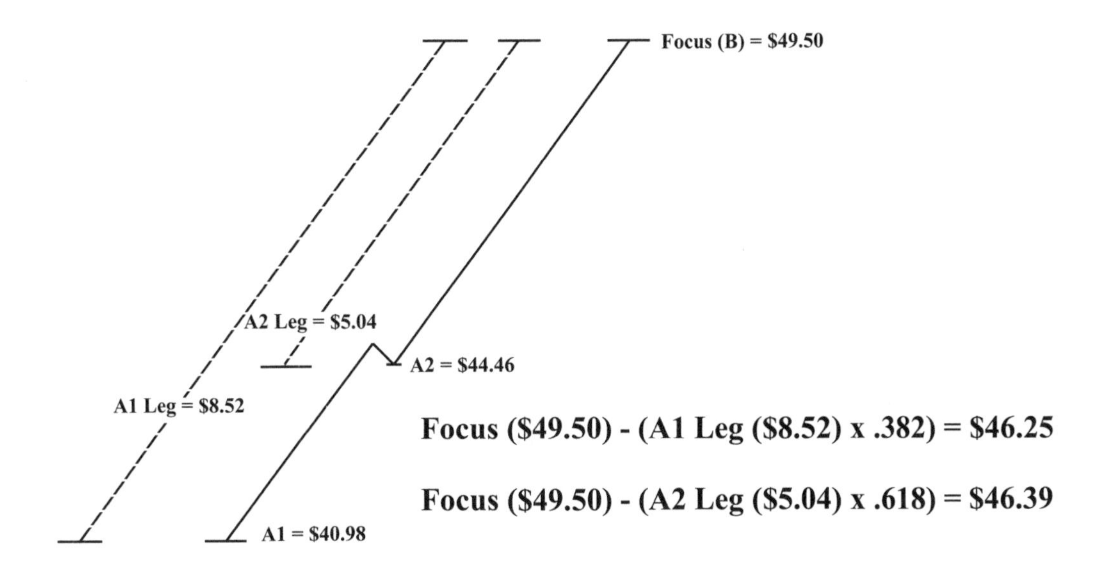

Figure AI-6

We've got our confluence numbers ($46.25 to $46.39) and these levels form the foundation for the staging area of our trade and by "staging area", I mean the area where we will focus on our entry, our stop and the stock's price activity, going forward.

We also take our confluence level and check to see if it is congruent with a previous swing point. If that's the case, confluence becomes even more powerful!

Now with confluence calculated, we identify optimal entry and stop points. Our entry would be anywhere above confluence and our stop should be on the other side of confluence as well as the other side of a previous swing point, if possible!

We identify an entry point of $46.40 and a stop of $44.76.

Risk/Reward

With entry and stop points identified, we calculate a risk/reward ratio.

Risk / Reward Calculation

Reward	Risk
A1 = $40.98 B = $49.50 A1 to B = $8.52 (Projected Expansion - Reward)	Target Entry $46.40 Stop - 44.76 Potential Loss = $ 1.64 (Risk)
"Risk/Reward Ratio" equals Reward divided by Risk $8.52 (Reward) / $1.64 (Risk) = 5.2 [Greater than 3 to 1]	

Figure AI-7

Our ratio comes up as 5.2-to-1 which is greater than 3-to-1, a good trade.

3x3 DMA & MACD

We turn to the 3x3 DMA and MACD for the final go-ahead. Looking at the 3x3 DMA we note that we are not quite on the right side of the trend; we wait. DD finally enters into the "bullish" side of the 3x3 DMA on January 27, 2005; we notice this as DD closes *above* the 3x3 DMA.

Dupont (DD)	Closing Price	Computed 3X3 DMA
January 27 (Price crosses into DMA "bullish side")	$ 46.97	$ 46.65
January 26	46.48	47.10
January 25 (Originally planned entry date)	46.58	47.36
January 24	46.01	
January 21	46.71	
January 20	47.23	
January 19	47.38	
January 18	47.49	

Figure AI-8

We take a look at the MACD and notice that the fast curve is fast approaching the slower curve and is about to make its crossover (it's O.K. to speculate that the crossover will occur, if it doesn't later on, you definitely want to get out of your trade). We aim for a good entry price and arrive at $47.00 which is 60 cents greater than our previously planned entry. From a risk/reward perspective we have given up 60 cents of reward and added 60 cents to our risk. Upon recalculation, our risk/reward ratio has moved from 5.2-to-1 down to 3.5-to-1, still above our 3-to-1 benchmark.

With everything looking good, and volume still behaving as expected, we enter the trade.

Before we shut down our computer though, we enter a sell order for our target price. More often than not, a stock will reach and surpass a target price point but not close above it; a sell order at your target will help make sure you're out when the price point is reached.

In the Trade

We've identified our trade, set it up and now we're in it. What now?

Price Projection

After turning around at confluence, Dupont begins its next move up, its C to D price projection. Volume during this phase picks up steam and stays fairly strong.

Mental Dynamics

We can't forget about mental dynamics. Much can go on in your head during this time (refer back to Chapter 17 - *In the Trade*). The most important thing is to definitely "stay cool"!

Success

Well, our stock seems to be getting close to its projection point, D. Volume has stayed strong and we're still in it. If Dupont reaches D, we're out. We've planned our trade and traded our plan. What's so bad about being right?

Let's take a look at what Dupont ended up doing:

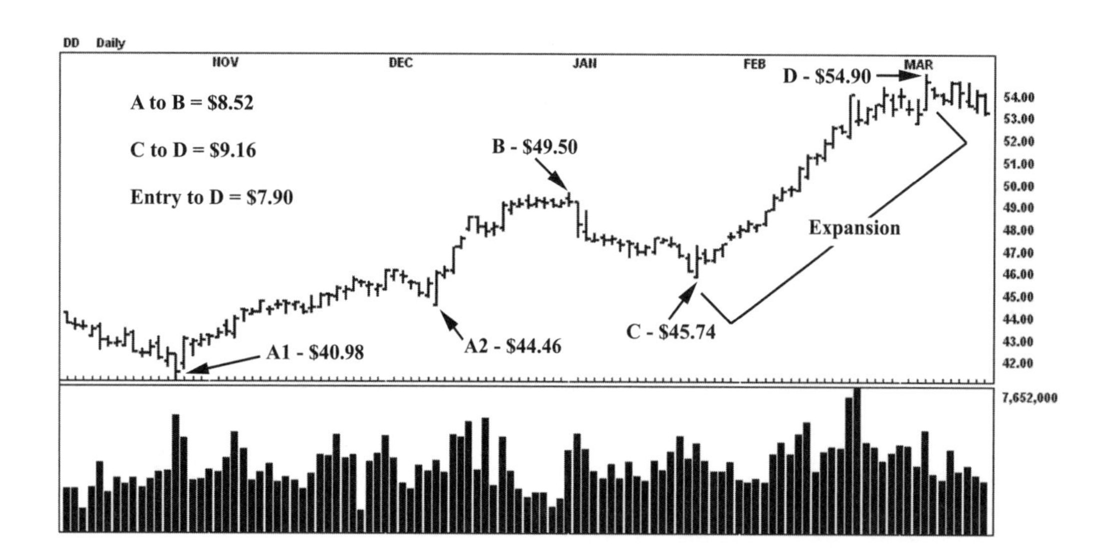

Figure AI-9

With our entry point equaling $47.00 and our projection point equaling $54.90, our actual expansion totaled $7.90, lower than the planned $8.52 (A to B) due to the simple reason that we waited for the appropriate entry signal from the 3x3 DMA & MACD and got in at a higher price. A good trade nonetheless!

Wow, what a ride! It's really a joy to take a look back on lessons learned and see how you can benefit from them - both in trading and in life. If you've absorbed the concepts in this book like a sponge takes to water, you should have easily assimilated this case study. Fortunately, Dupont worked out spectacularly and turned out to be a "textbook" example!

Appendix II

Drawdowns & ROI

There are two indispensable metrics I use to help me manage and gauge my trading performance: they are "drawdowns" and ROI (return on investment). These measurement tools are a critical component of practically all savvy traders' performance metrics and if it works for them, it will certainly work for you.

Drawdowns

A "drawdown" is a term used to describe the cumulative trading loss of money. If you start trading with $20,000 and you lose $1,000 on your very first trade, you have experienced a drawdown of $1,000. If you wish to express your drawdown in percentage terms, you simply divide your loss by your starting capital (in this case $20,000) and you arrive at 5%.

> ***Definition***: **drawdown** – the amount lost in a losing trade or losing trades; expressed as a dollar or percentage amount.

Unless you are the greatest and most infallible trader that has ever walked this planet, you will incur drawdowns; and while drawdowns are a certain reality in the world of trading, their quantification can help you gauge your performance as a trader and can even go so far as telling you if you're trading with the wrong system or should be trading at all.

To help you grasp the concept and importance of drawdowns, let's take a look at a hypothetical example. Let's suppose you have been trading for a year and have the following results:

Month	(A) Net Profit/(Loss)	(B) Cumulative Profit	(C) Running Drawdown	(D) Maximum Drawdown
January	$ 2,400	$ 2,400	$ —	$ —
February	500	2,900	—	—
March	(750)	2,150	(750)	(750)
April	850	3,000	—	(750)
May	(1,200)	1,800	(1,200)	(1,200)
June	(840)	960	(2,040)	(2,040)
July	680	1,640	(1,360)	(2,040)
August	(860)	780	(2,220)	(2,220)
September	1,850	2,630	(370)	(2,220)
October	(1,680)	950	(2,050)	(2,220)
November	2,250	3,200	—	(2,220)
December	2,860	6,060	—	(2,220)

Figure AII-1: *Drawdown Example*

(A) *Net Profit/(Loss)- This column is merely your total profit/(loss) for the given month.*

(B) *Cumulative Profit – This column keeps a running total of the profits and losses incurred to date.*

(C) *Running Drawdown – This column keeps a running total of your drawdowns which are offset by any gains; notice how drawdowns here are expressed as negative numbers – any compensating gains zero out the running balance.*

(D) *Maximum Drawdown – This column expresses the maximum running drawdown that you have experienced to date; notice how the amount increases in severity.*

The two important amounts to take note of in Figure AII-1 above are the ending figures (December's) for cumulative profit and maximum drawdown. According to your trading results, you made $6,060 for the entire year. However, your maximum amount of *losing* trades amounted to $2,220. If you take the approach that one trade will win or lose you a dollar, you had approximately three winners for every loser. Another way of looking at this relationship is that it took you $2,220 of losses to make $6,060; whichever way you look at it, the relationship of the two numbers will speak as to the effectiveness of your trading and/or trading system. Imagine if you incurred $6,000 of losses and made $6,000; now suppose you incurred a $1 loss and made $6,000 – at which end of this spectrum would you rather be?

The goal for any trader is to keep a tight rein on drawdowns, which by doing so controls maximum drawdowns, and keeps trading volatility (i.e., pronounced swings from profits to losses) at a minimum. Figure AII-2 below illustrates two curves representing the profits and losses of two different trading patterns. Movements to the upside represent profits, drawdowns are expressed to the downside and overall portfolio growth can be read by the slope of the entire curve.

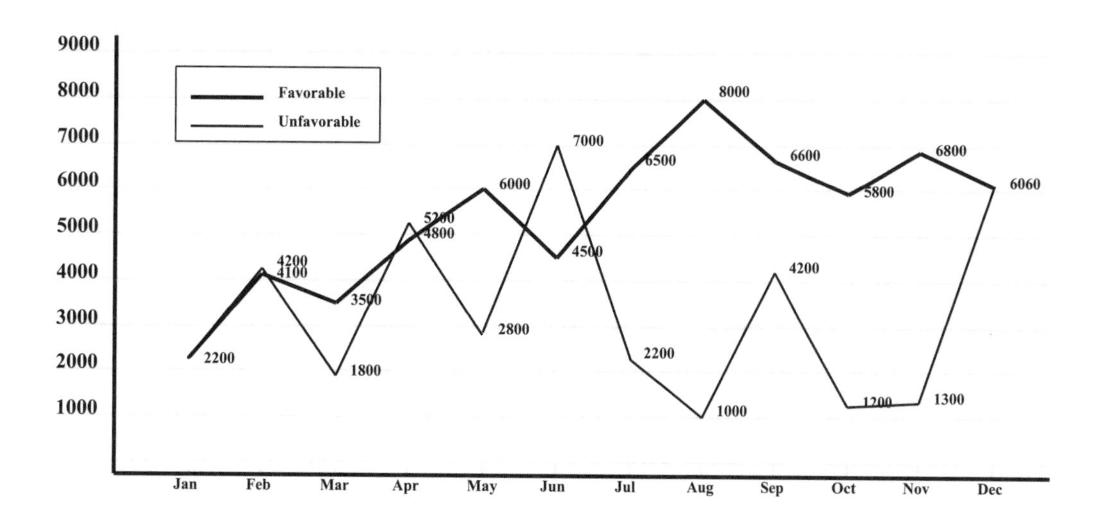

Figure AII-2: ***Effect of Drawdowns***
See how the thinner curve ("Unfavorable") is the more volatile with drawdowns dragging down the overall upward momentum of trading gains and "whipsawing" the trader into a frenzied state. The thicker curve ("Favorable") is obviously more desirable as drawdowns appear to be under control and portfolio growth seems relatively unimpeded. Both curves end up at the same amount ($6,060), but which represents better trading?

Although drawdowns are an inevitable consequence of trading, tracking them on a continual basis will keep you informed as to the success of your trading system (vis-à-vis consistency and volatility), which ultimately will lead you to better trading!

ROI (Return on Investment)

ROI or "return on investment" is used to quantify the amount made on a trade or trades, usually expressed as an annual percentage. Let's use a simple example:

Suppose you buy 1,000 shares of Microsoft (MSFT) at $24.00. You sit on your shares for three months and see MSFT hit $27.00. You sell your shares, enjoying a $3.00 per share profit. What's your ROI? Right off the bat, you made $3 on $24 invested, that's one-eighth or 12.5%. Not bad. But in annual terms your percentage will be much higher. Since you held the shares for three months, your return on an *annualized* basis is computed as follows:

ROI = percentage return x (no. of months in year / no. of months shares held)
= 12.5% x (12/3) = 50%

Fifty percent is your computed annualized ROI for the amount you *invested.* If you had more than $24,000 in your capital base (for example, you had $30,000 but invested only $24,000), your computed ROI would be less if you applied it to your entire capital base. Regardless how it's applied, ROI will tell you how efficiently your capital is being utilized.

ROI and Drawdowns Combined

When ROI is combined with drawdowns, you get a different angle for analyzing how effectively your trading behavior and/or trading system is impacting your overall trading performance from a risk/reward perspective. Let's further our examples:

Suppose your starting capital for trading is $24,000, your maximum drawdown for the period is $2,220 (on a percentage basis, this amounts to 9.25%) and your annualized ROI for your trades amounts to 50%.

From a risk/reward angle, you've been risking $9.25 to make $50. Breaking this further down, the ratio comes up to 5.4-to-1 ($5.40 reward for $1 of risk); not bad.

If your maximum drawdown had been $4,440, this would have doubled your maximum drawdown percentage to 18.5%, meaning you've been risking $18.50 to make $50, cutting your risk/reward ratio in half to 2.7-to-1. In my case, since 2.7-

to-1 is below my desired risk/reward parameter of 3-to-1, this would be a good sign telling me to reassess my trading approach and/or system(s).

ROI and drawdowns, when used individually and on a combined basis, will undoubtedly give you a clearer picture as to your trading behavior, system(s) and your overall trading success!

Appendix III

Glossary

ABC up (down) – a term used to describe and plot the price movement of a rising (falling) stock. The commencement of each leg is denoted with an A, B or C (see Chapter 5 - *ABCs*).

Accumulation phase – a period where an operator(s) will quietly build up an inventory of stock in anticipation of selling at higher prices; volume is relatively low and stable during this period (see Chapter 2 - *Quality Volume™*).

Cause – that which produces an effect or result; that from which anything proceeds, and without which would not exist; in the context of *Timing the Trade*, "cause" equals volume and can also equal time (see Chapter 3 - *Cause & Effect*).

Channel – a term used to denote a stock's apparent trading range perimeters and the associated levels of support and resistance (see Chapter 12 - *Channels*).

Coming back to ice – a term used by Richard Wyckoff to describe the price retracing behavior of a stock that has previously broken through a level of resistance or support or "jumped the creek" (see Chapter 13 - *Jumping the Creek, Coming Back to Ice*).

Consolidation – a term used to characterize price activity that is building cause for the next move (up or down).

Confluence – the price range sandwiched between the .382 retracement level of a trend and the .618 retracement of a related subtrend; confluence reveals powerful support & resistance levels (see Chapter 7 - *Confluence*).

Contraction theory – the concepts associated with price retracements and resulting price move behavior (see Chapter 6 - *Fibonacci).*

Distribution phase – a period where operators unload their inventory of stock at profitable prices; volume is relatively low during this phase (see Chapter 2 - *Quality Volume™).*

Doji – a candlestick charting symbol denoting a session in which the opening and closing prices are the same (or almost the same); usually represents a stalemate and potentially a change in the direction of the current trend. (see Chapter 4 - *Candlestick Charting*).

Drawdown – a reduction in trading capital due to trading losses (see Appendix II - *Drawdowns & ROI*).

Effect – a result or consequence; in the context of *Timing the Trade*, "effect" equals price (see Chapter 3 - *Cause & Effect).*

Engulfing pattern – a technical reversal pattern found in candlestick charting; typical engulfing patterns are the bullish, bearish and last engulfing patterns (see Chapter 4 - *Candlestick Charting*).

Expansion theory – the concepts associated with price moves (consistent with the current trend) that follow retracements (see Chapter 6 - *Fibonacci).*

Focus point – the highest high of an uptrend or the lowest low of a downtrend; also the B point of an ABC pattern; used to mark the end of an A to B leg for calculating contraction, expansion and confluence amounts (see Chapter 7 - *Confluence).*

Gap up (down) – occurs when there is a price range having no trades between two trading days' price ranges (see Chapter 11 - *Gaps*).

Hammer – typically a technical reversal candlestick line; a bullish indicator when appearing during a downtrend; similar in appearance to a hanging man (see Chapter 4 - *Candlestick Charting*).

Hanging man – typically a technical reversal candlestick line; a bearish indicator when appearing during an uptrend; similar in appearance to a hammer (see Chapter 4 - *Candlestick Charting*).

Jumping the creek – a term used by Richard Wyckoff to describe the price movement behavior of a stock breaking through a level of resistance or support (see Chapter 13 - *Jumping the Creek, Coming Back to Ice*).

Mark-down phase – a period where operator(s) will actively endeavor to push down prices of a particular stock in order to begin another accumulation phase (see Chapter 2 - *Quality Volume™*).

Mark-up phase – a period where operator(s) will actively endeavor to push up prices of a particular stock in order to be able to unload their inventory at higher prices (during the *distribution phase*); volume is relatively high and volatile during this period (see Chapter 2 - *Quality Volume™*).

Money management – the science behind the allocation of a capital base to a trading plan (see Chapter 18 - *Risk & Money Management*).

Moving average convergence/divergence (MACD) – a technical indicator that combines three exponentially smoothed moving averages (see Chapter 14 - *3x3 DMA & MACD*).

Operator – any individual trader or institution with the ability to manipulate a stock's price beyond the stock's natural price point (based on supply and demand) in order to gain an advantage in anticipation of a major price move; operators usually have more information than the individual investor. Richard Wyckoff coined a similar term: "composite man".

Overhead supply – ownership at higher prices, which in turn creates resistance (see Chapter 9 - *Support & Resistance*).

Passing B point with volume – occurs during a C to D point price projection when an equity passes its ABC structure B point with volume that is heavier than the B point's volume (see Chapter 5 - *ABCs*).

Price axis theory – a methodology for identifying a particular price point on a price spread or price move; the determination is dependent upon the current trend: top price in an uptrend and lowest price in a downtrend, i.e., "the highest highs and lowest lows" (see Chapter 6 - *Fibonacci*).

Price projection – a planned price move that follows a retracement; a component of expansion theory; also the C to D leg of an ABC structure (see Chapter 6 - *Fibonacci*).

Price spread – the difference between the high and low trading price of any given session.

Quality Volume™ – a term I have coined to characterize a pattern of strong volume followed by light volume accompanying a strong price move followed by a retracement, respectively (see Chapter 2 - *Quality Volume™*).

Real price – a term I have coined to denote the price point where there is an enormous amount of buying and selling activity, typically emphasizing a possible intersection of supply and demand curves for the related stock (see Chapter 2 - *Quality Volume™).*

Retracement – a stock's price movement behavior that "retraces" a previous trend or price move; retracements are an important component to contraction theory; also the B to C leg of an ABC structure.

Risk management – the science behind planning the potential loss of money in stock trading (see Chapter 18 - *Risk & Money Management*).

Risk/reward – a term used to denote the comparison between a planned potential loss and a planned potential gain; typically expressed as reward-to-risk (see Chapter 18 - *Risk & Money Management*).

ROI – acronym for "return on investment"; used to measure trading performance (see Appendix II - *Drawdowns & ROI*).

Shooting star – typically a technical reversal candlestick line; a bearish indicator appearing during an uptrend (see Chapter 4 - *Candlestick Charting*).

Stochastics – a technical indicator utilizing oscillating curves that signal overbought and oversold conditions.

Stop – a trading mechanism used to establish a price point to exit a trade; stops are also used to quantify risk (see Chapter 8 - *Stops*).

Support & resistance – the concepts associated with a stock's tendency to remain above or below certain price levels based on ownership (see Chapter 9 - *Support & Resistance*).

Swing point – a point in a stock's price movement where there is a sudden, significant turn in direction; this point becomes an important level of support or resistance (see Chapter 10 - *Swing Points).*

Test – the act or occurrence of a stock reaching a particular price point.

Three-by-three displaced moving average (3x3 DMA) – a technical indicator consisting of a three-day moving average that is shifted forward three days (see Chapter 14 - *3x3 DMA & MACD*).

Trailing stop – a trading mechanism used to establish a price point to exit a trade; typically used to protect profits; also used to quantify risk (see Chapter 8 - *Stops*).

Volume – the amount of shares bought and sold for any given stock or market during any given time frame (typically expressed as a daily amount, see Chapter 2 - *Quality Volume™*).

Volume off the top – term used to characterize heavy volume that accompanies a strong price move down immediately following a prolonged uptrend (see Chapter 2 - *Quality Volume™*).

YES – pseudo ticker symbol representing "Your Excellent Stock", a hypothetical stock used in various examples throughout this book.

Appendix IV

Stocks in Action

This appendix contains a listing of all stocks featured in *Timing the Trade* and is included to assist you in your own analyses. The listing is arranged by chapter and includes each stock's ticker symbol, time frame presented and figure number reference.

Chapter 1 – *Let's Get Cookin'*

1-1 General Electric (GE) – daily, (Jul 2004 – Dec 2004)

Chapter 2 – *Quality Volume*™

2-4 Hecla Mining (HL) – weekly, (Nov '00 – May '04)

2-5 Krispy Kreme Doughnuts (KKD) – weekly, (Aug '03 – Aug '04)

2-9 American International Group, Inc. (AIG) – daily, (Sept '04 – May '05)

2-11 Sears Holding Corp. (SHLD) – daily, (Nov '04 – Apr '05)

2-12 Exxon Mobil Corp. (XOM) – daily, (Jan '05 – Jun '05)

Chapter 3 – *Cause & Effect*

3-1 Hecla Mining (HL) – weekly, (Aug '00 – Aug '05)

3-2 Glamis Gold Ltd. (GLG) – weekly, (Jan '01 – Aug '03)

3-3 Hansen Natural Corp. (HANS) – weekly, (Jul '01 – Apr 05)

Chapter 4 – *Candlestick Charting*

4-3 Carnival Corp. (CCL) – daily, (Mar ’05 – Jun ’05)

4-4 Petroleum Development Corp. (PETD) – daily, (Aug ’04 – Dec 04)

4-7 Fording Canadian Coal Trust (FDG) – daily, (Apr ’05 – Jun ’05)

4-8 Ingersoll-Rand Company Ltd. (IR) – daily, (Sept ’03 – Dec ‘03)

4-10 McDonald’s Corp. (MCD) – daily, (Jan ’05 – May ’05)

4-11 Cardinal Health, Inc. (CAH) – daily, (Jan ’05 – Jun ’05)

4-13 3M Company (MMM) – daily, (Jun ’05 – Jul ’05)

4-14 Apollo Group, Inc. (APOL) – weekly, (Feb ’04 – Dec ’04)

Chapter 5 – *ABCs*

5-6 Phelps Dodge Corp. (PD) – daily, (Apr ’05 – Jul ’05)

5-8 Intel Corp. (INTC) – weekly, (Dec ’03 – Oct ’04)

5-9 Jabil Circuit, Inc. (JBL) – daily, (Aug ’04 – Apr ’05)

Chapter 7 – *Confluence*

7-3 Glamis Gold Lmt (GLG) – daily, (May ’05 – Jun ’05)

7-6 Toll Brothers, Inc. (TOL) – daily, (Jan ’04 – May ’04)

7-9 Caterpillar Inc. (CAT) – daily, (Jul ’04 – Nov ’04)

Chapter 9 – *Support & Resistance*

Chapter 10 – *Swing Points*

Chapter 11 – *Gaps*

Chapter 12 – *Channels*

Chapter 13 – *Jumping the Creek, Coming Back to Ice*

Chapter 14 – *3x3 DMA & MACD*

Chapter 15 – *Identifying the Trade*

Chapter 16 – *Setting up the Trade*

Appendix I – *Case Study*

AI-1 S&P 500 Index (SPX) – weekly, (Aug ’03 – Dec ’04)

AI-2 Dupont (DD) & Cyclical Index (CYC) – daily, (Aug ’04 – Nov ’04)

AI-3 Dupont (DD) – daily, (Feb ’03 – Dec ’04)

AI-4 Dupont (DD) – daily, (Sept ’04 – Jan ’05)

AI-5 Dupont (DD) – daily, (Oct ’04 – Jan ’05)

AI-9 Dupont (DD) – daily, (Oct ’04 – Mar ’05)

Index

D

E

F

G

H

I

J

K

L

M

N

O

P

Q

R

S

T

U

V

W

Y

Z

Always remember folks, the Bear can claw your heart out,
the Bull can run you over, and thank God there's always another trade!

~ Tom O'Brien

Tom O'Brien

Tom O'Brien is the President and founder of Tiger Financial News Network, Inc. He is the host of "The Tom O'Brien Show", a nationally syndicated radio show that also has one of the largest international audiences via the worldwide web. Tom is also the editor of two newsletters, the daily "Market Insights" and weekly "The Gold Report".

Tom is hailed as one of the foremost proponents and teachers of price & volume dynamics and their ability to move markets. Using his unique approach, he trades markets across the globe, tirelessly in search of Quality Volume™. Tom's ultimate purpose is to educate listeners so that they may take control of their financial destiny.